Hinduism as a Missionary Religion

Hinduism as a Missionary Religion

Arvind Sharma

SUNY PRESS

Published by State University of New York Press, Albany

Printed in the United States of America

For information, contact State University of New York Press, Albany, NY
www.sunypress.edu

Production by Kelli W. LeRoux
Marketing by Michael Campochiaro

Library of Congress Cataloging-in-Publication Data

Sharma, Arvind.
Hinduism as a missionary religion / Arvind Sharma.
p. cm.
Includes bibliographical references and index.
ISBN 978-1-4384-3212-0 (paperback : alk. paper)
ISBN 978-1-4384-3211-3 (hardcover : alk. paper)
1. Hinduism—Missions—Historiography. I. Title.

BL1243.32.S53 2010
294.5'72—dc22 2009052580

10 9 8 7 6 5 4 3 2 1

Contents

Preface

The title of this book provides the reason for writing it. None of the three words in its title—*Hinduism, missionary,* and *religion*—are Hindu words, although all three have been invoked in a Hindu context. It is a basic feature of all discourse that a thing must be described in terms other than what it is. The moment an object is described as a table, a cognitive distance has already been established between the word and the object it denotes. This provides a preliminary vision of how large a gap such a cognitive distance might assume if the facts of one religion or culture are presented in terms of another religion or culture.

To describe Hinduism as a missionary religion further lengthens the distance between the word and the reality. Three questions seem to be contained in this description: Is Hinduism an ism? Is it a religion? And is it a missionary religion?

This book is concerned with the exploration of the third dimension at a *substantive* level, although the issue has been posed as a nominal one. The question which is addressed is: In what ways and to what extent can Hinduism be described as a missionary religion in terms of available historical evidence?

The first of the three questions or propositions listed above has been under the lens of scholarly[1] investigation for some time now; so, also the second.[2] The aim of this book is to subject the third issue to scholarly scrutiny in the same spirit.

Chapter I

The Antiquity and Continuity of the Belief that Hinduism Is Not a Missionary Religion

I

From the earliest times, the Hindus have appeared to outside observers as a non-missionary people, that is, a people not interested in converting others to their religion. The earliest record of the contact of the Hindus with people outside India pertains to the Persians, as indicated by an examination of the Avestan and Vedic material.[1] The evidence does not suggest any missionary effort directed toward the Persians by the Vedic Hindus.[2] On the contrary, if there was any proselytizing going on, it was on the part of the Zoroastrians in relation to followers of the pre-Zoroastrian forms of religion,[3] which bore some affinity to Vedism.[4]

The Persians invaded India in the sixth century BC, and because of this event, the relation between the Zoroastrians and the Hindus becomes clearer.[5] Again, there is no suggestion that this forced contact led to any missionary activity on the part of the Hindus, even though an Indian contingent fought alongside the Persians in Greece.[6] There is, on the other hand, some evidence of Zoroastrian proselytising activity.[7]

The Macedonian invasion of India in the fourth century BC provides the next point of contact between the Hindus and the non-Hindus beyond India—this time with the Greeks. Again, any evidence of missionary activity on the part of the Hindus is lacking. But two incidents associated with Alexander's campaign seem to foreshadow emerging patterns of the relationship between the Hindus and the non-Hindus. The first incident consists of what is generally regarded as the earliest recorded account of the rite of *Satī*. When the leader of an Indian contingent with the Greeks died in Persia 316 BC, his two wives vied with each other in wanting to immolate themselves. The elder one, who was pregnant, was prevented from doing so, but the younger one was allowed to proceed with her resolve.

> The elder wife went away lamenting, with the band about her head rent, and tearing her hair, as if tidings of some great disaster had been brought her; and the other departed, exultant at her victory, to the pyre, crowned with fillets by the women who belonged to her and decked out splendidly as for a wedding she was escorted by her kinsfolk who chanted a song in praise of her virtue. When she came near to the pyre, she took off her adornments and distributed them to her familiars and friends, leaving a memorial of herself, as it were, to those who had loved her. Her adornments consisted of a multitude of rings on her hands, set with precious gems of diverse colours, about her head, golden stars about her head, not a few, variegated with different sorts of stones, and about her neck a multitude of necklaces, each a little larger than the one above it. In conclusion, she said farewell to her familiars and was helped by her brother onto the pyre, and there, to the admiration of the crowd, which had gathered together for the spectacle, she ended her life in heroic fashion. Before the pyre was kindled, the whole army in battle array marched round it thrice. She meanwhile lay down beside her husband, and as the fire seized her no sound of weakness escaped her lips. The spectators were moved, some to pity and some to exuberant praise. But some of the Greeks present found fault with such customs as savage and inhumane.[8]

We learn toward the end that the spectators "were moved, some to pity, some to exuberant praise." It is not clear whether the spectators referred to here are only Indians; it is likely that they included Persians and Greeks—and, if so, then some of them may have been moved to exuberant praise as well. But we are also told that some of the Greeks condemned the custom. It is unlikely, however, that, as a result of witnessing the rite of Satī, any Persian or Greek may have decided to convert to Hinduism. On the contrary.

The second incident, which may shed some light on the matter, is Alexander's encounter with the gymnosophists, especially with their leader Dandamis.

King Alexander, accordingly, when he heard of all this, was desirous of learning the doctrines of the sect, and so he sent for this Dandamis, as being their teacher and president. . . .

Onesicritus was therefore dispatched to fetch him, and when he found the great sage he said: "Hail to thee, thou teacher of the Bragmanes. The son of the mighty god Zeus, King Alexander, who is the sovereign lord of all men, asks you to go to him, and if you comply, he will reward you with great and splendid gifts, but if you refuse will cut off your head."

Dandamis, with a complacent smile, heard him to the end, but did not so much as lift up his head from his couch of leaves, and while still retaining his recumbent attitude returned this scornful answer:—"God, the Supreme King, is never the author of insolent wrong, but is the creator of light, of peace, of life, of water, of the body of man, and of souls. He alone is the God of my homage, who abhors slaughter and instigates no wars. But Alexander is not God, since he must taste of death; and how can such as he be the world's master, who has not yet reached the further shore of the river Tiberaboas, and has not yet seated himself on a throne of universal dominion? . . . Know this, however, that what Alexander offers me, and the gifts he promises, are all things to me utterly useless; but the things I prize, and find of real use and worth, are these leaves which are my house, these blooming plants which supply me with dainty food, and the water which is my drink, while all other possessions and things, which are amassed with anxious care, are wont to prove ruinous to those who amass them, and cause only sorrow and vexation, with which every poor mortal is fully fraught. But as for me, I lie upon the forest leaves, and, having nothing which requires guarding, close my eyes in tranquil slumber; whereas had I gold to guard, that would banish sleep. The earth supplies me with everything, even as a mother her child with milk. I go wherever I please, and there are no cares with which I am forced to cumber myself, against my will. Should Alexander cut off my head, he cannot also destroy my soul. My head alone, now silent, will remain, but the soul will go away to its Master, leaving the body like a torn garment upon the earth, whence also it was taken. I then, becoming spirit,

> shall ascend to my God, who enclosed us in flesh, and left us upon the earth to prove whether, when here below, we shall live obedient to his ordinances, and who will require of us, when we depart hence to his presence, an account of our life, since he is judge of all proud wrong-doing, for the groans of the oppressed become the punishments of the oppressors.
>
> Let Alexander, then, terrify with these threats those who wish for gold and for wealth, and who dread death, for against us these weapons are both alike powerless, since the Bragmanes neither love gold nor fear death. Go, then, and tell Alexander this: 'Dandamis has no need of aught that is yours, and therefore will not go to you, but if you want anything from Dandamis come you to him.' " Alexander, on receiving from Onesicritus a report of the interview, felt a stronger desire than ever to see Dandamis, who, though old and naked, was the only antagonist in whom he, the conqueror of many nations, had found more than his match.[9]

It is clear from this account that Dandamis had no desire to convert Alexander. This attitude is confirmed by the experience of Onesicritus, who met fifteen renunciants near Taxila. Upon telling them that the Greek king wanted to learn of their wisdom, he received the following reply from one of them: "No one coming in the drapery of European clothes—cavalry cloak and broad-brimmed hat and top-boots, such as Macedonians wore—could learn their wisdom. To do that he must strip naked and learn to sit on the hot stones beside them."[10] It was like asking Sir Winston Churchill to become a nakid fakir!

One should note that there is a willingness to impart instruction—but on one's own terms. But "you call us, we won't call you" is hardly an attitude consistent with a missionary spirit.

Further evidence from Greek sources only serves to confirm this view. Megasthenes is believed to have been the ambassador of Seleucus at the court of Candragupta Maurya, who founded the Mauryan Empire and ruled from circa 324–300 BC. His account of India is now lost, but it was freely drawn upon by later writers. The admittedly fragmentary evidence supplied by these references seems to confirm the overall picture. We are told that the Indians did not conquer lands beyond their borders: "A sense of justice, they say, prevented any Indian king from attempting conquest beyond the limits of India."[11] We are also told that "the Indian stands almost alone among the nations in never having migrated from their own country."[12] Because conquest and migration are two major ways in which a religion displays its missionary zeal—as illustrated by the history of Christianity and Islam—the presumption is strengthened that Hinduism was not a missionary religion, at least at the time.

II

After the Greek accounts, it is from the accounts of the Chinese travelers to India that we must determine whether Hinduism appeared to them to be missionary religion. Pre-eminent among the Chinese Buddhist monks, who visited India, are Faxian (Fa-hien), Xuanzang (Hiuen Tsang), and Yijing (I-tsing). Faxian traveled to India and Śrī Laṅkā between 399–414 AD, during the reign of the Gupta monarch Candragupta II Vikramāditya, though he does not mention the king by name.[13] The account left by him basically consists of Buddhist curiosities, but a few observations pertaining to Hinduism can be found scattered through the work. Faxian even mentions a region that may be seen as falling outside the pale of both Buddhism and Hinduism. He remarks, while describing the Deccan:

> At a very long distance from the hill there are villages, where the people all have bad and erroneous views, and do not know the Śramaṇas of the Law of Buddha, Brāhmaṇas, or (devotees of) any of the other and different schools. The people of that country are constantly seeing men on the wing, who come and enter this monastery. On one occasion, when devotees of various countries came to perform their worship at it, the people of those villages said to them, 'Why do you not fly? The devotees whom we have seen hereabouts all fly'; and the strangers answered, on the spur of the moment, 'our wings are not yet fully formed.'[14]

Faxian, however, makes no mention of either Buddhist or Hindu missionary activity taking place in the region.

Faxian's account testifies to the cordial relations between the Hindus and the Buddhists. He states at one point in his description of central India that, after the Buddha's *mahāparinirvāṇa,* "the kings and the heads of the Vaiśyas built vihāras for the priests and endowed them" and that these endowments were "engraved on plates of metal, so that afterwards they were handed down from king to king, without anyone daring to annul them, and they remain even to the present true."[15] While speaking of his own time he says: "When the monks have done receiving their annual tribute (from the harvests), the Heads of the Vaiśyas and all the Brahmans bring clothes and such other articles as the monks require for use, and distribute among them."[16]

Faxian, in the course of describing life in Magadha or modern Bihar, states that there resided in Pāṭaliputra (modern Patna) "a great Brahman, named Rādha-sāmi, a professor of the *mahāyāna,* of clear discernment and much wisdom. . . . He might be more than fifty years old, and all the kingdom looked up to him."[17] He also mentions "a Brahman teacher, whose name was Mañjuśrī," residing in another monastery "whom the Shamans of greatest virtue in the kingdom, and the mahāyāna Bhikshus honour and look up to."[18] It is noteworthy that these teachers were Brahmins. Faxian further states that, when the procession of images is celebrated "on the eighth day of the second month," images of the Buddha are included in the procession and ". . . the Brahmans come and invite the Buddhas to enter the city on that day."[19]

Any missionary activity on the part of the Hindus to reconvert the Buddhists seems inconsistent with this picture of amicable relations between the two.

On the other hand, it seems that the Hindu caste tabus were in operation in the Middle Kingdom, or *Madhya-deśa*. The *caṇḍālas* are mentioned by Faxian in a well-known passage, which contains a generally positive portrayal of the Middle Kingdom.

> Throughout the whole country the people do not kill any living creature, nor drink intoxicating liquor, nor eat onions or garlic. The only exception is that of the Chandalas. That is the name for those who are (held to be) wicked men, and live apart from others. When they enter the gate of a city or a market-place, they strike a piece of wood to make themselves known, so that men know and avoid them, and do not come into contact with them. In that country they do not keep pigs and fowls, and do not sell live cattle; in the markets there are no butchers' shops and no dealers in intoxicating drink. In buying and selling commodities they use cowries. Only the Chandalas are fishermen and hunters, and sell flesh meat.[20]

In the opinion of most scholars, because one can only be born[21] into a caste (and not be converted to it), the outcastes imply the existence of the caste-system, and the caste-system is inconsistent with proselytization—the implication seems to be that Hinduism was non-missionary.

When acts of charity are mentioned as being performed by Hindus, there is no suggestion that they were meant to attract converts.[22] This seems to hold true for Śrī Laṅkā as well.[23]

The next important Chinese traveler of note was Xuanzang[24] (Hiuen Tsang), whose travels in India extended from 629 to 645 AD. These "travels described in a work entitled Records of the Western World, which has been translated into French, English and German, is a treasure-house of accurate information indispensable to every student of antiquity, and has done more than any archaeological discovery to render possible the remarkable resuscitation of lost Indian history."[25] Xuanzang visited India at a time during the reign of Harṣa,[26] whose empire is usually[27] (though perhaps erroneously)[28] regarded as the last great empire of ancient India. Harṣa did however rule over much of north India. This fact imparts to Xuanzang's observation an added significance. Yet Xuanzang, while he does allude to Brahmanical opposition to Harṣa's patronage of Buddhism at one point, does not allude to missionary activity on the part of the Hindus. (His evidence, however, is significant enough for us to take up in more detail after the account of his successor Yijing had been presented.)

The last of the great Chinese Buddhist pilgrims to India was Yijing (I-tsing, 635–713 AD).[29] He was a junior contemporary of Xuanzang and "may have witnessed the 'noble enthusiasm of Hiuen Tsang' and probably also the grand ceremony of his funeral carried out under the special direction of the emperor, for his death occurred during I-tsing's stay in the capital," at Ch'ang-an.[30] Yijing was primarily concerned with the state of the monastic order and monastic rules, to whose proper observances he attached prime importance,[31] but whatever evidence can be gleaned from his account tends to confirm the impression that Hinduism must have appeared to him as a non-missionary religion. He states that the "teaching of the Buddha is becoming less prevalent in the world from day to day."[32] If this is not to be dismissed as an aside, then it should be noted that the geographical theater of the decline of Buddhism is global, not Indian, and further, that the paragraph ends with some measure of optimism: "it is to be hoped that we shall be more attentive in future."[33] Presumably the reference is to the observance of the rules of the order whose nonobservance, it seems to be implied, was the cause of this decline. It is also possible that the purpose of the statement of the decline is to attract attention, as the passage is didactic in nature. In any case, in no way is the alleged decline of Buddhism associated with Hindu missionary activity. Indeed, the translator comments that "there is no trace of Brahmanic hostility in our Record; this is in harmony with the dates of Kumārila Bhaḥṭa (about 750) and Śaḥkarācārya (about 788–820)."[34] A passage in the Record testified to the aloofness of the Brahmins, an attitude hardly consistent with a missionary spirit, although this aloofness is mentioned in the context of their relation to the other castes, as well as to their devotion to the cultivation of the Vedas:

> The Brahmans are regarded throughout the five parts of India as the most honourable (caste). They do not, when they meet in a place, associate with the other three castes, and the mixed classes of the people have still less intercourse with them. The scriptures they revere are the four Vedas, containing about 100,000 verses; 'Veda' hitherto was wrongly transcribed by the Chinese characters 'Wei-t'o;' the meaning of the word is 'clear understanding' or 'knowledge.' The Vedas have been handed down from mouth to mouth, not transcribed on paper or leaves. In every generation there exist some intelligent Brahmans who can recite the 100,000 verses.[35]

Moreover, two bits of evidence, somewhat contradictory in themselves, reinforce the same conclusion: that Hinduism was not missionary. On the one hand, Yijing observes about certain rules regarding dietic impurities that "this is the custom among both the rich and poor, and is not only a custom observed by us but even by the Brāhmans (Devas, gods)." The parenthetical gloss is a bit obscure, but if Brahmins are meant, then it is clear that Brāhmaṇas and Śramaṇas observed some rules in common, so that the divide between them is thereby reduced. On the other hand, one finds anticipations of an ethnocentric conceit on the part of Indians (Hindus?), which Albīrūnī (973–1048) was to excoriate in the eleventh century AD (though here too, as with Albīrūnī, it is balanced by the author's own self-regard!). The concerned passage runs as follows:

> Besides India, there are countries of the Pārasas (Persians) and the Tajiks (generally taken as Arabs), who wear skin and trousers. In the country of the naked people (Nicobar Isles) they have no dress at all; men and women alike are all naked. From Kaśmīra to all the Mongolic countries such as Suli, Tibet, and the country of the Turkish tribes, *the customs* resemble one another to a great extent; *the*

> *people in these* countries do not wear the covering-cloth (Skt. kambala), but use wool or skin as much as they can, and there is very little karpāsa (i.e. cotton), which we see sometimes worn. As these countries are cold, the people always wear shirt and trousers. Among these countries the Pārasas, the Naked People, the Tibetans, and the Turkish tribes have no Buddhist law, but the other countries had and have followed Buddhism; and in the districts where shirts and trousers are used the people are careless about personal cleanliness.
>
> Therefore *the people of* the five parts of India are proud of their own purity and excellence. But high refinement, literary elegance, propriety, moderation, *ceremonies of* welcoming and parting, the delicious taste of food, and the richness of benevolence and righteousness are found in China only, and no other country can excel her. . . .[36]

But whether it was cultural convergence between the Hindus and Buddhists within India, or the conceit of the Indians vis-à-vis foreigners, the implication of both for Hinduism being a missionary religion is obviously negative.

We revert now to a more detailed investigation of the evidence furnished by Xuanzang about the missionary, or otherwise, character of Hinduism during his visit to India. One salient feature of Xuanzang's account[37] is the fact that it shows Buddhism in decline. This is clear from his description of the various places he visited. On numerous occasions one encounters the remark: "adherents of the different non-Buddhist sects lived pell-mell,"[38] or a similar comment. It is even more significant that the Buddhists seemed to live in anticipation of the exhaustion of their own religion. Thus, we are told about a tope:

> The Buddha predicted that when this tope had been seven times burned and seven times rebuilt, his religion would come to an end. The Records of former sages stated that the tope had already been erected and destroyed three times. When Yuan-Chuang arrived he found there has been another burning, and the work of rebuilding was still in progress.[39]

The references to the dilapidated condition of many Buddhist structures and deserted Buddhist sites only confirms this general impression that Buddhism was on the decline and that the Buddhists seem to have been aware of it.

If the Buddhists were declining relatively to non-Buddhists, then one would expect some evidence of Hindu missionary activity as an element in the process. However, rather strikingly, references to cases of conversion to Buddhism abound! However, a close inspection reveals that, but for a few exceptions, the cases refer to conversion in the Buddha's lifetime or in the following centuries.[40] Cases of conversion during Xuanzang's lifetime to Buddhism are conspicuous by their absence, except in one particular case, that of Śīlabhadra. Xuanzang narrates the story about him as follows:

> Śīlabhadra was a scion of the Brahminical royal family of Samataṭa (in East India); as a young man he was fond of learning and of exemplary principles. He traveled through India seeking the wise, and in Nālandā he met Dharmapāla P'usa who gave him instruction, and in due time ordained him as a bhikshu. Then Śīlabhadra rose to be eminent for his profound comprehension of the principles and subtleties of Buddhism, and his fame extended to foreign countries. A learned but proud and envious Brahmin of South India came to Magadha to have a discussion with Dharmapāla. Śīlabhadra, at the time the most eminent of the disciples of Dharmapāla, although only thirty years of age, proposed to meet the Brahmin in controversy, and the offer was accepted. At the discussion the Brahmin was utterly defeated, and the king to mark his appreciation of the victor's success wished to endow him with the revenues of a certain city. But Śīlabhadra declined the gift saying: "The scholar with dyed garments is satisfied with the requisites of his Order; leading a life of purity and continence what has he to do with a city?" The king, however, urged him to accept the reward; "The prince of religion has vanished" he said, "and the boat of wisdom has foundered; without public recognition there is nothing to stimulate disciples: for the advancement of Buddhism be graciously pleased to accept my offer." Then Śīlabhadra, unable to have his own way, accepted the city, and built the monastery. Carrying out the rule of right to the end, he offered up [the revenue from] the inhabitants of the city for the proper maintenance of the establishment.[41]

Later on, while describing the immensity of Nālandā, the pilgrim gives

> the names of some celebrated men of Nālandā who had kept up the luster of the establishment and continued its guiding work. There were Dharmapāla and Chandrapāla who gave a fragrance to Buddha's teachings, Guṇamati and Sthiramati of excellent reputation among contemporaries, Prabhāmitra of clear argument, and Jinamitra of elevated conversation, Jñānachandra whose perfect excellence was buried in obscurity. All these were men of merit and learning, and authors of several treatises widely known and highly valued by contemporaries.[42]

It is clear, therefore, that the conversion of Śīlabhadra to Buddhism was more or less a contemporary event—as distinguished from numerous other instances of conversions, which belonged to the past.

There is, however, one case of some interest. Xuanzang mentions a lapse from Buddhism on the part of the people of Srughna.[43] He writes: "After the Buddha's decease the people of this country had been led astray to believe in wrong religions and Buddhism had disappeared. Then Śāstra-masters from other lands defeated the Tirthikas and Brahmins in discussions, and the five monasteries already mentioned were built at the places where the discussions were held in order to commemorate the victories."[44] Thus, although a movement away from Buddhism is admitted here, it is also pointed out that the lost ground was recovered.

It thus seems difficult to attest to Hindu missionary activity even from the account of Xuanzang, notwithstanding its detailed nature and the historical fact that Buddhism seems to have been on the decline during this period. On the other hand, instances of cordial relations between the Hindus and the Buddhists are often met with. The account of Xuanzang's first meeting with Harṣa is itself instructive in this respect. While Xuanzang was studying at Nālandā, he was invited by King Bhāskarvarman to Assam (Kāmarūpa). "Śīlabhadra convinced him that it was also his duty to go to Kāmarūpa on the invitation of its king who was not a Buddhist." Thus, here we have the case of a non-Buddhist king patronizing a Buddhist. In the meantime, King Harṣa decided to hold a great Buddhist assembly at Kanauj:

> Hearing of the arrival of the Chinese pilgrim at the court of king Kumāra he sent a summons to the latter to repair to him with his foreign guest. Kumāra replied with a refusal, saying that the king could have his head but not his guest. "I trouble you for your head," came the prompt reply.

> Thereupon Kumāra became submissive and proceeded with the pilgrim and a grand retinue to join Śīlāditya. When this sovereign met Yuan-Chuang, our text here relates, having made a polite apology to the pilgrim (literally, having said—I have fatigued you) he made enquiry as to Yuan-Chuang's native land, and the object of his travelling. Yuan-Chuang answered that he was a native of the great T'ang country, and that he was travelling to learn Buddhism.[45]

King Harṣa, who came from a family of sun-worshippers,[46] treated the Buddhist monk with great respect. The way Harṣa and Bhāskarvarman treated Xuanzang serves to highlight what seems to have been a general atmosphere of cordiality, which characterized the relations between the Hindus and the Buddhists,[47] even if Xuanzang's account at times must be taken with a grain of salt.[48]

Thus, it is difficult to state that Hinduism was a missionary religion on the basis of Xuanzang's account.

III

The suggestion hitherto has been that Hinduism is not a missionary religion, as it did not display any traits of being one to outside observers. None of these observers, however, *explicitly* stated that the Hindus were not a missionary people; consequently, one had to rely on inference rather than testimony. But *argumentum et silentio* can be a weak reed on which to rest such a major statement about the characteristic features of a religious tradition. The view that Hinduism is not a missionary religion, nevertheless, receives explicit and direct support from the statements made by Albīrūnī (973–1048 AD) in his famous work on India.[49] Albīrūnī, a contemporary of Maḥmūd of Ghazna, has been widely commended,[50] and even extolled,[51] for his just portrayal of the Hindus.

In the first chapter of his book, entitled "On the Hindus in General, as an Introduction to our Account of Them," he enumerates the difficulties, which render "it so particularly difficult to penetrate to the essential nature of any Indian subject."[52] In the course of enumerating these difficulties he remarks:

> Secondly, they totally differ from us in religion, as we believe in nothing in which they believe and vice versa. On the whole, there is very little disputing about theological

> topics among themselves; at the utmost, they fight with words, but they will never stake their soul or body or their property on religious controversy. On the contrary, all their fanaticism is directed against those who do not belong to them—against all foreigners. They call them *mleccha*, i.e., impure, and forbid having any connection with them, be it by intermarriage or any other kind of relationship, or by sitting, eating, and drinking with them, because thereby, they think, they would be polluted. They consider as impure anything which touches the fire and the water of a foreigner; and no household can exist without these two elements. Besides, they never desire that a thing which once has been polluted should be purified and thus recovered, as, under ordinary circumstances, if anybody or anything has become unclean, he or it would strive to regain the state of purity. They are not allowed to receive anybody who does not belong to them, even if he wished it, or was inclined to their religion. This, too, renders any connection with them quite impossible, and constitutes the widest gulf between us and them.[53]

Thus, herein we meet with an unequivocal statement that Hindus do not convert others to their religion. What makes the passage interesting is that both the tolerance and the non-missionary nature of Hinduism are referred to simultaneously. This pattern is repeated in the accounts of several outside observers of Hinduism.

In the passage cited above, Albīrūnī can be seen as making not one but two statements about the Hindus: that they do not allow conversion to Hinduism, and that they do not allow reconversion to Hinduism. This second point is singled out for emphasis elsewhere as well, when he writes:

> I have repeatedly been told that when Hindu slaves (in Muslim countries) escape and return to their country and religion, the Hindus order that they should fast by way of expiation, then they bury them in the dung, stale, and milk of cows for a certain number of days, till they get into a state of fermentation. Then they drag them out of the dirt and give them similar dirt to eat, and more of the like.
>
> I have asked the Brahmans if this is true, but they deny it, and maintain that there is no expiation possible for

> such an individual, and that he is never allowed to return into those conditions of life in which he was before he was carried off as a prisoner. And how should that be possible? If a Brahman eats in the house of a Śūdra for sundry days, he is expelled from his caste and can never regain it.[54]

Thus, the evidence from Albīrūnī further confirms the view that Hinduism was a non-missionary religion.[55]

Another foreign observer of the Indian scene, whose account may shed some light on the nature of Hinduism in medieval times is Ibn Batūtah (1304–1368/1369), who is regarded the most important of the foreign travelers who visited India during the fourteenth and fifteenth centuries.[56] Ibn Batūtah, who was born in Tangier and died in Fez, traveled through the Indian subcontinent from 1333 to 1347 AD,[57] during the reign of Muhammad ibn Tughlaq, one of the more controversial potentates of the Sultanate period.[58] Ibn Batūtah's account of his stay in India is an invaluable source of information on Hindu attitudes.[59]

It would be difficult to characterize Hinduism as a missionary religion on the basis of Ibn Batūtah's narrative.[60] The main community at this time toward which such efforts could be directed would be the Muslim community. Ibn Batūtah's account seems to leave little doubt that, whatever else the Hindu attitude towards the Muslims may have been, it was not missionary; if anything, it was hostile (although hostility does not necessarily exclude proselytization as the work of Christian missionaries was to prove later).[61] Islam was already well established in India,[62] and Ibn Batūtah's account does not suggest that its establishment was challenged by Hindu proselytization. Even when the Hindu attitude to Muslims is not depicted as hostile,[63] no effort to convert them to Hinduism is mentioned. Rather, the Muslims were segregated into a separate community. Drawing the picture of Hindu-Muslim relations, based on Ibn Batūtah's account, R.C. Majumdar writes:

> The segregation of the Muslim community was rendered necessary, at least to a large extent, by the social rules and habits of the Hindus who regarded the Muslims as unclean and impure (*mlechchhas*). The Hindus maintained no social intercourse with the other community by way of inter-dining and intermarriage. They were uncompromising in this respect, and regarded the touch of Muslims, or even a scent of their food, as pollution. Ibn Batūtah keenly felt all this when he passed through the Hindu States of Malabar, where

> Muslims were few and far between. He justly complains that no Hindu would give a vessel to a Muslim for drinking water of a well as he would do to another Hindu. "If one happens to be a Muslim he (Hindu) pours water into his (Muslim's) hands and leaves off when the latter makes him a sign or withdraws. It is the custom among the heathens in the Malabar country that no Muslim should enter their houses or use their vessels for eating purposes. If a Muslim is fed out of their vessels, they either break the vessels, or give them away to the Musalmans" (p. 182). These Hindu ideas of untouchability concerning the Muslims were not confined to Malabar, but extended all over India, and Ibn Batūtah draws refreshing contrast in this respect between the infidels of Ceylon and those of India. The infidels of Ceylon, we are told, were unlike the infidels of India who would neither admit even Muslim fakirs in their houses nor give them food and water in their own utensils (p. xxxiv).[64]

Significantly, R.C. Majumdar concludes his discussion by remarking: "Any one who reads Ibn Batūtah's account would be reminded of what Al-Bīrūnī said regarding the attitude of the Hindus towards the Muslims and vice versa; evidently things had not improved much even after the lapse of three hundred years."[65] Lest this be regarded as an idiosyncratic conclusion, another scholar reaches a similar conclusion and institutes a similar comparison between Albīrūnī's and Ibn Batūtah's remarks. He too is constrained to remark:

> Writing in 1030, before the full tide of conquest had begun, Al-Biruni spoke of how the Hindus differed from the Muslims in every respect, and, because of the raids by Mahmud of Ghazni, cherish the most inveterate aversion toward all Muslims. Nearly three centuries later another traveler, Ibn Battuta, remarked that Hindus and Muslims lived in entirely separate communities. For Hindus, there could be no intermarriage with Muslims nor even inter-dining. "It is the custom among the heathen of the Malabar country," he remarked, "that no Muslim should enter their houses or use their vessels for eating purposes. If a Muslim is fed out of their vessels, they either break the vessels or give them away to the Muslims."[66]

Thus, Ibn Batūtah's account confirms the general impression that Hinduism was a non-missionary religion in medieval times.

The fact that Hinduism was not missionary is further confirmed by what the Portuguese Duarte Barbosa (1500–1521),[67] has to say about the Vijayanagar Empire, which flourished from the early fourteenth to the early seventeenth century AD in South India.[68]

It is significant that the Vijayanagar Empire was a Hindu empire in the sense that its rulers were Hindus[69]—although the king, according to Barbosa, allowed "such freedom that every man may come and go and live according to his own creed without suffering any annoyance, and without enquiry, whether he is Christian, Jew, Moor or Hindu."[70] This meant that, by comparison with North India, which had passed under Muslim rule, the Hindus were not under any political pressure not to convert others to Hinduism, and yet, there does not seem to be any record of any conversion to Hinduism in the accounts of foreign observers of the Vijayanagar empire. It seems that, unlike the Muslims,[71] the Hindu rulers of Vijayanagar did not use their position to encourage or force conversions to Hinduism, even though politically the

> success of the early kings was phenomenal. Ibn Batuta, who was in India from 1333 to 1342, states that even in his day a Muhammadan chief on the western coast was subject to Harihara I, whom he calls 'Haraīb' or 'Harīb' from 'Hariyappa' another form of the king's name; while a hundred years later Abdur Razzāk, envoy from Persia, tells us that the king of Vijayanagar was then lord of all Southern India, from sea to sea and from the Dakhan to Cape Comorin—'from the frontier of Serendib (Ceylon) to the extremities of the country of Kalbergah. . . . His troops amount in number to eleven lak,' i.e. 1,100,000.[72]

Yet, there is no evidence that the rulers of Vijayanagar encouraged their Muslim subjects or subordinates to convert to Hinduism.[73] Rather, Abdur Razzāk testifies to the religious tolerance of the Vijayanagar kings.[74] The accounts the Portuguese chronicler Domingo Paes (c 1520–1522) and of Fernao Nuniz, a trader (1535–1537) also do not provide so much as a hint of conversions to Hinduism.[75]

IV

The accounts of the Greek, the Chinese, and the Muslim travellers to India have now been examined, and the overwhelming impression left by a perusal of these accounts is that Hinduism as a religion was non-missionary. The arrival of Vasco da Gama at Calicut in 1498[76] led to a restoration of Europe's direct links with India, and several Europeans came to travel through and even reside in India thereafter. The accounts of some of these Europeans have already been referred to, toward the end of the last section. With the passage of time, the connection between India and Europe grew closer, and from the seventeenth century onward, one has the observations and records of several Europeans to draw on. These become even more ample from the eighteenth century onward. It is to an examination of these accounts that we must now turn for whatever light they may shed on the question of whether Hinduism was a missionary religion.

Early English travelers to India have left behind interesting accounts of India, such as those left by Father Thomas Stephens (1579–1619), a Jesuit priest, and Henry Lord, who was the chaplain at the East India Company's factory at Surat around 1630.[77] Their accounts often refer to such characteristic Hindu practices as Satī[78] and the veneration of the cow,[79] and sometimes even contain statements of Hindu beliefs;[80] and, while it is difficult to identify explicit statements to the effect that Hinduism was non-missionary, there is also nothing in them to suggest that it was. If anything, the impression that it is non-missionary religion persists.

Indeed, one begins to wonder on reading the incident with which Thomas Coryat (1612–1617) concludes his account whether even the Moghul emperor himself may not have imbibed the Hindu attitude, or at least had been influenced by it! The incident relates to Jahāngīr, the Moghul emperor, having a man whipped for not preserving his integrity as a Christian! Jahāngīr "bade all men by his example take heed, that seeing he gave liberty to all religions, that which they choose and professe, they may sticke unto."[81]

One such European traveler, who has left behind an account of his travels through Moghul India in the seventeenth century, is the French traveler Francois Bernier.[82] An incident recorded in his book, *Travels in the Moghul Empire (AD 1656–1668)*,[83] seems to confirm the view that Hinduism is a non-missionary religion. It takes place as follows. The Hindus say their *sandhyā* prayers thrice, or as Bernier puts it: "The Beths (Vedas) render it obligatory upon every gentile (Hindu) to say his prayers with his face turned to the East thrice in twenty-four hours: in the morning, at noon, and at night."[84] Bernier goes on to observe that these prayers are to be preceded by ablutions, preferably "in running rather than stagnant water," which he thought was a sound practice for a country with India's climate.

He then goes on to say:

> This, however, is found an inconvenient law to those who happen to live in cold countries, and I have met in my travels with some who placed their lives in imminent danger by a strict observance of that law, by plunging into the rivers or tanks within their reach, or if none were sufficiently near, by throwing large pots full of water over their heads. Sometimes I objected to their religion that it contained a law which it would not be possible to observe in cold climates during the winter season, which was, in my mind, a clear proof that it possessed no divine original, but was merely a system of human invention. Their answer was amusing enough. 'We pretend not,' they replied. 'that our law is of universal application. God intended it only for us, and this is the reason why we cannot receive a foreigner into our religion. We do not even say that yours is a false religion: it may be adapted to your wants and circumstances, God having, no doubt, appointed many different ways of going to heaven.' I found it impossible to convince them that the Christian faith was designed for the whole earth, and theirs was mere fable and gross fabrication.[85]

The West, as was mentioned earlier, came into renewed contact with India with the arrival of Vasco da Gama at Calicut in 1498, but this contact between the West and India really became close in the eighteenth century, in the course of the tripartite struggle for the control of India among the British, the French, and the Dutch. And, with the establishment of British Raj in India after the Battle of Plassey (1757), India came into even closer contact with the West through its connection with Britain.

The accounts of Hinduism left by Western—and specially British—travelers, scholars, and Christian missionaries further strengthen the impression that Hinduism is not a missionary religion. In 1758, John Zephaniah Holwell (1711–1779) wrote a tract entitled *The Religious Tenets of the Gentoos*. Therein, he makes two observations, which bear on the subject under discussion. The first is:

> It is necessary to remark that the Bramins did not, indeed could not, seek this intercourse, for the principles of their religion forbade their travelling, or mixing with other nations; but so famed were they in the earliest known times

> for the purity of their manners, and the sublimity of their wisdom and doctrines, that their converse was sought after, and solicited universally by the philosophers, and searchers after wisdom and truth. For this character of them, we have the concurring testimony of all antiquity.[86]

This is reminiscent of Alexander's encounter, or rather nonencounter with Dandamis, and leaves room for suggesting that even if the Hindus, or more specifically the Brahmins, did not seek to set out on their own to spread their gospel, they were at least willing to share it with those who came to them. But, as soon as we try to pin down the point further and ask, "if, as a result of this audition someone wanted to become a Hindu would he be admitted to the fold?" the answer, it seems, would have to be in the negative. Holwell remarks:

> By the fundamental doctrines and laws of the Gentoos, they cannot admit of proselytes or converts, to their faith or worship; not receive them into the pale of their communion, without the loss, of their cast, or tribe; a disgrace, which every Gentoo would rather suffer death than incur; and although this religious prohibition, in its consequences, reduced the people to a slavish dependence on their Bramins; yet it proved the cement of their union as a nation; which to this day remains unmixed with any other race of people. These are circumstances which, to the best of our knowledge, remembrance, and reading; peculiarly distinguish the Gentoos, from all the nations of the known world, and plead strongly in favour of the great antiquity of this people, as well as the originality of their scriptures.[87]

The passage is also interesting for connecting the absence of a missionary spirit with the fact of Brahmanical dominance in Hinduism. Alexander Dow (1735/1736–1779) seems to confirm this impression when he writes:

> The books which contain the religion and philosophy of the Hindoos, are distinguished by the name of Bedas. They are four in number, and like the sacred writings of other nations, are said to have been penned by the divinity. Beda in the Shanscrita, literally signifies Science; for these books not only treat of religious and moral duties, but of every branch of philosophical knowledge.

> The Bedas are, by the Brahmins, held so sacred that they permit no other sect to read them; and such is the influence of superstition and priest-craft over the minds of the other Casts in India, that they would deem it an unpardonable sin to satisfy their curiosity in that respect, were it even within the compass of their power. The Brahmins themselves are bound by such strong ties of religion, to confine those writings to their own tribe, that were any of them known to read them to others, he would be immediately excommunicated. This punishment is worse than even death itself among the Hindoos. The offender is not only thrown down from the noblest order to the most polluted Cast, but his posterity are rendered for ever incapable of being received into his former dignity.[88]

The implication of the above passage for the prospect of Hinduism being a missionary religion is seriously negative for how is a religion to be spread if its fundamental scriptures are concealed, not only from outsiders but also from many of its own adherents? Alexander Dow narrates, in an interesting flash-back, the nature of the problem. He tells us that, when the catholic Akbar (1542–1605), the greatest ruler of the Moghul Dynasty, embarked on his plan to learn about other religions, he had little difficulty in the matter

> as almost all religions admit of proselytes, Akbar had good success in his enquiries, till he came to his own subjects the Hindoos. Contrary to the practice of all other religions sects, they admit of no converts, but they allow that every one may go to heaven his own way, though they perhaps suppose, that theirs is the most expeditious method to obtain that important end. They chose rather to make a mystery of their religion, than impose it upon the world, like the Mahommedans, with the sword, or by means of the stake, after the manner of some pious Christians.[89]

It is clear the whole tenor of the account suggests that Alexander Dow did not see Hinduism as a missionary religion at all.

Another observer of the Indian scene in the latter half of the eighteenth century, Nathaniel Brassey Halhead, seems to confirm the non-missionary character of Hinduism from a loftier point of view: "It is indeed an article of faith among the Bramins, that God's all merciful power would not have permitted such a number of different religions, if he had not found a pleasure in beholding their varieties."[90]

Bishop Heber (1783–1826), who traveled through northern India in the first half of the nineteenth century, leaves the reader with the same impression, though his more specific observations deal with the problem of the conversion of people from rather than to Hinduism.[91] However, one comment seems to confirm the close association of belonging to a caste with being a Hindu, and inasmuch as one is born into a caste, this would seem to support the view that Hinduism is a non-missionary religion. The remark is anecdotal in nature and concerns an exchange of two Hindu *sepoys* after they had suppressed a Hindu-Muslim riot in Benaras, which "began by the Mussalmans breaking down a famous pillar, named Śiva's walking-staff, held in high veneration by the Hindoos."[92] Bishop Heber reports:

> Respecting the pillar a tradition had long prevailed among the Hindoos, that it was gradually sinking in the ground, that it had been twice the visible height it then shewed, and that when its summit was level with the earth, all nations were to be of one caste, and the religion of Brahma to have an end. Two brahmin Sepoys were keeping guard in the mosque, where the defaced and prostrate pillar lay. 'Ah,' said one of them, 'we have seen that which we never thought to see, Siva's shaft has its head even with the ground; we shall all be of one caste shortly, what will be our religion then?' 'I suppose the Christian,' answered the other. 'I suppose so too,' rejoined the first, 'for after all that has passed, I am sure we shall never turn Mussulmans.'[93]

While Bishop Heber was touring northern India, Abbe J.A. Dubois was touring southern India. As with Bishop Heber, it is difficult to find a clear statement in his report[94] to the effect that Hinduism is not missionary. But the implication is clear. And what is intriguing is that the passage that contains the implication follows immediately after one attesting to tolerance. Dubois observes that people in India may migrate freely from one region to another. "Indeed, every native of India is quite free to take up his abode wherever it may seem good to him. Nobody will quarrel with him for living his own life, speaking what language he pleases, or following whatever customs he is used to. All that is asked of him is that he should conform generally to the accustomed rules of decorum recognized in the neighbourhood."[95] He remarks earlier of the people of Telegu origin living in Tamil Nadu or Mysore as follows: "They always carefully avoid following the peculiar usages of their adoptive country, yet they are invariably treated with the most perfect tolerance."[96]

The paragraph containing this indication of tolerance is followed by:

> The Brahmin caste has seemed to me to merit particular attention. It is the caste whose rules and practices are most scrupulously observed. All persons who have visited India or who have any notion of the character of the Brahmins, of the high esteem in which they hold themselves, and of the distant hauteur with which they treat the common people, will be able to appreciate the difficulties which anybody must encounter who would become intimate, or ever acquainted, with these proud personages. The hate and contempt which they cherish against all strangers, and especially against Europeans; the jealous inquietude with which they hide from the profane the mysteries of their religious cult, the records of their learning; the privacy of their homes: all these form barriers between themselves and their observers which it is almost impossible to pass.
>
> Nevertheless, by much diplomacy and perseverance I have succeeded in surmounting most of the obstacles which have turned back so many others before me, I therefore trust that the minute particulars which I have given in this work will be accepted as a record of all that it is useful to know about the religious ceremonies and ritual of the Hindus.[97]

It is clear that the content of the paragraph is inconsistent with Hinduism being a missionary religion in the overall context. The impression is confirmed by his remarks about caste and caste usages, whose "strict and universal observance forms practically their whole social law."[98] Dubois is more explicit on the question of reconversion to Hinduism after loss of caste. He writes:

> There are certain offences so heinous in the sight of Hindus, however, as to leave no hope of reinstatement to those who commit them.[99]

Then Dubois refers to circumstances in which caste cannot be regained, such as open cohabitation between a Brahmin and a Pariah woman or the eating of cow's flesh, "even supposing he had committed such an awful sacrilege under a compulsion."[100] That the impossibility of reconversion to Hinduism is implied thereby is clear from the next statement:

> It would be possible to cite several instances of strange and inflexible severity in the punishment of caste offences. When the last Mussulman Prince reigned in Mysore and sought to proselytize the whole Peninsula, he began by having several Brahmins forcibly circumcised, compelling them afterwards to eat cow's flesh as an unequivocal token of their renunciation of caste. Subsequently the people were freed from the yoke of this tyrant, and many of those who had been compelled to embrace the Mahomedan religion made every possible effort, and offered very large sums, to be readmitted to Hinduism. Assemblies were held in different parts of the country to thoroughly consider their cases. It was everywhere decided that it was quite possible to purify the uncleanness of circumcision and of intercourse with Mussulmans. But the crime of eating cow's flesh, even under compulsion, was unanimously declared to be irredeemable and not to be effaced either by presents, or by fire, or by the pancha-gavia.
>
> A similar decision was given in the case of Sudras who found themselves in the same position, and who, after trying all possible means, were not more successful. One and all, therefore, were obliged to remain Mahomedans.[101]

In 1818 AD, after the final defeat of the Marathas by the British, the British Empire in India was firmly established. This was followed by the introduction of English as the official language of India and by the considerable increase in Christian missionary activity. But it was after the suppression of the so-called Sepoy Mutiny in 1858, that British paramountcy in India was so solidly established as not to be seriously questioned until the rise of the Indian independence movement. This period saw the consolidation of Indology as a branch of study, of which the study of religion was an integral part. The accounts of Hindu doctrines and practices—left behind by scholars such as W.J. Wilkins, Monier Monier-Williams, and Max Mueller—seem to confirm the impression, now so firmly rooted in foreign observations of India that Hinduism is not a missionary religion.

W.J. Wilkins clearly states of the Hindus that they "cannot proselytize, because the blessings to be enjoyed through the Hindu religion can only be obtained by those who are born in Hindu families."[102] He then proceeds to connect this absence of the missionary spirit in Hinduism with its liberal spirit in religious matters:

> So far does the liberality of the Hindu go, that whilst believing in the divine origin of his own religion, he will admit that Mohamedanism and Christianity may be given by the same Being. And further, that it is the duty of all to continue in the system in which they were born. In the shops are pictures on sale which illustrate this phase of Hindu contemporary thought. There is a figure of a man with eight arms, each of a different colour, the representatives of Brahma, Vishnu, Siva, Rama, Kali, and Durga (the most popular of the Hindu deities) Mohamed with the Koran, and Jesus with the Bible. Only birth can admit a man into the privileged classes of Hindu society, therefore it would be casting pearls before swine to attempt to proselytize other nations. The Hindu does not therefore interfere with men of other religions, nor molest those who as Hindus may differ in creed from himself. He lets other people walk in their own way, whilst he asks that they will not disturb his religious beliefs. As the Christian child sings, "I thank the goodness and the grace that on my birth have smiled" in making me a Christian, the Hindu thanks the gods that he is a Hindu; and the best wish he can express on behalf of those not so highly privileged is that in some future birth they may appear on the earth as such.[103]

Monier Monier-Williams, "having been a student of Indian sacred literature for nearly fifty years, and having thrice travelled over every part of India, from Bombay to Calcutta, from Cashmere to Ceylon," is surely entitled to our attention on his views on the question of whether Hinduism was a missionary religion or not, and they are made known to us soon, in the preface to his well-known work, *Brahmanism and Hinduism*.[104] He writes:

> It is, indeed, a solemn thought that at least 200 millions of our fellow-subjects are adherents of that religion. And yet it is a remarkable characteristic of Hinduism that it neither requires nor attempts to make converts. Nor is it by any means at present diminishing in numbers. Nor is it at present being driven off the field, as might be expected, by being

> brought into contact with two such proselyting religions as Christianity and Muhammadanism. On the contrary, it is at present rapidly increasing, for a man becomes a Hindu by merely being born a Hindu; so that every day adds to the adherents of Hinduism through the simple process of the daily increase of births over deaths, which in India is everywhere considerable. And far more remarkable than this it will be seen from what I have written in Chapter iii, that another characteristic of Hinduism is its receptivity and all-comprehensiveness. It claims to be the one religion of humanity, of human nature, of the entire world. It cares not to oppose the progress of any other system. For it has no difficulty in including all other religions within its all-embracing arms and ever-widening fold.[105]

Monier-Williams, in the course of this passage and in the book, makes several interesting points regarding Hinduism as a missionary, or rather, a non-missionary religion. He points out that, if a religion is not missionary, it does not automatically mean that it is declining in numbers or even dying—a trap Max Mueller falls into. A religion can explode not merely militarily as Islam did in the seventh and eighth centuries AD but also demographically, as Hinduism has done in the nineteenth and the twentieth centuries. Secondly, like Wilkins, Monier-Williams connects the non-missionary spirit of Hinduism with its orientation towards religious tolerance, a connection which was made earlier by Alexander Dow and which will be made repeatedly.

A famous Indologist and comparative religionist,[106] who has expressed his views on the issue in question is Max Mueller (1823–1900).[107] Although Max Mueller never set foot on Indian soil,[108] he wrote extensively about Hinduism,[109] and in a lecture delivered on the evening of December 3, 1873 at the Westminster Abbey, he addressed the matter which concerns us here directly.[110] He began by noticing that "the number of religions which have attained stability and permanence in the history of the world is very small,"[111] and proceeded to list the following eight religions: "the Jewish, the Christian, the Mohammedan, the Brahman, the Buddhist, and the Parsi" and the "two religious systems of China, that of Confucius and Lao-tse."[112]

Max Mueller then went on to make the claim that "after a careful study of the origin and growth of these religions, and after a critical examination of the sacred books on which all of them profess to be founded, it has become possible to subject them all to a scientific classification, in the same manner as languages."[113] One such classification, according to Max Mueller, is their "division into Non-Missionary and Missionary Religions."[114] Then he goes on to say: "Among the six religions of the Aryan and Semitic world, there are three that are opposed to all missionary enterprise—Judaism, Brahmanism and Zoroastrianism; and three that have a missionary character from their very beginning—Buddhism, Mohammedanism, and Christianity."[115] Then, he goes on to compare the two kinds of religions, the Missionary and the Non-Missionary, and concludes: "The former are alive, the latter are dying or dead."[116]

It is clear, then, that, for Max Mueller, Hinduism was a non-missionary religion and was therefore dying. He establishes the fact of Hinduism being a non-missionary religion by comparing it with Judaism and Buddhism.[117] If it be asserted "that it is a mistake to suppose that the Hindu religion is not proselytizing" and that "any number of outsiders, so long as they do not interfere with established castes, can form a new caste, and call themselves Hindus and the Brahmans are always ready to receive all who submit to and pay them,"[118] then Max Mueller asks: "Can this be called proselytizing? Proselytizing consists on the part of the adherents of a religion in recognizing 'the duty of spreading the truth, of refuting error, of bringing the whole world to acknowledge the paramount, if not the divine, authority of their doctrines.' "[119]

Thus, Max Mueller leaves one in no doubt about the non-missionary character of Hinduism. He then goes on to say that it is dying:

> It is true there are millions of children, women, and men in India who fall down before the stone image of Vishṇu, with his four arms, riding on a creature half bird, half man, or sleeping on the serpent; who worship Śiva, a monster with three eyes, riding naked on a bull, with a necklace of skulls for his ornament. There are human beings who still believe in a god of war, Kārtikeya, with six faces, riding on a peacock, and holding bow and arrow in his hands; and who invoke a god of success, Gaṇeśa, with four hands and an elephant's head, sitting on a rat. Nay, it is true that, in the broad daylight of the nineteenth century, the figure of the goddess Kālī is carried through the streets of her own city, Calcutta, her wild disheveled hair reaching to her feet, with a necklace of human heads, her tongue protruded from her mouth, her girdle stained with blood. All this is true; but ask any Hindu who can read and write and think, whether these are the gods he believes in, and

> he will smile at your credulity. How long this living death of national religion in India may last, no one can tell: for our purposes, however, for gaining an idea of the issue of the great religious struggle of the future, that religion too is dead and gone.
>
> The three religions which are alive, and between which the decisive battle for the dominion of the world will have to be fought, are the three missionary religions *Buddhism, Mohamedanism, and Christianity.*[120]

A subsequent observer of the Indian scene, J.N. Farquhar, who died in 1929[121] and was himself a missionary, confirmed Mueller's diagnosis and saw in the various Hindu revivalist movements the sign of Hinduism's impending demise, similar to the pattern of the brief revival of pagan religions in Rome prior to the triumph of Christianity.[122] But, although he cites several cases of the influence of missionary methods on Hinduism[123] and points out that the "dominance, of Christianity in the religious development of the last hundred years may be clearly seen in this that, almost without exception, the methods of work in use in the movements have been borrowed from the missions";[124] yet, he does not assert that Hinduism itself may be said to have become a missionary religion as a result of these efforts. Rather than themselves turning missionary, the Hindus increasingly questioned Christian missionary activity itself.[125]

J.N. Farquhar, however, does draw attention to two developments which bear on the question of Hinduism being a non-missionary religion. He refers to the existence of the All-India Śuddhi Sabhā:

> In the nineties a movement arose in the Panjab for readmitting to the Hindu community people who had passed over to other faiths. Since a Hindu becomes impure through embracing another religion, the method adopted is to subject those who return to a purifying ceremony. Hence the name Suddhi Sabha, purification society. At a later date other provinces formed similar organizations; and now there is an All-India Suddhi Sabha, which holds an annual Conference. In 1913 the Conference was held at Karachi in the Christmas holidays. The Arya Samaj still take a large share in the work, but other bodies, and notably the Prarthana Samaj, are interested.[126]

A similar provision for "re-admission of repentant converts" was also to be found in the provisions of the National Social Conference.[127]

Does this not indicate a missionary spirit on the part of Hinduism? In answering this question one must once again repeat the question asked earlier in the context of the Arya Samaj: is reconversion to Hinduism comparable to the kind of conversion which is associated with Islam and Christianity? There is obviously a fundamental difference. In the former case, the lost members are reclaimed; in the latter case, new members are gained. The second point worth noting is the universalistic claims that some Hindu bodies had begun to make. J.N. Farquhar's account of this development deserves to be cited in full, especially as it highlights the point that such a development according to him, is not intrinsic to Hinduism but the result of Christian influence and, thus, not authentically Hindu. He describes the activities of the Mahāmaṇḍala:

> It is also worthy of notice that, although the purpose of the organization is to defend and maintain the ancient religion unchanged, the modern spirit shows itself in much of the work of the Association. First of all, like every other modem religious movement in India, the Mahamandala finds itself driven to set forth the Hindu system as the religion for all mankind. To defend a religion, which is, but the religion of the Hindus is felt to be impossible for the modem mind. Hence we have the extraordinary spectacle of this organization, created for the express purpose of defending the religion which in all its own sacred books is expressly restricted to the four highest castes—Brahmans, Kshayriyas, Vaisyas and Sudras,—making the following declaration: 'But the Sanatan Dharma is not marked by any such spirit of narrowness or exclusiveness. It is not a particular creed promising salvation to its followers alone; it is the universal Dharma for all mankind.' Again, in all the sacred literature of Hinduism the rule is laid down that the Vedas must not be made known to any one except initiated members of the three twice-born castes, Brahmans, Kshatriyas and Vaisyas. No woman, and no Sudra may hear the sacred words, not to speak of Outcastes and foreigners. This rule may be found thousands of times in all the great books, legal and philosophical. In the earliest of Hindu law-books we read:
>
> 'If a Sudra listens intentionally to a recitation of the Veda, his ears shall be filled with some molten tin or lac. If he recites Veda texts, his tongue shall be cut out. If he

> remembers them, his body shall be split in twain.' Yet this most orthodox movement, backed by the heads of all the greatest Hindu sects, sells copies of any part of the Vedas to any one who cares to buy them, and encourages their study, no matter what a man's caste may be. Clearly, the freedom as well as the universality of Christianity is working with irresistible force within the very citadel of Hinduism.[128]

It is clear, therefore, that, under the influence of modern forces and the example of Christianity, Hinduism in modern times may be seen as losing some of its frigidity towards gaining converts. It cannot, however, be said to have become missionary by construing reconversion to it constituting as a special type of missionary activity (if it may be so called) because its universalism does not necessarily involve conversion. According to Farquhar, such behavior on its part is an expression of Christian influence. It may also be borne in mind that a religion may be universal in spirit without being missionary—a claim often made on behalf of neo-Hinduism.[129]

Chapter II

The Neo-Hindu Conviction that Hinduism Is a Non-Missionary Religion

During the modern period,[1] that is, since 1800 AD, the general tendency within Hinduism has been to oppose conversion. In the main, this opposition has been directed at conversion *from* Hinduism, but it has often carried with it the implication that there may be no conversion *to* Hinduism either—though, on the latter point, it presents a less unified stand than on the former.

Raja Rammohun Roy (1772/74–1833) is generally regarded as the first representative Hindu figure of the modern period. There can be little doubt that he was opposed to conversion from Hinduism to Christianity. He witnessed the intensification of Christian evangelism in India and spoke out strongly against it. In 1823, he started pseudonymously a journal entitled, *The Brahmanical Magazine*; or, *The Missionary and the Brahmun;* subtitled *Being a Vindication of the Hindoo Religion against the Attacks of Christian Missionaries*.[2]

In one of the articles published therein, he points out how Bengal has been under the British "for a period upwards of fifty years," and that while "during the first thirty years," the British seemed to follow a policy of noninterference with the religion of their subjects, "during the last twenty years, a body of English gentlemen who are called missionaries are endeavoring in several ways to convert Hindoos and Mussulmans of this country to Christianity."[3] He then proceeds to specify three such ways: publications critical of Hinduism; public preaching; and "if any natives of low origin become Christians from the desire of gain or from any other motives, these gentlemen employ and maintain them as a necessary encouragement to others to follow their example."[4]

Roy acknowledges the fact the "apostles of Jesus Christ used to preach the superiority of the Christian religion to the natives of different countries," but he sees one important difference between the apostles and the modern missionaries. The apostles did not belong to the class of rulers of the countries they preached in.[5] Roy, therefore, says that he would be far more impressed with the zeal of the missionaries if they preached in say Turkey or Persia, where they were not rulers, rather than in India. As for their scurrilous attacks on Hinduism, Roy remarks: "It seems almost natural that when one nation succeeds in conquering another, the former, tho' their religion may be quite ridiculous laugh at and despise the religion and manners of those that are fallen into their power,"[6] and then proceeds to cite several examples.

It is clear, then, that Roy was opposed to conversion by Christians. Was he, however, equally opposed to conversion to Hinduism? This was hardly a realistic possibility in his time, but the theoretical possibility of this happening does seem to have entered his mind, as may be gauged from a tangential illustration he offers. Roy was present when the missionary Alexander Duff opened a school in 1930 and tried to "remove the prejudice which the Hindu students might have against reading the Bible."[7] On that occasion, he said: "Christians like Dr. H.H. Wilson have studied the Hindu Sastras and you know that he has not become a Hindu."[8] The statement seems to concede by implication the fact that it was possible to become a Hindu. It could also be that the possibility was entertained purely for rhetorical effect. That Roy was capable of converting people is clear from the fact that he "converted to Unitarianism the Scottish missionary with whom he was translating the New Testament into Bengali,"[9] an incident that led the missionaries to bemoan the event as the Second Fall of Adam, because the name of the person involved was Adam! It should also be borne in mind that, according to the trust deed of the Brahmo Samaj, the organization Roy founded, members of any religion could attend its functions. This is indicative of Hindu tolerance on the one hand; on the other hand, however, the statement does make it possible for non-Hindus to identify with this Brahmo version of Hinduism. On the whole, however, both by temper[10] and example,[11] Roy probably would not have encouraged conversion to Hinduism; in any case, he was more concerned with stopping conversion from it.[12]

A few other pieces of evidence further seem to suggest that Roy would not have looked upon any missionary enterprise on the part of Hinduism with favor. First of all, there is the negative argument that, in one context, he attributed the decline of the Hindus to casteism and pacifism[13] and does not specifically identify their unwillingness to make converts as a factor in the decline.[14] Second, in the passage quoted earlier, it is possible to detect anticipations of the position developed more fully subsequently: that the true end of religious activity or evangelical activity should not be to make a Hindu or a Muslim into a Christian but to make a Hindu a better Hindu, a Muslim a better Muslim and a Christian a better Christian—that we should "endeavour to improve our intellectual and moral faculties, relying on the goodness of the Almighty Power, which alone enables us to attain that which we earnestly and diligently seek."[15] Finally, Roy had already "struck a note of universalism which is heard again and again in the teachings of the Hindu prophets of the new age."[16] He wrote in 1831:

> It is now generally admitted that not religion only but unbiased commonsense as well as the accurate deductions of scientific research leads to the conclusion that all mankind are one great family of which numerous nations and tribes existing are only branches. Hence enlightened men in all countries feel a wish to encourage and facilitate human intercourse in every manner by removing as far as possible all impediments to it in order to promote the reciprocal advantage and enjoyment of the whole human race.[17]

It is true that such universalism in a religion need not necessarily be inconsistent with the missionary enterprise. Christianity and Islam are universalistic religions, as well as missionary religions, but in the Hindu case, a universalistic position usually goes hand in hand with an attitude that is critical of the missionary endeavor undertaken by any religion.

Thus, on balance, it seems fair to claim that Roy would have regarded Hinduism as a non-missionary religion. The same seems to hold true of his successors in the Brahmo Samaj movement, which he founded—though with a difference of degree. This difference is least in the case of Devendranath Tagore (1817–1905), who was actually greatly offended by Christian missionary activity and did his best to counter it. So, Tagore was squarely opposed to conversion to Christianity.[18] He too, like Roy, welcomed new members into the Brahmo Samaj, but given its nonsectarian and universalistic orientation, it is difficult to apply the word *conversion* to the kind of adherence involved. Keshub Chunder Sen (1838–1884) was the one least opposed to Christianity among the leaders of the Brahmo Samaj, but even he seems to have had only limited enthusiasm for its missionary aspect. It is noteworthy though that a conversation he had with Max Mueller in England seems to imply that he might have considered becoming a Christian but for the fact that he would lose all influence in public life if he publicly did so.[19] So, whether by precept or practice, all three—Roy, Tagore, and Sen—did not favor conversion to Christianity—or, for that matter, to Hinduism.

The next prominent Hindu whose views on this issue to be examined is Mahadev Govind Ranade (1842–1901). As in the case of Roy, it is difficult to identify a definite statement that indicated his position—but again as with Roy, the implications of his various pronouncements point clearly in the direction of the position that Hinduism was non-missionary. Some incidents of his life also tend to confirm this view. One such incident has been referred to rather appropriately by D.S. Sarma as "storm in the tea-cup."[20] The details of the incident are as follows: In 1890, some prominent gentlemen of Poona, including Ranade, were invited to a missionary meeting at which biscuits and tea were served. "Ranade only touched the cups formally and set them aside,"[21] but this implied dining with Christians and led to "an outcry on the part of the orthodox Brahmans of Poona, who condemned the action of the 'rebels' and threatened them with excommunication."[22] Ranade had to perform (along with B.G.Tilak, another national leader, who was also involved in the incident) the "necessary purificatory ceremonies" to "have the social boycott lifted. The purification was particularly humiliating to Ranade, as he was the leader of the reform party. But Ranade's object in consenting to undergo purification was to prevent people from thinking that social reform necessarily meant eating and drinking with men of their religions."[23] At least two points become clear from this incident: first, that Ranade was primarily concerned with social reform within Hinduism rather than with extending its frontiers, and second, that he could hardly have visualized the latter possibility if merely eating and drinking with members of other religions called for ritual purification. How could evangelical activity be carried out among non-Hindus with such an attitude, even if accepted under duress. While one can only guess at Ranade's attitude to conversion to Hinduism, his attitude about conversion from Hinduism was one of opposition to it. Ranade broke off from the Sadan when Tilak's efforts exposed the essentially proselytizing intent underlying the Sarada Sadan, founded by the famous Hindu-turned-Christian Pandita Ramabai. In Ranade's letter of resignation, he wrote: "If the Sadan is to be conducted as an avowed proselytizing institution we must disavow all connection with it."[24]

Some of the statements made by Ranade give the impression that he would have regarded Hinduism as a non-missionary religion. Firstly, he accepted wholeheartedly the Hindu tolerance of religious diversity. An iconoclastic spirit is characteristic of Islam, and to a lesser extent, of Christianity, both of which are missionary religions. In view of this fact, the following remarks by Ranade on the absence of it in Hinduism would also seem to imply the non-missionary character of Hinduism:

> The supremacy of one God, One without a second, was the first article of the creed with every one of these [Bhakti] saints, which they would not allow anybody to question or challenge. At the same time as observed above, the iconoclastic spirit was never characteristic of this country, and all the various forms in which God was worshipped were believed to merge finally into one Supreme Providence or *Brahma*. This tendency of the national mind was a very old tendency. Even in the Vedic times, Indra and Varuna, Marut and Rudra, while they were specially invoked at the sacrifices offered for their acceptance, were all regarded as interchangeable forms of the One and supreme Lord of Creation.[25]

It should be noted that, of the Semitic religions, it is Judaism alone which was generally regarded as non-missionary at the time.[26] It may not be entirely insignificant then that Ranade compared the lot of the Hindus to the Jews and remarked: "If the miraculous preservation of a few thousand Jews had a purpose, this more miraculous preservation of one-fifth of the human race is not due to mere chance."[27] But he also remarked: "I profess implicit faith in two articles of my creed. This country of ours is the true land of promise. This race of ours is the chosen race."[28] Judaic sentiments, very. As with Judiasm, a Hindu claim of being a chosen people need not imply that it is a proselytizing religion. The next representative figure of modern Hinduism is Swami Dayananda Sarasvati (1824–1883),[29] who founded the Arya Samaj in 1975.[30] Swami Dayananda is a special case of the general view being developed in this chapter, that Hinduism is non-missionary, for he took the view, unlike the other spokesmen of Hinduism during this period, that Hinduism should accept the conversion of those people back to Hinduism who had gone over to Islam or Christianity. This was to be brought about by a process which was called *śuddhi* (purification). Does this not compromise the view that Hinduism is non-missionary?

On the face of it does, for it makes Hinduism emerge as a proselytizing religion. In this case, however, two points need to be borne in mind: (1) Although *śuddhi* at the first glance implies conversion to Hinduism, a closer look reveals that it is really a case of *re*conversion to Hinduism. This is implied by the word *śuddhi*, which means purification. According to this view, those Hindus who became Muslims or Christians in former times thereby became impure and placed themselves outside the pale of Hindu society. Now, these former Hindus were to be welcomed back into the fold after being purified for this lapse. Thus, even Dayananda's provision for conversion to Hinduism turns out to be a case of reconversion and represents not a forward movement but rather a rearguard action. (2) Although this movement met with some success (notably among the Malkana Rajputs),[31] it was criticized by most of the other spokesmen of modern Hinduism, particularly by Mahatma Gandhi.[32]

Remarkably, Dayananda not only provided for reconversion to Hinduism but also departed from the traditional Hindu attitude of tolerance towards other religions by criticizing them vehemently.[33] This is significant in view of the fact that, within Hinduism, one usually finds religious tolerance and nonproselytization going hand in hand, even appearing at times like two sides of the same coin. That, in the case of Dayananda, the provision for reconversion should be accompanied by a sharp criticism of other religions seems to afford a parallel correlation. Just as tolerance and non-proselytization go hand in hand; so also intolerance and proselytization seem to go hand in hand. Dayananda's attacks on other religions were also criticized by Mahatma Gandhi. He wrote:

> I have profound respect for Dayananda Saraswati. I think that he has rendered great service to Hinduism. His bravery was unquestioned. But he made his Hinduism narrow. I have read the *Satyarthaprakash*, the Arya Samaj Bible. Friends sent me three copies of it whilst I was resting in the Yeravda Jail. I have not read a more disappointing book from a reformer so great. He has claimed to stand for truth and nothing less. But he has unconsciously misrepresented Jainism, Islam, Christianity and Hinduism itself. One having even a cursory acquaintance with these faiths could easily discover the errors into which the great reformer was betrayed.

> He has tried to make narrow one of the most tolerant and liberal of faiths on the face of the earth. And an iconoclast though he was, he has succeeded in enthroning idolatry in the subtlest form. For he has idolized the letter of the *Vedas* and tried to prove the existence in the Vedas of everything known to science. The Arya Samaj flourishes in my humble opinion not because of the inherent merit of the teachings of the *Satyarthaprakash*, but because of the great and lofty character of the founder. Wherever you find Arya Samajists there is life and energy. But having a narrow outlook and a pugnacious habit they either quarrel with people of other denominations and failing them with one another.[34]

Before one proceeds further, however, the attitude of Dayananda towards other religions needs to be clarified. Dayananda is believed to have been hostile towards religions other than Hinduism[35]—perhaps more so than any other leader of the Hindu renaissance—but his position needs to be analyzed with greater care than seems to have been bestowed on it.[36] He clearly states in his Autobiography that "my sole object is to believe in what is true and help others to believe in it. I neither accept the demerits of different faiths whether Indian or alien, nor reject what is good in them."[37] It is noteworthy that Dayananda "attacks what he calls 'untrue elements' in Islam or Christianity the same way as he does in regard to Hinduism. He shows no leniency to the latter on account of its being 'his own, or that of his forefathers' religion.' "[38]

It is well-known that Swami Vivekananda[39] attended the Parliament of World Religions in Chicago in 1893; however, it is not as well known that Swami Dayananda "went so far as to invite a conference of the representatives of all religions, on the occasion of the Delhi Durbar in 1877. Keshub Chandra Sen, Sir Syed Ahmad, and Munshi Alakhdhari were among those who responded to the invitation. Dayananda's proposal was premature, but his idea that the exponents of various faiths should put their heads together to evolve a formula of united activity was unique in those days."[40] In the introduction to the *Satyārthaprakāśa*, he writes:

> At present there are learned men in all religions. If they give up prejudices, accept all those broad principles on which all religions are unanimous, reject differences and behave affectionately towards each other, much good will be done

> to the world. The differences of learned people aggravate the differences among the common masses with the result that miseries increase and happiness is lost.[41]

It is also noteworthy that he concludes his statements of beliefs and disbeliefs with the following comment:

> In short, I accept universal maxims: for example, speaking of truth is commended by all, and speaking of falsehood is condemned by all. I accept all such principles. I do not approve of the wrangling of the various religions against one another for they have, by propagating their creeds, misled the people and turned them into one another's enemy. My purpose and aim is to help in putting and end to this mutual wrangling, to preach universal truth, to bring all men under one religion so that they may, by ceasing to hate each other and firmly loving each other, live in peace and work for their common welfare. May this view through the grace and help of the Almighty God, and with the support of all virtuous and pious men, soon spread in the whole world so that all may easily acquire righteousness, wealth, gratification of legitimate desires and attain salvation, and thereby elevate themselves and live in happiness. This alone is my chief aim.[42]

It should be noted, however, that this one religion under which all were to live in harmony seems to have had for him both a moral and a revelatory component. Men of all religions could act together on the moral plane, but if they were to belong to one true religion, it had to be the Vedic revelation.[43] In order to accomplish this latter goal it was the duty of the Arya Samaj "(a) to recall India to the forsaken *Vedic* paths and (b) to preach the Vedic gospel throughout the whole world."[44] This latter approach, however, did not prove as effective as the former.

As a result of all these considerations, one may have to modify the widely held view that Swami Dayananda represented a departure from the cosmopolitan temper of modern Hinduism. He did represent a point of departure in one respect: he advocated the reconversion of Hindus who had formerly been converted to religions other than Hindu—primarily Islam and Christianity—and were now willing to return to the Hindu fold. But does this make Hinduism a missionary religion in the same sense as Islam and Christianity? The reclaiming of members of one's religion lost to other religions needs to be clearly distinguished from seeking fresh converts. When it is recognized that, what Swami Dayananda advocated was reconversion and not conversion the position of Swami Dayananda seems to represent less of a departure from than a refinement of the more general view that Hinduism is non-missionary. It must be conceded, however, that his position represents a special case of the general view that Hinduism is non-missionary.[45]

The attitudes of Raja Rammohun Roy, M.G. Ranade, and Swami Dayananda Sarasvati among the spokesmen of modern Hinduism have hitherto been examined on the question of whether Hinduism was a missionary religion or not. One may now turn to the Theosophical Society and examine its view on this point. Some readers will doubtless wonder whether the Theosophical Society is to be regarded as a Hindu body. Whether in itself Hindu or not, there can be little doubt that the Theosophical Society constituted an element in the evolving neo-Hindu worldview. To be sure, it was founded in New York in 1875 by Madame Blavatsky and Colonel Olcott,[46] but its headquarters were moved to Adyar, near Madras, in 1882.[47] It seems desirable, therefore, that the Theosophical position on the question of the missionary character of Hinduism be examined in some detail, especially in view of its impact on Hinduism. As D.S. Sarma has observed:

> Even Farquhar, the Christian Missionary writer, who has given an extremely unfavorable account of the Theosophical Society in his *Modern Religious Movements in India,* admits the service rendered by the society to Hinduism and Buddhism. He says that 'for several decades Hindu and Buddhist thought and civilization were most unjustly depreciated and unmercifully condemned by Missionaries, by Europeans in general and even by some Hindus,' and so there was good reason for such a crusade in defense of them as was undertaken by the Theosophists.[48]

The position of the Theosophical society on both conversion to and from Hinduism is quite clear. If the stated objects of the Society are any guide, it was clearly opposed to conversion *from* Hinduism. One of these was "to counteract as far as possible the efforts of the missionaries to delude the so-called 'Heathens' and 'Pagans' as to the real origin and dogmas of Christianity, . . ."[49] so that it may be safely assumed it was opposed to Christian missionary activity. We meet with the following unambiguous pronouncement by Annie Besant

(1847–1933) on the question of whether Hinduism itself was a missionary religion:

> And if Hindus do not maintain Hinduism who shall save it? If India's own children do not cling to her faith, who shall guard it? India alone can save India, and India and Hinduism are one. No one in a Western body can do what you can do. No love of mine for India, no fullness of service, no completeness of devotion, can do in this alien body what you, India's sons, can do. A Hindu is born, he is not made. No amount of service to Hinduism, no practice of Hindu teachings, no training in Hindu wisdom, can make a non-Hindu into a Hindu. Hence, even those of us who have Hindu hearts, and have past Hindu lives behind us, can only help you, the main work you must do for yourselves.[50]

It is also significant that membership in the Theosophical Society did not involve severing connections with one's ancestral faith. Indeed the claim was made that a Theosophist was enabled to penetrate to the heart of his or her own religions tradition. Thus Annie Besant wrote:

> No man in becoming a Theosophist need cease to be a Christian, a Buddhist, a Hindu; he will but acquire a deeper insight into his own faith, a firmer hold on its spiritual truths, a broader understanding of its sacred teachings. As Theosophy of old gave birth to religion, so in modern times does it justify and defend them. It is the rock whence all of them were hewn, the hole in the pit whence all were digged. It justifies at the bar of intellectual criticism the deepest longings of the human heart; it verifies our hopes for man; it gives back ennobled our faith in God.[51]

The passage seems to reflect the standard neo-Hindu position that the religious task was not to make a Muslim of the Hindu or a Christian of the Muslim—but to make a Hindu a better Hindu, a Muslim a better Muslim, and a Christian a better Christian.

Thus—in its origin, aspirations, and influence—the Theosophical Society seemed to share the neo-Hindu ethos in which the nondesirability of conversion in general, and the non-missionary character of Hinduism in particular, are important ingredients.

No discussion of the neo-Hindu attitude to conversion can afford to omit the position adopted towards this issue by Ramakrishna Paramahamsa (1836–1886) and his famous disciple, Swami Vivekananda (1869–1902).

Ramakrishna is a familiar figure in the study of modern Hinduism, and several accounts of his life are now available. Most of these writings basically recapitulate the facts and arguments of three lengthy hagiographies: *Sri Ramakrishna: The Great Master* by Swami Saradananda, a disciple's attempt to present a comprehensive interpretation of Ramakrishna as an *avatara*; *The Gospel of Sri Ramakrishna* by Mahendranath Gupta, a householder devotee's ostensibly stenographic record of many of Ramakrishna's conversations with his followers; *Life of Sri Ramakrishna Compiled from Various Authentic Sources*, a comprehensive source of historical facts about Ramakrishna. But despite these efforts, work by recent scholars indicates that much remains to be done in analyzing the relationships between Ramakrishna's life, his message, and the central elements of Indian culture and religion.

While some ambiguities may surround some aspects of Ramakrishna's life and teachings, there is no gainsaying the fact, that the range of his mystical experiences was unusually versatile, and that as a result of these experiences, he came to the conclusion that all religions are true.

A survey of the religious experiences of Ramakrishna reveals that, although himself a Hindu, he had mystical visions of Christ and Muhammad. Ramakrishna had the Bible read to him and had pictures of Jesus in the parlor, one of which was of the child Jesus in his mother's lap. His biographer records:

> The Master used to say that he sat one day in that parlour and was looking intently on that picture and thinking of the extraordinary life of Jesus, when he felt as if the picture came to life and effulgent rays of light, coming out from the bodies of the mother and the child, entered into his heart. . . .[52]

The biographer also records that on the third day of his devotion to Jesus

> the Master saw, while walking under the Panchavati, that a marvelous god-man of very fair complexion was coming towards him, looking steadfastly at him. As soon as the Master saw that person, he knew that he was a foreigner.

> He saw that his long eyes had produced a wonderful beauty on his face, and the tip of his nose, though a little flat, did not at all impair the beauty . . .
>
> Very soon the person approached him and from the Master's pure heart came out the words with ringing sound, "Jesus, Jesus the Christ, the great Yogi, the loving son of God and one with the Father, who gave his heart's blood and put up with endless torture in order to deliver men from sorrow and misery!"[53]

Similarly, Ramakrishna also had a vision of the Prophet. He was initiated into Islamic practices by a Hindu convert, Govind Rai, and

> engaged himself in practicing Islam according to its prescribed rules. The Master said, "I then devotionally repeated the holy syllable 'Allah,' wore cloth like the Muslims, said Namaz thrice daily and felt disinclined even to see Hindu deities not to speak of saluting them, inasmuch as the Hindu mode of thought vanished altogether from my mind. I spent three days in that mood, and had the full realization of the result of the practices according to that faith." At the time of practicing Islam the Master at first had the vision of an effulgent, impressive personage with a long beard . . .[54]

Ramakrishna had undergone several phases of Hindu religious practices before he turned to experimenting with non-Hindu religions. Two such experiences of his are of capital importance from the point of view of this book. His first major mystical experience was a vision of Kali—the goddess. He describes it in these words:

> I was then suffering from excruciating pain because I had not been blessed with a vision of the Mother. I felt as if my heart were being squeezed like a wet towel. I was overpowered by a great restlessness, and a fear that it might not be my lot to realize Her in this life. I could not bear the separation any longer: life did not seem worth living. Suddenly my eyes fell on the sword that was kept in the Mother's temple. Determined to put an end to my life, I jumped up like a madman and seized it, when suddenly the blessed Mother revealed herself to me, and I fell unconscious

> on the floor. What happened after that externally, or how that day or the next passed, I do not know, but within me there was a steady flow of undiluted bliss altogether new, and I felt the presence of the Divine Mother.[55]

This experience obviously corresponds to the theistic type of mystical experience. Ramakrishna had several such experiences. Towards the end of 1865, however, he was coached in the monistic approach to reality. Ramakrishna again describes his experiences in his own words as follows:

> After the initiation my guru began to teach me the various conclusions of the Advaita Vedanta and asked me to withdraw the mind completely from all objects and dive into the Atman (self). But in spite of all my attempts I could not cross the realm of name and form, and bring my mind to the unconditioned state. I had no difficulty in withdrawing the mind from all objects except one, the all too familiar form of the Blissful Mother—radiant and of the essence of Pure Consciousness—which appeared before me as a living reality preventing me from passing beyond the realm of name and form. Again and again I tried to concentrate my mind upon the teachings of Advaita (non-dualism), but every time the Mother's form stood in my way. In despair I said to the guru, "It is hopeless. I cannot raise my mind to the unconditioned state and come face to face with the Atman (Self)." He grew excited and sharply said, "What! You can't do it! But you have to." He cast his eyes round, and, finding a piece of glass, took it up; then, pressing the point between my eyebrows, he said, "concentrate the mind on this point!" Then with a stern determination I again sat to meditate and as soon as the gracious form of the Divine Mother appeared before me, I used my power of discrimination as a sword and with it severed her form in two. There remained no more obstruction to my mind, which at once soared beyond the relative plane, and I was lost in samadhi (super-consciousness).[56]

Thereafter Ramakrishna returned to normal consciousness only after great effort. In the description which follows one sees the reemergence of the theistic element after the monistic experience.

> After his guru had left Dakshineswar, Sri Ramakrishna was determined to remain in a state of absolute identity with Brahman. He accordingly meditated and entered into nirvikalpa samadhi again. Referring to this period of his life, he used to say, "For six months at a stretch I remained in that state whence ordinary men can never return—the body falling off after twenty-one days like a seared leaf. I was not conscious of day and night, flies would enter my mouth and nostrils just as they do in a dead body, but I did not feel them; the hair became matted with accretions of dust. There was no chance for the body to survive, and it would certainly have perished but for the kind ministrations of a monk who was present at Dakshineswar at the time. He realized the state of my mind and also understood that this body must be kept alive at any cost since it was to be of immense good to the world. He therefore busied himself in preserving this body. He would bring food regularly to me and try various ways to bring my mind down to the consciousness of the relative world, even by beating me with a stick. As soon as he found me to be a little conscious, he would press some food into my mouth, only a bit of which reached the stomach; and there were days in which all his efforts would be in vain. Six months passed in this way. At last I received the Mother's command, 'Remain on the threshold of relative consciousness (bhavamukha) for the sake of humanity.' Then I was laid up with a terrible attack of dysentery; an excruciating pain in the stomach tortured me day and night; it went on for six months. Thus only did the mind gradually come down to a lower level and to consciousness of the body. I became a normal man; but before that at the slightest opportunity the mind would take a transcendental flight and merge in the nirvikalpa samadhi. . . ."
>
> Sri Ramakrisha . . . had thus gone through the whole range of Hindu disciplines in the course of twelve years, from his eighteenth year to his thirtieth. He had become a Paramahamsa.[57]

What are we to make of conversion from one religion to another in the light of these experiences of Ramakrishna? As Huston Smith has pointed out, "out of these experiences came a set of teachings on the essential unity of the great religions which comprise Hinduism's finest voice on this matter."[58] He then cites several statements of Ramakrishna, some of which are reproduced below.

> God has made different religions to suit different aspirants, times, and countries. All doctrines are only so many paths; but a path is by no means God Himself. Indeed, one can reach God if one follows any of the paths with whole hearted devotion. One may eat a cake with icing either straight or sidewise. It will taste sweet either way.
>
> As one and the same material, water, is called by different names by different peoples, one calling it water, another eau, a third aqua, and another pani, so the one Everlasting-Intelligent-Bliss is invoked by some as God, by some as Allah, by some as Jehovah, and by others as Brahman.
>
> As one can ascend to the top of a house by means of a ladder or a bamboo or a staircase or a rope, so diverse are the ways and means to approach God, and every religion in the world shows one of these ways.
>
> As the young wife in a family shows her love and respect to her father-in-law, mother-in-law, and every other member of the family, and at the same tine loves her husband more than these, similarly, being firm in thy devotion to the deity of thy own choice, do not despise other deities, but honor them all.
>
> Bow down and worship where others kneel, for where so many have been paying the tribute of adoration the kind Lord must manifest himself, for he is all mercy.
>
> The devotee who has seen God in one aspect only, knows him in that aspect alone. But he who has seen him in manifold aspects is alone in a position to say, 'All these forms are of one God and God is multiform.' He is formless and with form, and many are his forms which no one knows.
>
> The Saviour is the messenger of God. He is like the viceroy of a mighty monarch. As when there is some disturbance in a far-off province, the king sends his viceroy to quell it, so wherever there is a decline of religion in any part of the world, God sends his Saviour there. It is one and the same Saviour that, having plunged into the ocean of life, rises up in one place and is known as Krishna (the leading Hindu incarnation of God), and diving down again rises in another place and is known as Christ.

> People partition off their lands by means of boundaries, but no one can partition off the all-embracing sky overhead. The indivisible sky surrounds all and includes all. So common man in ignorance says, "my religion is the only one, my religion is the best." But when his heart is illumined by true knowledge, he knows that above all these wars of sects and sectarians presides the one indivisible, eternal, all-knowing bliss.
>
> As a mother, in nursing her sick children, gives rice and curry to one, and sago arrowroot to another, and bread and butter to a third, so the Lord has laid out different paths for different men suitable to their natures.
>
> Dispute not. As you rest firmly on your own faith and opinion, allow others also the equal liberty to stand by their own faiths and opinions. By mere disputation you will never succeed in convincing another of his error. When the grace of God descends on him, each one will understand his own mistakes.[59]

The final implication of Ramakrishna's experiences and sayings for the issue of conversion is best presented in his own words:

> Every man should follow his own religion. A Christian should follow Christianity, a Mohamedan should follow Mohammedanisrn, and so on. For the Hindus the ancient path, the path of the Aryan sages, is the best.[60]

In other words: neither convert nor be converted. The implication clearly is that Hinduism, and indeed all religions, should not proselytize.

This message was carried to the West by his disciple Swami Vivekananda. When he addressed the World Parliament of Religions in Chicago in 1893, his entire speech, which was much applauded, was shot through with references to the religious tolerance of the Hindus. Almost the entire address, which was brief, is a plea for religious toleration, as the following passages demonstrate.

> I am proud to belong to a religion which has taught the world both tolerance and universal acceptance. We believe not only in universal toleration, but *we accept all religions as true.* I am proud to belong to a nation which has sheltered the persecuted and the refugees of all religions and all

> nations of the earth. I am proud to tell you that we have gathered in our bosom the purest remnant of the Israelites, who came to Southern India and took refuge with us in the very year in which their holy temple was shattered to pieces by Roman tyranny. I am proud to belong to the religion which has sheltered and is still fostering the remnant of the grand Zoroastrian nation. I will quote to you, brethren, a few lines from a hymn which I remember to have repeated from my earliest boyhood, which is every day repeated by millions of human beings: "*As the different streams having their sources in different places all mingle their water in the sea, so, O Lord, the different paths which men take through different tendencies, various though they appear, crooked or straight, all lead to Thee.*"
>
> The present convention, which is one of the most august assemblies ever held, is in itself a vindication, a declaration to the world of the wonderful doctrine preached in the Gita: "Whosoever comes to Me through whatsoever form, I reach him; all men are struggling through paths which in the end lead to me." Sectarianism, bigotry, and its horrible descendant, fanaticism, have long possessed this beautiful earth. They have filled the earth with violence, drenched it often and often with human blood, destroyed civilization and sent whole nations to despair. Had it not been for these horrible demons, human society would be far more advanced than it is now. But their time is come, and I fervently hope that the bell that tolled this morning in honour of this convention may be the death-knell of all fanaticism, of all persecutions with the sword or with the pen, and of all uncharitable feelings between persons wending their way to the same goal.[61]

If, "all religions are true" then conversion from one religion to another makes little spiritual sense.

> Plainly, if all religions are true, there would be no point in exchanging one true religion for another. Conversion, then, must be vigorously resisted since it means the violent uprooting of the convert and unnecessary distress both for him and for those near and dear to him whom he has left behind. "Do I wish that the Christian would become a Hindu?" he exclaims, "God forbid. Do I wish that the Hindu

> or Buddhist would become a Christian? God forbid. . . . The Christian is not to become a Hindu or a Buddhist, nor a Hindu or a Buddhist to become a Christian."[62]

It is clear, therefore, that neo-Hinduism, as represented by Ramakrishna and Vivekananda, clearly looked upon Hinduism as a non-missionary religion. In fact they seemed to go a step further and questioned the value of the missionary enterprise on anyone's part.

Another leading figure of modern India is Rabindranath Tagore (1861–1941), whose understanding of the nature of Hinduism must now be taken into account. Rabindranath Tagore was above all an author and poet, but[63]

> Tagore was more than a poet, he was also one of, the most famous Indians of his generation. The award of the Nobel Prize in 1913 for his poetry made him a world figure and gave him enormous prestige in India. This meant that, whatever his own inclinations might be, he had to relate himself to the nationalist movement then gaining momentum. Profoundly patriotic, he desired India's political freedom; at the same time he was repelled by many features of the nationalist movement. It seemed to him that Indian nationalism threatened India with the same evils that were destroying the West, and he refused to give his wholehearted support to the Indian National Congress. This led him into conflict with some of the nationalist leaders, but the greatest of them, including Gandhi, recognized that his opposition arose from the splendor of his vision of India's role in the world, not from any attachment to British rule. He did not stress, as had Vivekananda, the materialism of the West over against the spirituality of India, but he saw India's destiny as the creator of a new order of civilization and culture. A narrow and parochial nationalism, he believed, would make this impossible; therefore, India should strive to keep open the channels of spiritual communication with all the world. Although his vision fades with the passing years, he remains as one of the most attractive exponents of a vital element of the Hindu tradition.[64]

In his exposition of the Hindu tradition, Tagore emphasized its universality over its ethnicity. A classic illustration of this is provided by his famous novel *Gora*.

In his *Gora* he has given us his impartial criticism of the Brahmo Samaj as well as of Hindu orthodoxy. He has painted a faithful picture of the parent community and its Protestant sect as they appeared to him at the time. In this novel there is an unforgettable scene in which the heroine, the good Sucharita, who was brought up in a strict Brahmo family, rebels against the sectarian intolerance and self-righteousness of the Brahmo preacher, Haran Babu, who had hopes of marrying her. Haran comes one morning to her, while she was frying vegetables in her kitchen, and severely taxes her for her conduct in encouraging her "sister" Lalita to marry Vinoy, who does not belong to the Brahmo Samaj. In reply to all his stinging remarks, Sucharita keeps exclaiming, "I am a Hindu," "I know I am a Hindu," "I can tell you one thing, I am a Hindu," "The Lord of my heart knows about my religion and I do not propose to discuss it with anyone. But you can be certain of one thing, namely, that I am a Hindu." As against this, we have at the end of the novel the words of the hero, Gora, to Paresh Babu, the saintly Brahmo householder, when he found that the bottom of all his enthusiastic championship of Hindu orthodoxy throughout the novel was knocked out by the revelation that he was himself a foundling of Irish Parentage and thence technically, according to Hindu orthodoxy, an outcaste:

"Today give me the mantram of that Deity who belongs to all, Hindu, Mussalmin, Christian and Brahmo alike, the doors to whose temple are never closed to any persons of any caste whatever, He who is not only the God of the Hindus, but who is the God of India itself." Thereupon the hero and the heroine join hands. The lesson that Tagore wants to teach through these situations is obvious.[65]

Tagore emphasized the universal not merely in his prose writings but also in his poetry. Firstly, his poetry is essentially in line with the tradition of medieval devotional poets like Kabir, some of whose works he translated into English. This devotional poetry expressed the religious sentiments of the masses and was for the masses—as distinguished from the intellectual tradition of Hinduism, which was confined to the higher classes.[66] These devotional songs are addressed to God the Supreme Person, not to the Impersonal Absolute. In this respect, Tagore was obviously influenced by the Bauls of Bengal. He writes:

> I mention in connection with my personal experience some songs which I have often heard from wandering village singers, belonging to a popular sect of Bengal, called Bauls, who have no images, temples, scriptures, or ceremonials, who declare in their songs the divinity of Man, and express for him an intense feeling of love. Coming from men who are unsophisticated, living a simple life in obscurity, it gives us a clue to the inner meaning of all religions. For it suggests that these religions are never about a God of cosmic force, but rather about the God of human personality.[67]

The concept of God as a person is much more popular than that of God as an impersonal being, so that to begin with Tagore strikes a more universal chord. Secondly, Tagore's devotional poetry dispenses with "mythological symbols and sectarian names and forms. He uses the universal language of man."[68] Finally, nature mysticism plays a much more significant role in Tagore's poetry than has usually been the case.[69] Human beings may differ in culture, but they may differ much less in relation to nature. All these elements combine to impart to Tagore's religious vision a universal dimension.

Tagore articulated this universal vision in his well-known work *The Religion of Man*. Therein, he asserts that religion basically relates to man as such,[70] a thesis with obviously universal overtones. The fact that the world has possessed several cultures or has passed through different historical phases should not obscure the fact of their unity and common humanity. He writes about these cultures:

> The civilizations evolved in India or China, Persia or Judea, Greece or Rome, are like several mountain peaks having different altitude, temperature, flora and fauna, and yet belonging to the same chain of hills. There are no absolute barriers of communication between them; their foundation is the same and they affect the meteorology of an atmosphere which is common to us all. This is at the root of the meaning of the great teacher who said he would not seek his own salvation if all men were not saved; for we all belong to a divine unity, from which our great-souled men have their direct inspiration; they feel it immediately in their own personality, and they proclaim in their life, "I am one with the Supreme, with the Deathless, with the Perfect."[71]

Similarly, if one takes the simplistic view that the history of humanity really consists of two major revolutions, the agricultural and the industrial, then one can relate easily to Tagore's view that the industrial revolution has the potential of generating a world community, just as the agricultural revolution created national communities in place of tribal ones.[72]

A poet-philosopher with such a vision is hardly likely to approve of proselytization and conversion, rather the opposite. If, as Yeats says, Rabindranath Tagore represents a "tradition where poetry and religion are the same thing,"[73] the purpose of the passages that follow is obvious. The first one could easily be addressed to one who fanatically clinged to his own tradition, the second to one who discovers that turning to another tradition may only be a prelude to coming home.

> I sat alone in a corner of my house, thinking it too narrow for any guest, but now when its door is flung open by an unbidden joy I find there is room for thee and for all the world.[74]
>
> The traveler has to knock at every alien door to come to his own, and one has to wander through all the outer worlds to reach the innermost shrine at the end.[75]

What religion would a humanist like Tagore convert from, and to which religion may he convert to? He can only rise from the lower to the higher level of spirituality and universality.[76]

The attitude of Mahatma Gandhi (1869–1948) towards the question—is Hinduism a missionary religion?—may now be examined. It is clear from the foregoing discussion that the Hindu tolerance of other religions has been connected by many neo-Hindu figures with the fact of its being a non-missionary religion. Mahatma Gandhi regarded Hinduism as "the most tolerant of all religions."[77] In response to a question regarding the word *Hinduism,* Mahatma Gandhi explained its original usage as signifying "the inhabitants of the country to the east of Sindhu" and went on to add:

> The religion of these inhabitants became Hinduism and as they knew it, it was a most tolerant religion. It gave shelter to the early Christians who had fled from persecution, also to the Jews known as Beni-Israel as also to the Parsis. He was proud to belong to that Hinduism which was all-inclusive, and which stood for tolerance. Aryan scholars

> swore by what they called the *Vedic* religion and Hindustan was otherwise known as Aryavarta. He had no such aspiration. Hinduism of his conception was all-sufficing for him. It certainly included the Vedas, but it included also much more. He could detect no inconsistency in declaring that he could, without in any way whatsoever impairing the dignity of Hinduism, pay equal homage to the best of Islam, Christianity, Zoroastrianism, and Judaism. Such Hinduism will live as long as the sun shines.[78]

Similarly, on the question of conversion, Mahatma Gandhi was quite explicit: he was opposed to conversion *from* Hinduism;[79] he was opposed to conversion *to* Hinduism; and he was opposed to conversion in general.

Gandhi's opposition to conversion *from* Hinduism is best illustrated by his own life. The question of conversion cropped up at several points in his autobiography,[80] but one illustration should suffice. When he was in South Africa, he seems to have come under some pressure to convert at the Wellington Convention of Christian Protestants. Mahatma Gandhi writes:

> This Convention was an assemblage of devout Christians. I was delighted at their faith. I met the Rev. Murray. I saw that many were praying for me. I liked some of their hymns, they were very sweet. The Convention lasted for three days. I could understand and appreciate the devoutness of those who attended it. But I saw no reason for changing my belief—my religion. It was impossible for me to believe that I could go to heaven or attain salvation only by becoming a Christian. When I frankly said so to some good Christian friends they were shocked. But there was no help for it.[81]

Gandhi's opposition to conversion to Hinduism is illustrated by his negative attitude towards the *śuddhi* movement of the Arya Samaj, which aimed at reconverting Hindus who had ceased to be so and become Muslims or Christians. According to Gandhi, Swami Dayananda "unconsciously misrepresented Jainism, Islam, Christianity and Hinduism itself."[82] In his opinion, Swami Dayananda "tried to make narrow one of the most tolerant and liberal faiths on the face of the earth."[83] As for the *śuddhi* movement carried out by the Arya Samaj, Gandhi had this to say:

> In my opinion there is no such thing as proselytism in Hinduism as it is understood in Christianity or to a lesser extent in Islam. The Arya Samaj has, I think, copied the Christians in planning its propaganda. The modern method does not appeal to me. It has done more harm than good. Though regarded as a matter of the heart purely and one between the Maker and oneself, it has degenerated into an appeal to the selfish instinct. The Arya Samaj preacher is never so happy as when he is reviling other religions. My Hindu instinct tells me that all religions are more or less true. All proceed from the same God, but all are imperfect because they have come down to us through imperfect human instrumentality. The real *shuddhi* movement should consist in each one trying to arrive at perfection in his or her own faith. In such a plan character would be the only test. What is the use of crossing from one compartment to another, if it does not mean a moral rise? What is the meaning of my trying to convert to the service of God (for that must be the implication of *shuddhi* or *tabliqh*) when those who are in my fold are every day denying God by their actions.[84]

The rhetorical question with which this citation ends serves well to explain why Gandhi was opposed to any conversion altogether—namely, that "character counts for more than belief" and that adherents of every religion should be engaged in perfecting their moral lives rather than in bringing others into their fold. T.M.P. Mahadevan distinguishes between vertical and horizontal conversion, and this distinction illustrates Gandhi's position quite neatly. "Real conversion is vertical—i.e. from the lower to the higher conception of God, and not horizontal—i.e. from one formal faith to another."[85] For Gandhi, it was more important that Hindus become better Hindus, Muslims better Muslims and Christians better Christians than that Hindus should become Muslims or Muslims Christians. Let each individual take "the path which leads up life's mountain from his own culture; those who circle the mountain trying to bring others around to their paths are not climbing."

Moreover, Mahatma Gandhi believed in the equality of all religions and specially believed that India, his motherland, had clung to this spiritual insight with greater tenacity than any other country. Both these themes appear in the following statement made in 1937:

> There is in Hinduism room enough for Jesus, as there is for Mohammed, Zoroaster and Moses. For me the different religions are beautiful flowers from the same garden, or they are branches of the same majestic tree. Therefore they are equally true, though being received and interpreted through human instruments equally imperfect. It is impossible for me to reconcile myself to the idea of conversion after the style that goes on in India and elsewhere today. It is an error which is perhaps the greatest impediment to the world's progress towards peace. "Warring creeds" is a blasphemous expression. And it fitly describes the state of things in India, the mother, as I believe her to be, of Religion or religions. If she is truly the mother, the motherhood is on trial. Why should a Christian want to convert a Hindu to Christianity and vice versa? Why should he not be satisfied if the Hindu is a good or godly man! If the morals of a man are a matter of no concern, the form of worship in a particular manner in a church, a mosque or a temple is an empty formula; it may even be a hindrance to individual or social growth, and insistence on a particular form or repetition of a credo may be a potent cause of violent quarrels leading to bloodshed and ending in utter disbelief in Religion, i.e. God Himself."[86]

The twin themes—those of equality of religions and the mother metaphor—can be further developed. Mahatma Gandhi was quite willing to be regarded as a Muslim or a Christian[87] on the strength of the equality of world religions. T.M.P. Mahadevan has perspicaciously shown how this follows logically from Gandhi's definition of Hinduism itself:

> Hinduism was once defined by Gandhi as "search after Truth through non-violent means." It may be said that this is no definition of Hinduism, since the statement would be true of every religion. But that is exactly what Hinduism claims, viz., that the truth of every religion is the same. Gandhi acknowledged without any reservation his indebtedness to other Scriptures and teachers like the Sermon on the Mount and Tolstoy. In fact, many a Christian admirer of Gandhi has characterized him as "Christ returned to earth." The Mahatma's religious outlook was universal. Yet he was convinced that for him the best mode of approach

> to God lay through Hinduism. Denominations do not matter. There is no meaning in a superficial change of labels in religion. To each man his religion is the best. But the love of his own faith should not make him blind to the fact that there is truth in other religions also. Gandhi was one of the latest, not only to preach but also to practice the universalism of the Hindu faith.[88]

The mother metaphor may also be further developed, not in relation to India but to one's own religious tradition. A message was received from Gandhi at a Parliament of Religions which met in Calcutta in 1937, which was couched in the form of the following question: "What will the Parliament of Religions say in respect of all religions? Are all religions equal, as we hold, or is any particular religion in the sole possession of truth and the rest either untrue or a mixture of truth and error as many believe? The opinion of the Parliament in such matters must prove a helpful guidance."[89] The response of Sir Francis Younghusband in this respect is interesting. He said:

> To Mahatma Gandhi's question I would add another question. Are all mothers equally good? All mothers are not equally good, but each would think his own mother as the best in the world. Similarly, each one would regard his own religion as the best in the world. At any rate, that was certainly the impression that he gained at the World Congress of Faiths last year. Each one did honestly believe that his religion was the best. I have come in very close contact with people of diverse faiths and have discovered a fundamental unity among all these religions. It is this fundamental unity which I desire this Congress to realize and deepen and make it permanent and abiding.[90]

To this, Kakasaheb Kalelkar added, extending the simile: "Indeed every one of us regards his own mother as the best, but does he, therefore, expect or ask others to give up their own mothers and adopt his own?" In other words, just as one's own mother is *best for oneself*, so is every one's religion the best, each for himself; just as one's own country is *best for oneself*, every one's religion is best, each for himself. The equality of all religions lies in each being adequate or best for its respective adherents."[91]

It is clear, then, that for Mahatma Gandhi, Hinduism was a non-missionary religion.

The next leading figure of neo-Hinduism whose views, stated or implied, on the issue of Hinduism as a missionary religion must be taken into account is Aurobindo Ghosh (1872–1950). If Tagore's vision was universal, Aurobindo's vision was cosmic, and it is difficult to locate direct references bearing on the question of conversion, or on the nature of Hinduism as a missionary religion (or otherwise), in his writings. But the general scale of his vision and the nature of his thought leaves little room for doubt that conversion from one religion to another—either to or from Hinduism—would hardly have been meaningful to him. The one conversion Aurobindo does speak of, while emphasizing India's spirituality, involves a spiritual transformation. He writes.

> It must therefore be emphasized that spirituality is not a high intellectuality, not idealism, not an ethical turn of mind or moral purity and austerity, not religiosity or an ardent and exalted emotional fervor, not even a compound of all these excellent things; a mental belief, creed or faith, an emotional aspiration, a regulation of conduct according to a religious or ethical formula are not spiritual achievement and experience. These things are of considerable value to mind and life, they are of value to the spiritual evolution itself as preparatory movements disciplining, purifying or giving a suitable form to the nature; but they still belong to the mental evolution, the beginning of a spiritual realization, experience, change is not yet there. Spirituality is in its essence an awakening to the inner reality of our being, to a spirit, self, soul which is other than our mind, life and body. An inner aspiration to know, to feel, to be that, to enter into contact with the greater Reality beyond and pervading the universe which inhabits also our own being, to be in communion with It and union with It, and a turning, a conversion, a transformation of our whole being as a result of the aspiration, the contact, the union, a growth or waking into a new becoming or new being, a new self, a new nature.[92]

That Aurobindo would not support missionary activity of the usual kind on the part of any religion is further supported by his *Essays on the Gita*.[93] Robert Lawson Slater quotes from this work to support his position on what he calls Hindu relativism:[94]

> 'There is undoubtedly a Truth one and eternal which we are seeking, from which all other truth derives," says Sri Aurobindo. "But precisely for that reason it cannot be shut up in a single trenchant formula. . . . Nor has it been wholly found by us if our view of it necessitates the intolerant exclusion of the truth underlying other systems." It is, he says, the merit of the Bhagavad Gita that "it does not cleave asunder, but reconciles and unifies. . . . It maps out, but it does not cut up or build walls or bridges to confine our vision."[95]

And Hindu relativism is inimical to conversion as the "vision is seen to be realized by, or given to, men who travel different ways and sometimes unexpected ways—all, or most of these ways, should be left open and none, or few, forbidden."[96] He goes on to say that "the very reason why Hindus are hesitant about closing any road or marking it forbidden is the fear lest the vision whereby man lives may be lost. And looking out on the wider world today, and not least on our Western world, there are Hindus who believe there is indeed ground for this fear."[97]

The attitude of S. Radhakrishnan (1888–1975)[98] on the question of the missionary or otherwise nature of Hinduism may now be examined, especially as Radhakrishnan's interpretation of Hinduism is generally regarded as having been particularly influential with the English-educated elite of India.[99] This interpretation, though in a sense starting with his Master's thesis,[100] was particularly developed in a series of lectures delivered in England and the United States in 1926[101] and since. In these, if one chooses to look at them from the point of view of Hinduism as a missionary religion, "Especially significant has been his argument that Hinduism finds a place within itself for all the varieties of religious experience, thus creating a religion of tolerance, while Christianity and Islam, the inheritors of Judaism, display 'the intolerance of narrow monotheism.' "[102] The passage in which the above lines occur runs as follows:

> Hinduism does not support the sophism that is often alleged that to coerce a man to have the right view is as legitimate as to save one by violence from committing suicide in a fit of delirium. The intolerance of narrow monotheism is written in letters of blood across the history of man from the time when first the tribes of Israel burst into the land of Canaan.

> The worshippers of the one jealous God are egged on to aggressive wars against people of alien cults. They invoke divine sanction for the cruelties inflicted on the conquered. The spirit of old Israel is inherited by Christianity and Islam, and it might not be unreasonable to suggest that it would have been better for Western civilization if Greece had molded it or this question rather than Palestine. Wars of religion which are the outcome of fanaticism that prompts and justifies the extermination of aliens of different creeds were practically unknown in Hindu India. Of course, here and there were outbursts of fanaticism, but Hinduism as a rule never encouraged persecution for unbelief. Its record has been a clean one, relatively speaking.[103]

This Semitic exclusiveness and Hindu tolerance[104] stand out in sharp contrast in the vision of Radhakrishnan.

Like other major figures of neo-Hinduism, Radhakrishnan emphasizes the tolerant spirit of Hinduism:

> Hinduism is wholly free from the strange obsession of some faiths that the acceptance of a particular religious metaphysic is necessary for salvation, and non-acceptance thereof is a heinous sin meriting eternal punishment in hell. Here and there outbursts of sectarian fanaticism are found recorded in the literature of the Hindus, which indicate the first effects of the conflicts of the different groups brought together into the one fold; but the main note of Hinduism is one of respect and good will for other creeds. When a worshipper of Viṣṇu had a feeling in his heart against a worshipper of Śiva and he bowed before the image of Viṣṇu, the face of the image divided itself in half and Śiva appeared on one side and Viṣṇu on the other, and the two smiling as one face on the bigoted worshipper told him that Viṣṇu and Śiva were one. The story is significant.[105]

When one brings to bear such a catholicity of outlook on the question of conversion, then naturally the case of conversion from one religion to another comes off secondbest. Conversion may be hard to justify even if it be accepted that one religion is better than another.

> For as students are proud of their colleges, so are groups of their gods. We need not move students from one college

> to another, but should do our best to raise the tone of each college, improve its standards and refine its ideals, with the result that each college enables us to attain the same goal. It is a matter of indifference what college we are in, so long as all of them are steeped in the same atmosphere and train us to reach the same ideal; of course there will be fanatics with narrow patriotism holding up Balliol as the best or Magdalene as modern, but to the impartial spectator the different colleges do not seem to be horizontal levels one higher than the other, but only vertical pathways leading to the same summit. We can be in any college and yet be on the lowest rung of the ladder or be high up in the scale. Where we are does not depend on the college but on ourselves. There are good Christians and bad Christians even as there are good Hindus and bad Hindus.[106]

It is clear, therefore, that according to S. Radhakrishnan, not only is Hinduism a non-missionary mission; its attitude in this respect may even be worthy of emulation by other religions. What is more, Professor Radhakrishnan asserts the hospitable as opposed to the missionary character of Hinduism[107] in relation to other religions—not as a piece of mere intellectual observation but as a fragment of lived reality as a Hindu. Thus, he writes in his autobiographical fragment known as *My Search for Truth*:

> Our age is a sophisticated one. In its superior fashion it laughs at gods and ghosts, values and ideals. It is too clever to take these outworn superstitions seriously, but the illiterate Hindus who are foolish enough to perceive that these things are the symbols of thoughts beyond the reach of our rational minds do not merit our derision. I know that the people of India are the victims of paralyzing superstitions, but I cannot believe that they are devoid of religious sense. Every mother teaches her child that if he is to grow up religiously, he must love God, abstain from sin, and be full of sympathy and help to those who are in trouble. We have invented innumerable ways of spending the time allotted to us. May it not be that the way of the primitive Hindu is not the least wise of these? To dwell on the contemplation of eternal ideas, to struggle to behold the divine with the eye of the mind and to feed, on the shadows of perfection, is that an ignoble life?

> My religious sense did not allow me to speak a rash or a profane word of anything which the soul of man holds or has held sacred. This attitude of respect for all creeds, this elementary, good manners in matters of spirit, is bred into the marrow of one's bones by the Hindu tradition, by its experience of centuries.[108]

The view that Hinduism is a non-missionary religion continues to be vindicated even when we take some of the comparatively lesser known figures in modern Hinduism into account.

Ramana Maharshi (1879–1905) is one such figure.[109] He was born in Tiruchuzhi in Tamil Nadu. After a mystical experience soon after his sixteenth birthday, he left home.[110] After a short stay in a temple at Tiruvannamalai, he finally took up his abode on the Arunacala Mountain near the city. He started living there in 1898 and "never left Arunacala again."[111] He is usually regarded as an Advaitin and has been called "an incarnation of pure Advaita."[112]

The fact that he was opposed to conversion is illustrated by several incidents. For instance, a Britisher, F.H. Humphreys by name, became his disciple. He is regarded as his first Western devotee.[113] "He was in the police service and Ramana Maharshi advised him to attend to his service and meditation at the same time. For some years he did so and then he retired. Being already a Catholic and having understood the essential unanimity of all the religions, he saw no need to change but returned to England where he entered a monastery."[114] The question of his converting to Hinduism never arose. F.H. Humphreys offers the following statement on Ramana Maharshi's views on the question of the relationship among religions—a view hardly conducive to a missionary enterprise on the part of any religion, least of all Hinduism:

> It is useless to speculate, useless to try and take a mental—or intellectual grasp and work from that. That is only religion, a code for children and for social life, a guide to help us to avoid shocks, so that the inside fire may burn up the nonsense in us, and teach us, a little sooner, common sense, i.e. a knowledge of the delusion of separateness.
>
> Religion, whether it be Christianity, Buddhism, Hinduism, Theosophy, or any other kind of "ism" or "sophy" or system, can only take us to the one point where all religions meet and no further.

> That one point where all religions meet is the realization—in no mystical sense, but in the most worldly and everyday sense, and the more worldly and everyday and practical the better—of the fact that God is everything, and everything is God.[115]

Another religious figure who precedes Ramana, though he flourished in the same part of India, is Ramalinga Svami (1823–1874),[116] who—like "Dayananda and Paramahamsa . . . had no English education"[117]—and like Vivekananda was not a Brahmin. Ramalinga Svami was a Śaiva who preached in Tamil, and his collected works are known as *Thiruvarutpa*. In these, and in his life, he taught the ethical doctrine of compassion for all (*jivakarunyam*) and the metaphysical doctrine of the oneness of the soul of all beings (*Anmaneya Orumaippadu*).[118] One of the objectives of the Samarasa Śuddha Sanmarga Sangam, which he founded in 1865, was "casting away jati and varna differences and bringing about unity among people of all creeds by making them realize the oneness of all souls in love (Anmaneya orumaippadu)."[119] He tried to bring people around to following a common religion.

> Many a kind of religion and many a creed has thus far spread as sinful tenets. They have been hindrances for attaining true knowledge. Therefore, discard hereafter the evil path and embrace the new nectar, flowing from the common religion.[120]

T. Dayanandan Francis has pointed out that Ramalinga's "main contribution to the religious life of the Tamils is his concept of *suddha sanmarga* or the True Path. It points to a way of life which transcends the conventional patterns of religion. Ramalinga claims this path as being distinct from and higher than the Saiva Siddhanta concept of Sanmarga as well as the Samarasa Sanmarga or equality of all religions propagated in Tamil Nadu chiefly by the Saiva saint Thayumanavar."[121]

It is apparent that conversion from one religion to another, and least of all to Hinduism, is hardly consistent with such an approach, which even goes beyond the call for merely respecting the equality of all religions.

Ramalinga Svami preached in Tamil Nadu. Soon after him, what is now the neighboring state of Kerala was to become the theater of the reforming activity of another religious figure known as Narayana

Guru (1854–1928).[122] Narayana Guru was born among the untouchable Ezhava caste of Kerala, but despite this handicap, he rose to be one of the great religious leaders of Kerala. It is significant that "he was born a Hindu and remained a Hindu until his death," when some other untouchable Hindus, Dr. B.R. Ambedkar prominent among them, converted to other religions. Narayana Guru steadfastly held the view that conversion from one religion to another was not advisable. Thus he "never mentioned Hinduism, Vedanta, or any other religion as the salvation of all mankind."[123] He said:

> All religions aim at one thing, when rivers join the sea they lose their separateness. The function of religion is to turn the hearts of men upward, onward: when that is accomplished they will discover the truth for themselves. For the seeker of truth religions are the finger posts. But to those who have already attained the truth, religion is no authority. They are the authors of religion.[124]

V.T. Samuel infers from such statements that

> For Narayana Guru, religion was not static, but ever growing and changing. Therefore, conversion to another religion was meaningless. According to him, religion has two sides—the inner and the outer. Change of the outer religion is a social conversion. Among the thoughtful people the religion of the heart goes on gradually changing. The change is brought about by cultural growth and increasing experience of life.[125]

This is a statement with which the reader should be familiar by now. It is another way of saying that the aim of religious life should be to make a Hindu a better Hindu, a Muslim a better Muslim, and a Christian a better Christian, rather than that of making a Hindu out of a Muslim or a Muslim out of a Christian.

Chapter III

Hinduism as a Missionary Religion

The Evidence from Vedic India

I

Hinduism in India is said to have evolved through the movements in chronological order of the following peoples: the Negrito; the Proto-Australoid; the Dravidian; and the Aryan.[1] The Negritos were absorbed by the Proto-Australoids,[2] the latter being known as Niṣādas to the Aryans.[3] If the Indus Valley culture is tentatively identified as Dravidian,[4] then it is possible to detect connections between the Hindu religious tradition and the Proto-Australoid culture, as well as the Dravidian culture.

S.K. Chatterji identifies some elements of Hindu culture as Austric in origin. In this connection, he refers to the idea of taboo, to "certain remarkable agreements between the cosmogony of the Polynesians and that of the *Nāsadīya* hymn in the Ṛig Veda (X.129)," to "the enumeration of the days by the phases of the moon—the *tithis*," and to the adoption of Austric names for two phases of the moon "by Sanskrit (*rākā* = full moon and *kuhu* = new moon)."[5] He points out even more interestingly that

> in the domain of myth and legend, a number of Austric notions and tales appear to have survived in the myths of the Purāṇas and of the popular Hinduism. The legends of the creation of the world from an egg or eggs, or the *Avatāras* or incarnations of Vishṇu, e.g. that of the tortoise incarnation, of the princess smelling of fish (*matsya-gandhā*), of the Nāgas as serpent spirits of the waters and the underworld, and many more, which do not form part of the Aryan or Indo-European inheritance in Hinduism, and do not seem

> to have come from the Dravidian world either, can reasonably be expected to have been derived from the Austric or Proto-Australoid world.[6]

It is virtually impossible, however, on the basis of such evidence, which suggests connections, to argue for the conversion of the type one may associate with a missionary religion. This point is hard to establish without further concrete evidence. When we come to the Indus Valley culture, which is regarded as coming after the movements of the "Austric-speaking proto-Australoid people" in India, the situation is no better. The Indus script remains undeciphered.[7] Once again, there is evidence of continuities, this time between the Indus Valley culture and the Hindu religious tradition as we know it.

> Indus religious interests seem, in summary, to have revolved around the worship of male animals raised to sacred status, the parallel worship of a horned male figure represented as Lord of (male) creatures, worship of the *lingam* as the supreme symbol of male powers, and a conservative emphasis on order, restraint, and purification by bathing. Worship of the female powers of fertility and fecundity may have constituted a subsidiary cult at the popular or domestic level.[8]
>
> Many, if not all of these elements, including additional ones, are attested to in present-day Hinduism.[9]

It is when we come to the *ṚgVedic* period, as represented by the movement of the Indo-Europeans into India,[10] that the issue of whether Hinduism is a missionary religion or not can really be examined with some degree of confidence for the first time. In fact, we encounter a definite opinion on this point. Pratima Bowes,[11] who observed in a footnote that the "concept of conversion does not exist in the Hindu religions,"[12] remarks regarding the advent of the Aryans:

> The Aryan religion was not a proselytizing one, as polytheistic religions generally are not, and the Aryans made no attempt to convert everyone to their faith. Instead, in course of time Aryan beliefs and practices assimilated a great deal from other strands of thought and practice, both Dravidian and aboriginal, and some Vedic ritual and philosophy percolated down to the masses through sheer coexistence. The common culture now called "Hinduism"' was gradually

born—through spontaneous processes of social functioning rather than through deliberate preaching or teaching on a mass scale, since Hinduism does not have institutions through which mass preaching can be carried on.

Indeed, the Vedic Aryans were not even interested in mass conversion. On the contrary, they were quite reluctant to share their religion with the non-Aryan common people of India, who were branded as sudras and thought not to be fit for the Vedas.[13]

II

Is it so? Was Vedic Hinduism really nonproselytizing? Pratima Bowes seemed to argue that Vedic Hinduism cannot be regarded as a proselytizing religion because:

1. it was not avowedly missionary, as the Aryans were not interested in mass conversions;
2. they had no institutions through which mass preaching and presumably mass conversion could be carried out;
3. the non-Aryan people of India were branded as *śūdras*, people who could not study the Vedas. This is surely the negation of proselytization;
4. the Aryan religion is a polytheistic one, and polytheistic religions generally do not proselytize.

Let us now examine each of these arguments in the light of historical evidence.

Firstly, it is not true to say that the Aryans were totally lacking in missionary motivation. One verse of the *ṚgVeda* (IX. 63.5) contains the following exhortation: "Making the world Aryan" (*kṛṇvanto viśvamāryam*).

It could be suggested that the word *ārya* here should be taken in the sense of "noble," as indicating conversion to a nobler way of life than to becoming an Aryan. As a parallel one could urge that the call to make the whole world Christian is really an exhortation to suffuse the world with Christian ethics rather than convert it to Christianity. Ironically, the support for this view comes from the writings of Swami Dayananda,[14] who is said to have introduced proselytization into modern

Hinduism! Although the view that the verse embodies a missionary spirit has been accepted by some modern scholars, others feel that such a reading is far-fetched. However, there is certainly a reference involved to the Aryan way of life, either directly or by implication.[15]

The second argument does not seem to be very sound from the point of view of comparative religion. Islam does not possess an institutionalized machinery for conversion, and it has even been claimed that it does not have a word for a " 'missionary," but could it, on that account, be regarded as a nonproselytizing religion? The fact is however, that the Aryans did possess institutions which aided conversion and one of them was the *yajña*[16] (sacrifice). Later we hear of a rite of mass reconversion (*vrātyastoma*).[17]

The *ṚgVeda* distinguishes between the Aryans and the non-Aryans, who are called Dāsas or Dasyus or both.[18] The non-Aryans did not practice the sacrificial religion, which was organized primarily around the worship of Indra.

> A whole passage occurring in the seventh book of the ṚgVeda consists of a string of adjectives such as *akratūn, aśraddhān* and *ayajñān* applied to the Dasyus to emphasize their non-sacrificing character. Indra is asked to discriminate between the sacrificing Aryans and non-sacrificing Dasyus. They are also called *ayajvānaḥ*. The word *anindra* (without Indra) is used at several places, and presumably refers to the Dasyus, Dāsas and perhaps some Āryan dissenters.[19]

Thus, the way to convert to the Aryan way of life would be to patronize, perform, or participate in a sacrifice. A mode of conversion to the Aryan way of life was, thus, available. This seems to have actually happened.

> Priestly acceptance of gifts from the Dāsa chiefs such as Balbūtha and Tarukṣa earned them unstinted praises, through which they gained in status in the new order. That the Dāsas were in a position to make gifts and were looked upon as liberal donors can be deduced from the very meanings of the root *das* from which the noun Dāsa is derived. The process of assimilation went on in later times, for the later literature records the tradition that Pratardana Daivodāsi went to the world of Indra, who was historically the titular ruler of the Āryan invaders.[20]

When masses of people fell away from the Aryan way of life—as distinguished from non-Aryans being brought into the fold—the rite of *vrātyastoma* provided for their reentry into the Aryan fold. A *vrātya* was one who had ceased to observe the Aryan sacraments and thus ended up as an outcast. Such people could be readmitted into the Aryan fold proper by undergoing the rite of *vrātyastoma*.[21]

The third argument is more forceful. If the non-Aryans were not allowed to study the Vedic texts, then this is hardly consistent with a proselytizing spirit. It should be noted that this argument contains two parts: the non-Aryans are to be equated with the *śūdras*, and the *śūdras* are then denied access to the Vedas. Therefore, so runs the argument: because non-Aryans are denied access to the Vedas, the Vedic religion cannot be regarded as proselytizing.

Both the steps in the argument, however, are vulnerable to criticism. First of all, it is not at all certain that *only* the non-Aryans became *śūdras*. As Ram Sharan Sharma has pointed out:

> The one obstacle in the way of the correct interpretation by brāhmaṇical commentators of such Vedic texts as have direct bearing on social relations has been the tendency to look ahead to later developments. An example is the meaning of the words *ārya* and *dāsa* in the Ṛg Veda. Sāyaṇa takes *ārya* as the member of the first there varṇas, and *dāsa* as the śūdra; this is obviously based on the later division of society into four varṇas, which Sāyaṇa's interpretation is meant to justify. Likewise in the Atharva Vedic reference under discussion Sāyaṇa *explains ārya* as a member of the three varṇas, which naturally makes *śūdra* the representative of the fourth. But it becomes very hard to interpret earlier texts, if they are approached with the later conception of ārya and śūdra as developed in the Dharmaśāstras.[22]

This objection becomes particularly strong when it is realized that, the *śūdras* themselves were at least in some measure Aryans. The *Puruṣasūkta*, which deals with the genesis of the so-called caste system, contains the sole reference to the word *śūdra* in the *ṚgVeda*, depicts the *śūdras* as parts of the same *puruṣa* from which the *brāhmaṇas*, the *rājanyas* and the *vaiśyas* emerge. All of them, including the *śūdras*, are depicted as emerging from the same *puruṣa*. The claim that all the *dāsas* and *dasyus*, who were non-Aryans, became *śūdras* is also difficult to substantiate. R.S. Sharma finds it more probable that they were accommodated, in accordance with their status in their own society—as *brāhmaṇas, kṣatriyas, vaiśyas* and *śūdras*—and not merely as *śūdras*.[23] Otherwise, such facts that Vṛtra, the mortal enemy of Indra, was a *brāhmaṇa* become really hard to explain.[24] As a further point, it may be noted that one could possibly distinguish between the Dasyus and the Dāsas.[25] The Dasyus were virtually wiped out,[26] while the attitude to the Dāsas may have been "tempered with moderation"[27] as there are indications that "they were more amenable to the Aryan way of life than the Dasyus."[28] Moreover, it has been suggested that "the Dāsas were probably an advance guard of mixed Indo-Aryan peoples who came to India at the time when the Kassites appeared in Babylonia (c. 1750 BC)."[29]

The second part of the argument consists of the claim that the *śūdras* did not have access to the Vedas. However, it was only "towards the end of the Vedic period" that "there set in the tendency to exclude the śūdra from the *upanayana* and consequently from education."[30] "The first clear exclusion of the śūdra is found in a late Śrauta-sūtra"[31]—the *Satyāṣāḍha Śrautasūtra*. There seems to have been no such prohibition in the *ṚgVeda*. On the contrary, the *śūdras* are often included in Vedic invocations. Attention may be drawn here to the Yajur Vedic hymn[32] which expressly mentions the *śūdras* and implies their participation in the sacrifice.

Moreover, as P.V. Kane has pointed out, there are "faint traces that in ancient times" the prohibition of Vedic study on the part or the *śūdras* "was not so absolute or universal as the smṛtis make it"[33] and *Chāndogya Upaniṣad* IV 1–2 may be read as a case of knowledge being imparted to the *śūdra*. What makes the instance interesting is that the *Chāndogya Upaniṣad* itself forms part and parcel of the Vedas![34] It may also be added that, according to Bādari, all the four *varṇas* were entitled to perform the Veda sacrifices.[35]

Finally, it has been argued that the Aryan religion was polytheistic, and polytheistic religions are not proselytizing. One may here wish to avoid a scholarly squabble over whether *henotheism* or *polytheism* is the right word to use in the context of the *ṚgVeda* at this stage[36] and prefer to make the point that Indra provided such a central focus of *ṚgVedic* worship that monotheistic elements begin to emerge in relation to him. He is 'the most prominent divinity'[37] in the *ṚgVeda*, who is often referred to as *eka deva* or "one God."[38] And if one is inclined to associate monotheism with conflict even among the worshippers of the same god, then it is perhaps not without interest that in the *ṚgVedic* period the Indra-worshipping tribes seem to have been divided into two rival groups. One of these included the Sṛiñjayas and their allies the Bharatas, both lauded by the priestly family of the Bhāradvājas. To the other group belonged the Yadus, Turvaśas, Druhyus, Anus, and Pūrus who are found frequently in alliance with indigenous tribes. The first two tribes of the second group are branded as *Dāsas* in one passage of the Ṛig-Veda, and of the remaining three, the Pūrus are styled *mṛidhravāchah*, 'of hostile speech,' an epithet otherwise applied only to the non-Aryan *Dasyus*.[39]

III

Not only can the arguments adduced by Pratima Bowes in support of the thesis that Hinduism in the *ṚgVedic* period was nonproselytizing be negated, positive evidence can be adduced to support the view that, in point of fact, people were converted to the Aryan way of life. Let us first establish the possibility of this happening and then suggest some ways in which it may have come about. R.S. Sharma had drawn attention to the fact that, in *ṚgVeda* VI.22.10, Indra is described as converting the Dāsas into Āryas and, in *ṚgVeda* X.43.9, he is said to have deprived the Dasyus of the status of Ārya.[40] It is clear, therefore, that one could become or cease to be an *ārya*; one need not always be born as one.

This creates room for examining R.S. Sharma's general perspective on the assimilation of the non-Aryans by the Aryans in some detail. He writes:

> Despite the paucity of information reasonable hypotheses may be made about the social adjustment between the Aryans and survivors of Harappa society and other peoples. In the first flush of the Aryan expansion the destruction of the settlements and the people such as the Dasyus seems to have been so complete that very few people in northwestern India would remain to be absorbed into the new society.
>
> But this may not have been the case in the succeeding stages of their expansion. While the majority of the survivors and especially the comparatively backward peoples would be reduced to helotage, the natural tendency would be for the *viś* of the Āryan society to mix with the lower orders

> and for the Āryan priests and warriors to mix with the higher classes of earlier societies.[41]
>
> That the Vedic *ṛṣis* are a mixed lot lends support to this view.
>
> In origin the rishis came from diverse stock. Some were brāhmins, like the brahmaṛishis; some kshattriyas like the rajaṛishis; *many were of pre-Aryan*, of native origin such as Kratu and Pulaha. *Pulaha* married Kshamā and became the father of three sons, Kardama (himself a mahaṛishi), Arvarīvat and Sahishṇu. Pulaha, though often included with the brahmaṛishis, was the ancestor of several outcaste tribes and is not regarded as having produced true brahmin stock. In later legends he was said to have been a fly in a temple of Śiva, reborn as Pulaha. A number of other great ṛishis were of Indo-Persian origin, such as Atharvan and Aḥgiras.[42]

It has already been mentioned that Vṛtra was a Brahmin.[43] Similarly, local chieftains were probably absorbed as *kṣatriyas*, especially as the Aryans were also fighting among themselves and were presumably looking for military support.[44] Moreover, when the Aryans conquered their other Aryan enemies, there "is no indication of the treatment of these conquered Aryans, but essentially it might have been the same as in the case of the non-Aryans."[45] The way in which one group of Aryan tribes—the Yadus, Turvaśas, Druhyus, Anus and Pūrus—are found frequently in alliance with indigenous tribes has been referred to already. The following account of the rise of the Bharatas sheds further light on the situation. "The Bharatas were at first admittedly inferior to their foes and were shorn of their possessions . . . but Vasishtha became their family priest, and the people of the Tritsus prospered." Tritsu seems to have been the name of the ruling dynasty of the Bharatas, the most famous representatives of which were Divodāsa, and his son or grandson Sudās. Opposed to the Tritsus and the allied tribe of the Śriñjayas stood the Yadus, Turvasas, Druhyus, Anus and Pūrus. It is clear that the Bharatas and their allies did not like the idea of being permanently shorn of their possessions by their enemies. The result was that the two rival groups of tribes engaged in a deadly struggle with one another. In one of these contests, the Śriñjayas scattered the forces of the Turvasas and their allies, the Vrichīvats. In another and a more famous conflict, known as the Battle of the Ten Kings, Sudās, the Tritsu king, defeated the hostile tribes, who were joined on the Parushṇī River by the Śivas, Pakthas, and associate tribes from the northwest.

The Bharatas now definitely established their preeminence among the Aryan folks, and a late Vedic text—the *Śatapatha Brāhmaṇa*—refers to an old *gāthā*, which describes "the greatness of the Bharatas neither the men before nor those after them attained." More important than the internal conflicts of the Aryans were their struggles with the non-Aryans, which gradually led to a considerable extension of the Aryan dominion towards the east. To Divodāsa belongs the credit of fighting against a Dāsa chieftain named Śambara. His policy was continued by Sudās who crushed a hostile combination of indigenous tribes on the banks of the Jumnā. Under the guidance of a priest named Viśvāmitra, the Bharatas even seem to have entertained designs against the Kīkaṭas, a non-Aryan people traditionally associated with South Bihar. In the campaign against the Dāsas, the Bharatas were ably seconded by their rivals the Pūrus, one of whose kings bore the significant name of Trasadasyu, i.e. "terror to the Dasyus."[46]

The Aryans, and among the Aryans, the Bharatas emerged triumphant. But, in that process of annihilation, assimilation also seems to have been involved at various levels and in various ways. The absorption or the lower strata of the pre-Aryan people into the lower strata of the Aryan people may also have similarly come about.

If this line of reasoning has any element of truth in it, then it should serve to explain the paradox that the very so-called caste system, on the basis of which the existence of the proselytizing character of Hinduism is denied, may itself have been the very instrument of such conversion. And, if it is recalled that the nonadmissibility or the Gāyatrī mantra to the *śūdras* is a later development, then the suggestion made by Benjamin Walker may not turn out to be as implausible as it may have appeared at first sight—that the Gāyatrī mantra "was composed by the non-brahmin sage Viśvāmitra, and may have represented the confession of faith of non-Aryan converts to the new Aryan religion."[47]

IV

At this point it could be protested that the *ṚgVeda* adopts an attitude of religious toleration towards various beliefs and practices, as epitomized in the oft-quoted *ṚgVedic* verse (I.164.46): *ekam sad viprā bahudhā vadanti* (The Real is one; sages call it variously).[48] And that the whole idea of conversion would be repugnant to a people with such a point of view. This view has considerable force. As H. Aguilar observes:

> Already from the Vedic period the way in which the ṛṣis preserve the tradition without creasing to re-interpret it enables the kind of religious pluralism, which has become typical of later Hinduism and which in some people's opinion constitutes one of its grandeurs. What has been said of Hinduism in general—that rather than being a religion it is a sea of religions—could also be applicable to the earlier period to a considerable extent.[49]

However, when this tolerance for religious pluralism is placed alongside the undeniable fact of Aryan expansion in India, to be documented subsequently, then one is driven to the conclusion that this attitude affected not the *fact* but the *nature* of conversion to the Aryan way of life. That is to say, local beliefs and practices, perhaps after an initial period of hostility, were subsequently incorporated within the religious framework of the Aryans. This fact is too widely acknowledged to require further substantiation.[50] What needs to be emphasized is that such an attitude of religious tolerance did not prevent the Aryans from expanding their frontiers, and conversion probably accompanied such conquest, though it may well have been the kind of conversion that allowed various forms of religious beliefs and practices to coexist.

That the Aryan expansion did occur is hardly in doubt. The extent of the country reflected in the *ṚgVedic* hymns is "Afganistan, the Punjab, parts of Sind and Rajputana, the North-West Frontier Province, Kashmir, and Eastern India up to Sarayu."[51] But

> a review of the subsequent Aryan settlements leading up to the close of the Vedic period make it clear that the period of the later Saṅhitās, Brāhmaṇas, Upanishads, and Sūtras is characterized by a spirit of adventure and expansion, and the advancing Aryans were spreading in every direction, colonizing the east, south, and north. The Gangetic Doāb was completely occupied by the Aryans and the adventurous Bharatas and Videghas led expeditions along the Yamunā, the Sarasvatī, and the Sadānīrā. Towards the east Kosala, Videha, Magadha, and Aṅga came under Aryan occupation during this period. In the north and the north-west, we come across the Uttaramadras, Bāhlīkas, Mahāvṛishas,

> and Mūjavants, showing the expansion along Kashmir and the Himālayas. Towards the south the Vindhya appears for the first time in the *Kaushītaki Upanishad* (II.8), and the Kuntīs and Vītahavyas seem to have penetrated further south, and the Narmadā and Vidarbha also were within the Aryan fold.[52]

Or to put it simply, "in the *ṚgVedic* period the Aryan tribes had spread over the whole country from the Kabul to the upper Ganges,"[53] but by the end of the Vedic period, that is, "down to the period of the Upanishads," "the territory comprised within the sphere of Aryan influence"—may be "roughly described as the whole of India to the north of the Narmadā, and some regions even to the south of that river."[54]

It may be suggested at this point that these developments represent a case of political and cultural expansion rather than the expression of missionary zeal on the part or the Aryans. But, if it can be admitted that the "religion of Islam was spread by the conquests of the Arabs"[55] and that the missionary expansion of Christianity over the last three centuries followed in the wake of the European political expansion over the globe—and neither Islam nor Christianity are any less missionary for that—then it seems logical to suppose that the Aryan religion also spread along with the extension of Aryan political power. And this fact should not make it any less missionary.

Chapter IV

Hinduism as a Missionary Religion

The Evidence from Classical India

I

It could be maintained that while Hinduism may have been a missionary religion in Vedic times, it ceased to be so in post-Vedic times—the times to which alone the term *Hinduism*, according to one view, may be properly applied.[1] Such a position leaves us with a problem: we know that Hinduism ultimately came to embrace the whole of India, but by the post-Vedic period, it seems to have penetrated only as far as the Deccan. How then did it spread to the rest of peninsular India, right up to Śrī Laṅkā,[2] if it was not in some sense a missionary religion?

Some scholars believe that the Hindu epics—the *Rāmāyaṇa* and the *Mahābhārata*—contain allusions to this forward march of Hinduism.

> The Epics relate the acceptance of new tribes and their gods into the old family circle. The clash of cults and the contact of culture do not, as a rule, result in a complete domination of the one by the other. In all true contact there is an interchange of elements, though the foreign elements are given a new significance by those who accept them. The emotional attitudes attached to the old forms are transferred to the new, which is fitted, into the background of the old. Many tribes and races had mystic animals, and when the tribes entered the Hindu society the animals which followed them were made vehicles and companions of gods. One of them is mounted on the peacock, another one the swan, a third is carried by the bull, and the fourth by the goat. The enlistment of Hanumān, the monkey-general in the

> service of Rāma signifies the meeting-point of early nature worship and later theism. The dancing of Kṛṣṇa on Kālīya head represents the subordination, if not the displacement, of serpent worship. Rāma's breaking of the bow of Śiva signifies the conflict between the Vedic ideal and the cult of Śiva, who soon became the god of the south (Dakṣināmūrti). There are other stories in the Epic literature indicating the reconciliation of the Vedic and the non-Vedic faiths. The heroized ancestors, the local saints, the planetary influences and the tribal gods were admitted into the Hindu pantheon, though they were all subordinated to the one supreme reality of which they were regarded as aspects. The polytheism was organized in a monistic way. Only it was not a rigid monotheism enjoining on its adherents the most complete intolerance for those holding a different view.[3]

This may[4] or may not[5] be true but the fact that Hinduism did extend itself to cover South India is not open to doubt, only the manner in which this may have come about is. K.A. Nilakanta Sastri has pointed out that the southward extension of Hinduism, or the Aryanization of the South, is recognizable even in the *Manusmṛti*.[6]

This is supported by not only by Sanskrit but Tamil traditions as well. These "have plausibly been interpreted as reminiscent of historical occurrences" and relate to the figures of Agastya,[7] Kauṇḍinya, and Murugan. The Vedic Agastya has a miraculous birth like many other "heroes of nations," but otherwise K.A. Nilakanta Sastri regards him "as a historical person, as real as the king and tribes mentioned in the ṚgVeda; he composes hymns, has a wife and sister, and perhaps also a son. His life story receives full treatment in the two epics of the *Mahābhārata* and the *Rāmāyaṇa* and many new legends are recorded about him; the Purāṇas and the Tamil tradition mark still further stages of this development."[8] According to K.A. Nilakanta Sastri, "three achievements" ascribed to him are of "particular significance to the story of progressive Aryanization of South India and the East:" (1) Agastya's association with the Vindhyan mountain: He prevailed upon Vindhya mountain to cease growing in height; (2) Agastya's destruction of the Rākṣasa brothers, Ilvala and Vātāpi, who hated the Brahmins, and (3) Agastya's drinking up the waters of the ocean. "These three achievements have been understood to represent respectively the crossing of the Vindhyas into the Deccan by the bearers of the Indo-Aryan culture to that region, the initial opposition to the culture on the part of the indigenous people of the South, which, however, soon died away and gave place to a more propitious attitude, and the spread of the culture to the eastern lands across the sea."[9] Furthermore, according to one tradition, Agastya is also the author of the first Tamil grammar.[10] Agastya is also important as a *gotra*-name[11] This name, Indo-Aryan *gens*, is of frequent occurrence in the south. The importance of Kauṇḍinya is similar in this respect:

> Another name that bears an equally close connection with the Aryanization of South India and of East is that Kauṇḍinya, which is also, like Agastya, the name of *gotra* (Indo-Aryan *gens*). There are in existence quite a number of stone and and copper plate inscriptions in the South Indian languages regarding land gifts to members of the Kauṇḍinya *gotra,* among others, in different parts of the country from different dynasties of rulers. Much earlier than these is a full dress description of the daily life of religion and sacrifice observed in a Brahmin household of the Kauṇḍinya *gotra* (Kauniyan in Tamil) in the village of Pūñjāṟṟūr in the Tanjore District of the second or third century A.D. The prominence of the name of Kauṇḍinya in the foundation myths of the different kingdoms forming the Hindu colonies of Southeast Asia is well known and need not be reviewed here in detail. There can thus be no doubt that the Agastyas and the Kauṇḍinyas were very prominent among the adventurous leaders of Indo-Aryan society who spread its culture in lands originally non-Aryan.[12]

Murugan[13] is important as representing one particular way in which the Aryanization proceeded. "The undoubted antiquity of his cult is attested by the discovery at the pre-historic urn-field at Ādiccanaltūr of bronze cocks, iron spears and mouthpieces of gold leaf similar to those employed by modern worshippers of Murugan when they are on a pilgrimage carrying the *Kāvaḍi* in fulfillment of a vow."[14] In due course, the cult of Murugan became associated with the mythos surrounding Śiva and Pārvatī, thus blending the Aryan and non-Aryan elements.[15] This process of syncretization also seems to have proceeded at the level of the Little tradition.[16]

The point briefly is this: if the "whole of India including the extreme south had been Aryanized by the fourth century BC, if not earlier,"[17] then could this have been accomplished by the Aryans without engaging in some form of missionary activity?[18] For here the Aryanization cannot even be directly associated with conquest, as was the case with the spread of the Aryans from Northwestern to North India.

II

One may now turn from geographical to historical considerations. The rise of Buddhism and Jainism, inasmuch as they posed a challenge to Hinduism, created a new situation for Hinduism.[19] The patronage of these religions, notably of Buddhism by Aśoka[20] and of Jainism by Samprati,[21] seems to have put Hinduism on the defensive. But the fall of the Mauryan dynasty "was accompanied also by the gradual decline of Buddhism and the corresponding consolidation of popular Hinduism. When Puṣyamitra Śuṅga established himself as the ruler of Magadha after having overthrown his Mauryan master, he signalized his victory by performing the Brahmanic Aśvamedha sacrifice,"[22] though this should not be taken to mean the revival of Vedic ritualism in general.[23] All scholars are not agreed on the nature and extent of the Hindu revival after the Mauryas[24] but that something of this kind took place seems hard to deny. Later, while the "fall of the Śuṅgas marked the beginning of a period a kind of uncertainty in the fortunes of Hinduism,"[25] when "in the early forth century AD the Guptas came to power, Hinduism attained a truly classical efflorescence."[26]

R.N. Dandekar sees this efflorescence of Hinduism under the Guptas as characterized by tolerance, employment of Sanskrit pan-Indianism, and missionary activity.[27] This last is of special interest as the theme of this book and his comment on this aspect of Hinduism in Gupta times may be quoted in full:

> And, finally, Hinduism had then assumed a positive missionary role. The movement of the spread of Hinduism in foreign lands had already begun in the earlier period, and there is ample evidence of its expansion over the whole of South-East Asia, from Burma to Java and Bali, from at least the second century onwards, though many indications in this connections have been partially observed by Buddhism which had preceded and had then again followed Hinduism. Indeed, a Hindu mission is known to have penetrated into the Hellenistic world and to have advanced as far as Egypt at a very early date. This activity as well as that of the Hinduisation of foreign tribes, which came to India,

> continued with equal zeal even in the classical period of the history of Hinduism.[28]

In the passage just cited, R.N. Dandekar alludes to the spread of Hinduism outside India, especially in Southeast Asia. This fact needs to be emphasized in the context of the discussion of Hinduism as a missionary religion. Louis Renou makes this his starting point for far-reaching observations on the status of Hinduism as a missionary religion which are cited below in extenso.

> The diffusion of Vaiṣṇavite and Śaivite ideas outside India is enough to show that Hinduism, too, was a missionary religion; at a very early date a Hinduist movement took root in the Hellenistic world and penetrated as far as Egypt. The decline of Hinduism after the Moslem period must not be allowed to obscure this fact. The old lawgivers say that to be Hindu, or, more exactly, to belong to one of the three Aryan classes means to have been born in a certain area of Hinduism, the *Āryāvarta* (or homeland of the Aryas); but this assertion need not be taken literally. Hinduism long ago advanced beyond the limits assigned to it by the laws of Manu, by means of conquest or peaceful absorption, by marriage, and by adoption. Hinduism has no word to express the process of conversion so frequently referred to in Buddhist and Jaina apologetics, books written by the converted for those to be converted; but passages can be cited from the *Mahābhārata* which show that people of low caste, enemies and foreigners were received into the Hindu fold. Many people wanted to raise their status and be admitted to *Ārya* society; others fell away from it through marriage outside its ranks and by transgressions and misfortunes. A passage of Patañjali attests that the Śakas and the Yavanas could perform sacrifices and accept food from an Ārya without contaminating it; the fact is that Hinduism is a way of life, a mode of thought that becomes second nature. It is not so much its practices that are important, for they can be dispensed with; nor is it the Church, since it has no priesthood, or at least sacerdotal hierarchy. The important thing is to accept certain fundamental conceptions, to acknowledge a certain "spirituality," a term much abused in current parlance. For many Hindus it would be

> quite legitimate to take Jesus as *iṣṭadevatā,* without even regarding Him as an *avatāra,* so long as Indian tradition were acknowledged.[29]

III

If it is accepted that Hinduism, for want of a better word, did spread over the rest of India beyond its Vedic limits, and even beyond India, and that such a spread seems necessarily to involve some form of missionary activity apart from the passive presence of trading communities, then the question arises: how is this fact to be reconciled with the evidence provided internally by the Hindu scriptures and externally by the Greek chroniclers? Do not some texts recommend the pouring of molten lead down the ears of those *śūdras* who hear the Vedas, and are not the Greek accounts conspicuously silent on the question of conversion to Hinduism?

The question of the Hindu scriptures will be examined first. I will begin with the *Manusmṛti* itself. Surely the attitude depicted in the following passage is not consistent with missionary spirit in a religion.

> The list of the disabilities of the śūdras and pañchamas (outcasts of still more abject status) is a catalogue of human folly that is unique in history, many nations have at certain periods perpetuated atrocities against their fellows, but no nation can match the disgraceful record of Brahmin arrogance and bigotry against their co-religionists, which was maintained for centuries and buttressed up by every resource of religious force and social sanction.
>
> The Śūdra was barred from religious sacrifices. He could not partake of the sacred soma drink. He was no longer entitled to the initiation ceremony of rebirth. He dared not hear the scared scriptures recited. If he listened to a recitation of the Vedas his ears were to be filled with molten lead; if he recited the sacred texts his tongue was to be torn out; and if he remembered them his body was to be split in twain. In effect he could not be taught the precepts of his own religion.[30]

It should be noted, however, that although the *śūdra* could not study the Vedas in post-Vedic times, he was *not* debarred form hearing the *smṛtis,* or from attaining salvation.[31] According to the *Bhāgavata*

Purāṇa (I.4.25) "as the three Vedas cannot be learnt by women, śūdras and brāhmaṇas (who are so only by birth), the sage (Vyāsa) composed the story of the Bhārata:—i.e. the Mahābhārata—out of compassion for them."[32] And the exclusive reliance on Manu in the matter of *śūdras* is dangerous, especially as it may have been composed during a period of "social convulsions made worse by foreign invasions" which may account in part for the extreme form of brahmanical fanaticism displayed by Manu.[33] In the *smṛti* literature, for "the first time the Śānti Parvan declares that all the four varṇas ought to hear the Veda . . . such injunctions are in sharp contrast to Manu which provide very severe punishment in such cases."[34]

The foregoing discussion is deliberately apologetic in nature for two reasons. Firstly, the other side of the coin needed to be presented to balance the picture, to show that the religious needs of the *śūdras* were also catered to, lest Manu leave one with a contrary impression. But secondly, and more importantly, attention needed to be drawn to the fanatically Brahamanical nature of the *Manusmṛti*, which is often regarded as a narrow-minded Brahmin-serving law-book.[35] If one could establish the missionary character of Hinduism on the basis of work such as the *Manusmṛti*, which seems so antithetical to that kind of an enterprise on the face of it, then surely the case of Hinduism being a missionary religion will have to be taken seriously. This is precisely what is attempted below.

The *Manusmṛti* (II. 17–20) clearly enshrines a global vision for Hinduism, or more particularly the Brahmins, the value-bearers of Hinduism. The verses are translated by Bühler as follows:

> That land, created by the gods, which lies between the two divine rivers Sarasvatī and Drishadvatī, the (sages) call Brahmāvarta
>
> The custom handed down in regular succession (since time immemorial) among the (four chief) castes (varṇa) and the mixed (races) of that country, is called the conduct of virtuous men.
>
> The plain of the Kurus, the (country of the) Matsyas, Pāñcalas, and Śūrasenakas, these (form), indeed, the country of the Brahmarṣhis (Brahmanical sages, which ranks) immediately after Brahamāvarta.
>
> From a Brahman, born in that country, let all men on earth learn their several usages.[36]

It needs to be emphasized that the term used for earth is *prthvī*, and for men, *mānavāḥ*. If any doubt be expressed that *mānavaḥ* may not mean all men, it is preceded by the word *sarva* in the compound—"all men."

But this raises the question: How are the Brahmins to deal with all men of the earth, who are outside the pale of the *varṇa* system? How could they possibly be converted to the Brahmanical mode of life? The answer is provided by *Manusmṛti* itself. Firstly, everyone who has not undergone the *upanayana* ceremony, whether he be a *brāhmaṇa*, a *kṣatriya*, or a *vaiśya* is a śūdra until he undergoes the ceremony.[37] Lest this statement be considered an exaggeration, the following verses should be considered.

> (He who has not been initiated) should not pronounce (any) Vedic text excepting (those required for) the performance of funeral rites, since he is on a level with the śūdra before his birth from the Veda [II.172][38]

In other words one is, strictly speaking, not born as a *dvija* or twice-born; one becomes one.

Thus inasmuch as all men are born without initiation they are on par with *śūdras*, and they could theoretically be initiated into Vedic studies and thus become a member of the higher caste. Only those who are actually born as *śūdras* within the Hindu society are excluded from this privilege! Lest this be considered an exaggeration it should be recalled that many people whom Hindus would regard as foreigners—such as the Greeks, the Chinese, etc.—according to Manu (X.43.44), are to be considered degraded *kṣatriyas*!

> 43. But in consequence of the omission of the sacred rites, and of their not consulting Brāhmaṇas, the following tribes of Kshatriyas have gradually sunk in this world to the condition of Śūdras;
>
> 44. (Viz.) the Pauṇḍrakas, the Koḍas, the Draviḍas, the Kambojas, the Yavanas, the Śakas, the Pāradas the Pahlavas, the Cīnas, the Kirātas, and the Daradas.[39]

As degraded *kṣatriyas*, they are eligible for reconversion to the Hindu fold as *vrātya*s. The origin of the *vrātyas* is explained thus (II.38–40):

> 38. The (time for the) Sāvitrī (initiation) of a Brāhmaṇa does not pass until the completion of the sixteenth year

> (after conception), of a Kshatriya until the completion of the twenty-second, and of a Vaiśya until the completion of the twenty-fourth.
>
> 39. After those (periods men of) these three (castes) who have not received the sacrament at the proper time, become Vrātyas (outcasts), excluded from the Sāvitrī (initiation) and despised by the Aryans.
>
> 40. With such men, if they have not been purified according to the rule, let no Brāhmaṇa ever, even in times of distress, form a connection either through the Veda or by marriage.[40]

Indeed, the *vrātyas* are used to explain the origin of several tribes found in India.[41] The following provision may be interpreted as one for readmitting a *vrātya* (XI.191):

> Those twice-born men who may not have been taught the Sāvitrī (at the time) prescribed by the rule, he shall cause to perform three *kṛcchra* (penances) and afterwards initiate them in accordance with the law.[42]

The difficulty is that it is not entirely clear whether only the person who has failed to obtain initiation can be thus admitted or his descendants as well. If the latter are deemed to be disallowed by Manu, a *smṛti*, then they can be readmitted by the rite of *vrātyastoma* which is laid down in the *Tāṇḍya Brāhmaṇa*,[43] a *śruti* text which takes precedence over a *smṛti* text.[44]

To summarize: according to the worldview of the *Manusmṛti* virtually all foreigners are lapsed Hindus, who can be readmitted into the fold by the performance of proper rites. Technically, there is no conversion into Hinduism according to the *Manusmṛti*, only reconversion. Actually, it amounts to conversion, reconversion really only being a piece of canonical fiction.[45]

IV

One may next turn to another text which specifically deals with the attitude of the Hindu towards foreigners by contrast with *Manusmṛti*, which is regarded as a conservative sacerdotal text.[46] This is the

Bhāgavata Purāṇa, a liberal devotional text. [47] The net result is the same: foreigners may be admitted to Hinduism.

The *Bhāgavata Purāṇa* contains the following verse (II.4.18):

> Kirāta-hūṇāndhra-pulinda-pulkaśā
> ābhīra-śumbhā yavanāḥ khasādayaḥ
> ye'nye ca pāpā yad-apāśrayāśrayāḥ
> śudhyanti tasmai prabhaviṣṇave namaḥ

> Kirāta, Hūṇa, Āndhra, Pulinda, Pulkaśa, Ābhīra, Śumbha, Yavana and the Khasa races and even others who are addicted to sinful acts can be purified by taking shelter of the devotees of the Lord due to His being the supreme power. I beg to offer my respectful obeisances unto Him.[48]

At this point, one may ask: is there any evidence to support the view that foreigners were actually converted to Hinduism? Part of the evidence is circumstantial. Many foreign tribes such as the Hūṇas did invade India in the past but lost their identity before long, merging as it were in Hinduism.[49] Other tribes and people can also be mentioned.[50]

Fortunately, however, not all the evidence is circumstantial. At least some of it is epigraphic, specially in relation to the spread of the Bhāgavata cult. [51] One piece of evidence, which is of special interest from the point of view of the missionary character of Hinduism, comes from Besanager in old Gwalior State in the form of an inscription placed in the last quarter of the second century BC.[52] It refers to a "*garuḍa-dhvaja* (column surmounted by the figure of Garuḍa conceived as an emblem or *vāhana* of Vishṇu) at Vidiśā in honour of Vāsudeva, the *deva-deva* (the greatest god) by his Yavana or Greek devotee Heliodorus, and inhabitant of Takshila in Gandhara, who calls himself a worshipper of Bhāgavata (Vāsudeva-Vishṇu)."[53] U.N. Ghosal cites this case as of adoption of an Indian religion by a Greek and adds: "It is also probable that he was versed in the Mahābhārata, for an ethical text quoted in the inscription closely corresponds to a couple of verses in the Great Epic."[54] The inscription is also seen as "of value in the history of Indian religions as giving an early date for the *bhakti* cult of Vāsudeva, and as proving that people with Greek names and in the service of Greek kings has become the follower of Hindu gods."[55] It suggests the further conclusion that "while foreigners like Heliodorus were ready to adopt Indian gods, the Indians were slow to worship Greek deities." Thus, the "tendency was for Indo-

Greek princes and people to become Hinduized, rather than for the Indian Rajas and their subjects to become Hellenized. The Brahmans were able to take care of themselves and to keep at arm's length any foreign notions which they did not wish to assimilate."[56]

The inscription of Heliodorus dates back to the second century B.C. while the *Bhāgavata Purāṇa* has been placed anywhere from the "first half of the sixth century" to the middle of the tenth century.[57] Despite this chronological gap, it seems reasonable to assume that the Bhāgavata verse echoes the historical memory of the conversion of foreigners to Bhagavatism. If the use of the word *pāpayonayaḥ* in *Bhagavadgītā* IX.32 is taken to include people of "unclean descent" like "the Kirātas and the Hūṇas," as has been suggested,[58] then we almost have a literary piece of evidence of the process contemporaneous with the epigraphic, as the *Bhagavadgītā* is now usually placed in the second century B.C.[59]

It is clear, then, that whether we adopt a strict Brahmanical approach along the lines of the *Manusmṛti*, or a liberal devotional approach as espoused by the *Bhāgavata Purāṇa*, the missionary character of Hinduism is difficult to deny.

V

This conclusion is fortified by another consideration. Buddhism arose in India, spread in India and then disappeared from India. The extent of its spread,[60] as well as the chronology of its disappearance, are matters of the debate,[61] but the fact of its emergence and disappearance are not. This naturally raises the question: could this reversal in the fortunes of Buddhism have been accomplished without missionary activity on the part of Hinduism? Although Jainism, unlike Buddhism, did not disappear from India, similar questions are raised by its fluctuating fortunes in India as well.

The most detailed account of such missionary activity as can be gleaned comes from the rise of the Bhakti movement in Tamil Nadu, particularly from the accounts of the lives of the Vaiṣṇava Āḻvārs and the Śaiva Nāyanārs.

The early Āḻvārs—Poygai, Pūdam, and Pēy—are "altogether free from an intolerant sectarian outlook." But the poems of Tirumaḻiśai "exhibit a more controversial tone," and by the time we come to Tirumangai, "one of the most celebrated among the *āḻvārs*," he is "said to have stolen from the *vihāra* of Nāgapaṭṭinam an image of the Buddha of solid gold to pay for the renovation of the temple of

Ranganātha in Śrīrangam." He is placed in the middle of the eight century A.D. and his "hymns, the most numerous in the Canon, are equally full of good poetry and attacks on Buddhism and Jainism." One of the twelve Āḻvārs was "also Toṇḍar-aḍip-poḍi (the dust of the feet of the devotees)," "whose intolerance of Buddhism and Jainism was nearly as great as that of Tirumangai."[62]

From among the sixty-three Nāyanārs, "the three great men whose hymns are collected together in the Devāram,"[63] namely Tirunāvukkaraśu, Ñānasmambandhar, and Sundaramūrtti, are of more than average interest for helping identify the missionary character of Hinduism.

The events of the life of Tirunāvukkaraśu, also known as Appar, provide an interesting clue to the missionary activity of Hinduism in the seventh century.

> He belonged to a Vellal family of South India. Left an orphan at an early age, he was looked after by a devoted elder sister who instructed him in the ways of Śaiva faith. To her disappointment and grief, Appar joined the Jains and became a religious leader. His conversion to Jainism did not last long, for he came back to the Śaiva fold, thanks to the earnest prayers of his pious sister. Henceforth he was a zealous apostle of Śiva-bhakti, in spite of persecutions from the Jains, and converted many people to Śaivism, including the king of his own land. He went about the temples of South India, singing the praise of Śiva and the marvels of divine grace, and contributed a great deal to the revival of Śaivism. Sambandhar, though older then he, was a close friend; the two joined battle against Buddhism and Jainism and succeeded in wiping out these religions from the Draviḍa country.[64]

Sambandhar, whose name is also written as Tiruñāna Campantar (the man related to divine wisdom) "became a mystic poet, singing the praise of Śiva and his blessings and arousing people to religious fervour and devotion through the length and breadth of the Tamil country. While the king of Madurai, with many of his subjects, embraced Jainism, his queen consort, Maṅgaiyarkkaraśi, and her prime minister who remained faithful to their Śaivism, requested Campantar to save the country from the peril of Jainism." He also argued the case of Śaivism against the Jains in the presence of the king and reconverted him.[65] He said to have been born "according to

Śaivite tradition, in answer to the prayers of his parents that the Lord Śiva might bless them with a son who would win over to the Śaiva fold those who has abandoned their ancestral religion and embraced Buddhism or Jainism."[66] It is also said that he had eight thousand Jains put to death.[67]

No such drive against the non-Hindus seems to be associated with the name of Sundarar, but the situation is different in the case of Māṇikkavāśagar (one whose speech is ruby) "who flourished in the ninth century."[68] He is said to have "debated the Buddhists from Ceylon at Cidambaram and to have utterly vanquished them."[69] According to Mariasusai Dhavamony, the "immense output of mystical writings from the Śaivite Nāyanmārs and Vaiṣṇavite Āḻvārs in the Tamil century, which contributed to the revival of Hinduism against the currents of Buddhism and Jainism, reached its climax in the *Tiruvācakam* of Māṇikkavācakar, the last of the Tamil Śaivite poet-mystics."[70]

It is clear, therefore, that considerable missionary activity was involved on the part of Hinduism to combat Buddhism and Jainism in Tamilnadu. It is not the poems of Āḻvārs alone, which may be "said to have sung the 'atheistic' Buddhists and Jains out of southern India,"[71] for the Nāyanārs must not be overlooked. It seems that until about the fifth century AD, interreligious rivalry was not a marked feature of religious life in the South,

> But soon a great change came particularly in the Tamil country and people began to entertain fears of the whole land going over to Jainism and Buddhism. At any rate, worshippers of Śiva and Vishṇu felt the call to stem the rising tide of heresy. The growth, on the one hand, of an intense emotional *bhakti* to Śiva or Vishṇu and, on the other, of an outspoken hatred of Buddhists and Jains, are the chief characteristics of the new epoch. Challenges to public debate, competition in the performance of miracles, test of the truth of doctrines by means of ordeal, became the order of the day. Parties of devotees under the leadership of one gifted saint or another traversed the country many times over, singing, dancing and debating all their way. This great wave of religious enthusiasm attained its peak in the early seventh century and had not spent itself in the middle of the ninth.[72]

The above account should also serve to correct any misunderstandings about the extent to which the low status of the *śūdra* should be seen as disproving the missionary character of Hinduism or at least handicapping it. It should be noted about the Tamil poet-saints that Tirumaḻiśai was "brought up as *śūdra*"[73]; Tiruppāṇ was "a minstrel of low caste, who was not allowed to enter the temple at Śrīrangam"[74]; Nammāḻvār belonged to "a Vellala family"[75]; Nandan was "a pariah"[76]; and Tirunāvukkaraśu, a Vellala.[77] This inclusive attitude is in keeping with the spirit of the *Bhāgavata Purāṇa,* which is seen by most scholars as originating in this part of the country around this time. The *Bhāgavata Purāṇa* takes a positive view of Śūdrahood in relation to Bhakti.[78]

VI

No account of missionary activity in Hinduism during the classical period can be complete without a discussion of the missionary activity attributed to Śaṅkara (788–820 A.D.), the famous formulator of Advaita Vedānta. His case is particularly important because his philosophical doctrine of *māyā* has often been interpreted as life-negating[79] and his rigid Brahmanical stance in relation to the *śūdras* as reactionary.[80] According to legend, this great preacher of unity of all being asked a *cāṇḍāla* to move out of his way in a street of Benaras for fear of pollution.[81] Notwithstanding all this, he has been hailed as a great missionary, especially of the Advaita school of thought. "There are several traditional biographies of this great man, but few details of his life are known beyond doubt." The paucity of biographical data[82] contrasts with the magnitude of his influence. He is accepted as "great" even by his modern critics[83] and his interpretation of the Hindu scriptures has "so dominated Indian intellectual life, and has become so well-known in the West, that his work has become almost synonymous with Vedanta."[84] His teachings soon became the standard philosophy of intellectual Hinduism[85] and—although several schools of Vedanta developed after him—it can even be claimed that if "Vedanta is the dominant philosophy of India today, the credit is due almost entirely to the genius of Shankara"[86]. "One measure of his influence is that it is very difficult for anyone either Hindu or non-Hindu to read Indian religious texts without unconsciously seeing them through the general interpretation given by Shankara,"[87] which should serve both as a tribute to him and a warning to students of Hindu religious texts. An important question arises at this point. If Śaṅkara died at the age of thirty-two, as is generally believed,[88] then how did he become so influential in a short time? One answer that has been proposed to this question is through intense missionary activity.

> In his relatively short life he traveled all over India propagating his new philosophy and achieving triumphs in public debates with the protagonists of rival doctrines. He reorganized the ascetic order of sanyasis perhaps borrowing points from the organization of the Buddhist Sangha, and founded a number of *maṭhas* in different parts of India for the continued study and propagation of his doctrine. The best known of these *maṭhas* are those at Śṛngeri where he himself is believed to have spent several years, Dvārakā, Badrināth, Puri and Kāñcī. Within a short time of his death, a pupil of his, Śivasoma by name, was spreading his philosophy in distant Kambuja across the seas.[89]

The following seem to have been the ingredients of Śaṅkara missionary approach: founding of monasteries, an idea perhaps suggested by Buddhism; organizing orders of monks; public debating with religious opponents; composing commentaries on Hindu texts, and reform of Hinduism. He is said to have "established four great maṭhas or monasteries, one each at Badrināth in the Himālayas, Purī in the east, Dvārkā in the west, and Śṛingeri in the south in Mysore. These pontifical seats were to be occupied by his followers who, like Śaṅkara, sent out missionaries to propagate his teachings all over India."[90] There is some epigraphical evidence, though late, which can be adduced in support.[91] It is said that ten orders of Advaita sannyāsins arose after him. These are the orders whose members bear a name ending in *tīrtha, āśrama, vana, araṇya, giri, parvata, sāgara, sarasvatī, bhāratī,* and *purī.*[92] "These ten orders are said to be the pupils, in succession of the four disciples of Śaṅkara, i.e. the first two of Padmapāda, the next two of Hastāmalaka, the next three of Troṭaka (or Toṭaka) and the last three of Sureśvara."[93] Public debates, called *śāstrārthas,* were standard procedure in Hindu circles for establishing one's point of view and according to tradition Śaṅkara embarked on a polemical world conquest of which accounts are found in texts known as *Śaṅkara-dig-vijaya* or their variants.[94] There are no doubt exaggerated accounts of these debates, some even fanciful to the point of being risqué,[95] but there should be some truth underlying them as they are fully in keeping with the traditional pattern of sectarian interaction. His commentaries on the *Upaniṣads,* the *Bhagavadgītā* and the *Vedāntasūtra* have been called "marvels in metaphysical writing. They are clear (*prasanna*) and yet deep (*gambhīra*), penetrating as well as broad-based. Not only are the followers of Śaṅkara indebted to him, but also those teachers of Vedānta who differed from him. He set the model for subsequent metaphysical thinking, and gave a new direction to the course of philosophical history in India."[96] He is also believed to have composed such popular manuals of Advaita Vedānta as *Vivekacūdāmaṇi* and *Upadeśasāhasrī*.[97]

His commentaries and manuals are studied to this day. A less known aspect of his work is his attempt to reform Hinduism as well. He "opposed the grosser manifestations of Śaiva and Śākta worship. He ruthlessly suppressed the unclean worship of Śiva in his dog aspect in the name of Mallāri, and the pernicious practices of the Kāpālikas."[98] It may come as a surprise to those who regard this celibate monk as a misogynist that it is believed in "Kerala or Malabar that the great teacher Śaṅkara laid down 64 ācāras, among which are the prohibition of the sale of girls, prohibition of sati, etc."[99] It is also worth mentioning that all such missionary and reforming zeal was expressed by Śaṅkara within a basic framework of religious tolerance. The Buddha is lauded in one of the hymns ascribed to him as an incarnation of Viṣṇu (without the Puranic digs),[100] and *pañcāyatana pūjā* or the worship of the five deities: Sūrya, Durgā, Viṣṇu, Ganeśa and Śiva, is said to have been popularized by him.[101] Alternatively he "is said to have re-established six different religious cults (*ṣaṇmatasthāpakācārya*)."[102]

It could be suggested at this point that the missionary spirit exhibited by Śaṅkara is not intrinsic to Hinduism but the result of the influence of Buddhism (or even Islam).[103] After all, Śaṅkara has been dubbed a crypto-Buddhist in other ways. In Louis Renou's colorful phrase, "in fact Śaṅkara Brahmanizes the Great Vehicle"![104]

For such suggestions to be viewed in a larger perspective, it is important to consider the possibility that he was responding at least in part to the challenge posed by Buddhism—and it is hoped that enough evidence has been adduced to demonstrate the missionary character of Hinduism itself.

Louis Renou refers to the period from 700–1200 as "the time of the great commentators, chief among them Kumārila and Śaṅkara. To them is due the final defeat of Buddhism in a campaign inaugurated in the South, by the zeal of the Tamil 'saints,' the Vaiṣṇavite Āḻvārs and the Śaivite Nāyanārs."[105] Their role, as well as that of Śaṅkara, has now been discussed but something also needs to be said about Kumārila[106]—especially as he belongs to North India just as Śaṅkara belonged to South India. According to a somewhat romantic account: once the princess of Kāśī (Banaras) was drying her hair in the sun in the upper terrace of the palace and bemoaning the lot of Hinduism, then under siege by Buddhism and Jainism. She is believed to have composed a hemistich, which meant: "who is going to save the

Vedas from these attacks." The fact that a lady should express this sentiment is remarkable in itself, as women by then apparently did not have the right to study the Vedas (though one has to be aware of exceptions, as in the case of the wife of Maṇḍana Miśra). According to the account, the ascetic Kumārila happened to be passing by and upon overhearing this lament instantly provided a morale-lifting second hemistich: "Fear not, O fair lady, for Kumārila is still on this earth." This glamorized story would probably be of no account but for the fact that it was invented.[107] It may give us some idea of how high feelings might have been running on some issues and how these could fuel missionary activity.

> To move from the apocryphal to the authentic, Kumārila took serious issue with the Buddha. Kumārila (who flourished somewhere about 650 to 750 A.D.) did not admit that he was an avatāra. In his Tantravārtika Kumārila-bhaṭṭa says that the Śākya texts were promulgated by Buddha and others that had strayed from the path of the three Vedas and that acted contrary to the Vedas and asks the question "what assurance is there that one, who, himself being a kṣatriya, transgressed the dharma laid down for kṣatriyas and betook himself to the profession of a religious teacher and accepted gifts, would impart instruction in dharma that would not lead to confusion? It has been said 'one should leave at a distance a person who does act contrary to the other world. How can one who deceives himself confer benefit on another'?"[108]

The evidence for the zeal, even excesses, exhibited by Kumārila seems to be somewhat less substantial than in the case of Śaṅkara, but the general mood of opposition to Buddhism and the promotion of Hinduism is clear enough for us to discern a missionary character in his activities.

VII

It is clear, that even during the classical period, when Hinduism had to contend with the heterodoxies of Buddhism and Jainism, it did not cease to display a missionary character. To what else, indeed, is one to attribute its success in containing and then overcoming these avowedly proselytizing religions?

Chapter V

Hinduism as a Missionary Religion

The Evidence from Medieval India

I

Medieval India is distinguished by the singular fact of Muslim domination of the sub-continent.[1] The establishment of Muslim rule was a gradual process, but by 1200 AD, Islam had established itself as a major if not the paramount power on the subcontinent—a dominance which was to wane only in the eighteenth century.[2] It should also be added that Muslim power was first established in North India and then subsequently extended into the south.[3]

Almost all scholars of Hinduism realize that something radically different happened on the religious scene of India with the arrival of Islam in India. For "Islam did not in general offer a system of thought or a religious philosophy that could be appropriated by Hindus; it offered instead a radical alternative to Hinduism: submission to Allah as the one true God."[4] Hinduism had encountered proselytizing religions before, for both "Buddhism and Jainism were proselytizing religions, but since both believed fervently in the principle of *ahiṁsā*, that is, that it is clean contrary to *dharma* to injure any living creature, their propaganda on behalf of their faiths was on the whole pacific,"[5] but "war against the Hindus was regarded as a sacred duty, for Islam, though tolerant of the 'people of the Book,' that is, the Jews, Christians and Zoroastrians who were considered to be recipients or true revelation, abominated idol-worship which was scathingly denounced in their sacred book, the Koran. Moreover, war against the unbelievers, if they refused conversion, was a sacred duty."[6] Thus—while the missionary activities of Buddhism and Jainism were generally pacific, and with the Hindu theistic philosophical renaissance in South India missionary activities had become more or less subdued—Islam was more aggressive inasmuch as, put negatively, it sought to exterminate Hinduism; on the positive side, it aimed at the conversion of the Hindu population to Islam.[7]

It is also important to bear in mind that, while Hinduism had evolved a policy of even-handedness in the matter of dealing with different religious communities,[8] Islam insisted "on the assumption of political order."[9] Thus, the assumption of political power by Islam in India was an extremely significant development, as it meant a departure from the policy of the neutrality of the state, by and large, in religious matters, to which the Hindus were accustomed. This attitude of neutrality had even been extended to Islam itself, when political power rested with the Hindus.

> Two instances may be here cited from Arab writers themselves in confirmation of the kind of treatment accorded to Musalmans by Hindu rulers: Idrisi, in the eleventh century, noted that the Arab traders who frequent Anhilvara in large numbers "are honourably received by the king and his ministers, and find protection and safety." M. Ufi records that, when the Muslims at Cambay were attacked by the Hindus, Sidharaj (1094–1143 AD) punished his own offending subjects and subsidised the Musalmans in building a mosque by way of compensation.[10]

How is one to assess the missionary character of Hinduism in such a situation, when it is threatened by a religion of great vigor and force? For the Hindus, it was a fight for survival, and an effort of imagination is required to sense their demoralization.[11] If, even in such a political climate, instances of missionary activity on the part of the Hindus could be cited, then it would surely be difficult to deny its missionary character. It should also be noted that, when a religion is losing its adherents to another religion, reconversion of those who were converted away might as much be a proof of missionary zeal as the conversion of new members to the religion.

II

The earliest Islamic incursion into India is represented by the Arab invasion in Sind.[12] "The conquest of Sind was effected by Muhammad ibn Qasim in AD 712, and thenceforth for centuries that country remained under Arab rule."[13] The Hindu king, Dahir, died resisting the raid[14]. Two points are of interest here about this raid. Firstly, the "privilege of the Zimmi (Hebrews and Christians) were extended to the Hindus and Buddhists of Sind"[15] by the Muslims, even if for reasons of practical accommodation rather than ideological conviction, though it meant the levying of the *jizya,* a poll tax on non-Muslims. This is sometimes referred to as "the Brahmanabad settlement."

> The basic principle was to treat the Hindus as "the people of the book," and to confer on them the status of the zimmis (the protected). In some respects the arrangements were even more liberal than those granted to "the people of the book" by the later schools of Islamic law. It appears, Hajjaj wrote, "that the chief inhabitants of Brahmanabad had petitioned to be allowed to repair the temple of Budh and pursue their religion. As they have made submission, and have agreed to pay taxes to the Khalifa, nothing more can properly be required from them. They have been taken under our protection, and we cannot in any way stretch out our hands upon their lives or property. Permission is given them to worship their gods. Nobody must be forbidden and prevented from following his own religion. They may live in their houses in whatever manner they like."[16]

The other great Islamic incursion, prior to the founding of Muslim rule in India proper, is represented by the seventeen raids of the iconoclast Maḥmūd of Ghazna, who ruled from 997 to 1030 AD. Maḥmūd was a capable general,—and once the back of Hindu resistance was broken after the defeat of Jayapāla in 1001 AD[17] and the establishment of a national confederacy at Peshawar in 1008 AD—his expeditions into India became "almost winter sport." Apart from his raids, the other point of interest of his reign is the fact that "the most distinguished ornament of Sultan Mahmūd's reign was the profound scholar commonly called Alberuni,"[18] who wrote a masterly exposition of Hindu culture, which has long excited the admiration of scholars.

Albiruni[19] comments on the attitudes of Hindus towards those who have ceased to be so. In Chapter I of his book, otherwise known as *Alberuni's India,*[20] he remarks that the Hindus "never desire that a thing which once has been polluted should be purified and thus recovered, as, under ordinary circumstances, if anybody or anything has become unclean, he or it would strive to regain the state of purity."[21]

What he subsequently says of the attitude of the Hindus towards ex-Hindus follows as a natural consequence of this attitude. The following passage has been cited earlier in the book and reproduced here for convenience.

> I have repeatedly been told that when Hindu slaves (in Muslim countries) escape and return to their country and religion, the Hindus order that they should fast by way of expiation, then they bury them in the dung, stale, and milk of cows for a certain number or days, till they get into a state of fermentation. Then they drag them out of the dirt and give them similar dirt to eat, and more of the like.
>
> I have asked the Brahmans if this is true, but they deny it, and maintain that there is no expiation possible for such an individual, and that he is never allowed to return into those conditions of life in which he was before he was carried off as a prisoner. And how should that be possible? If a Brahman eats in the house of a Sudra for sundry days he is expelled from his caste and can never regain it.[22]

It seems, however, that Albiruni's statements are contradicted by the evidence available from other sources on this point.[23]

The passage which is cited above is quoted by Professor Mohammad Habib in support of his argument that "face to face with the social and economic provision of the 'shariat' and the Hindu 'Smrtis' as practical alternative the Indian city worker preferred the Shariat."[24] Buddha Prakash criticizes Professor Habib's reliance on Albiruni's statement and remarks that "this information is of a hearsay nature and Albiruni was not sure of it, as he himself admits. He depended on the reports of persons, whom he visited, which were somewhat exaggerated and fantastic. He also consulted orthodox hackneyed texts, that were doctrinaire and dogmatic in their approach to social problems."[25]

Buddha Prakash's remarks on the hearsay nature of the evidence of Albīrūnī seem to be justified, but as Albīrūnī does not base the passage under consideration on any text, there seems to be no need to criticize him on that score. What Buddha Prakash has written in general on the issue, however, seems relevant:

> There is always a world of difference between theory and practice. Whereas theory stagnates, practice oversteps it and gives it a new light and interpretation. Though the Brāhmaṇa informant of Albīrūnī told him that no expiation was possible for a person, who was taken away by the Mlecchas, and he could never be allowed to return to his original fold if he got an opportunity, the *Devalasmṛti*, the *Atrisaṁhitā* and other kindred texts supported and sanc-

tioned the reconversion activity. The sage Devala sitting on the banks of the Sindhu permitted the *śuddhi* of those who were forcibly enslaved by the Mlecchas and compelled to slaughter the cows and other animals and eat their flesh together with the leavings or their food or to dine and mix with their women after a simple expiatory and purificatory rite. Even women kidnapped and ravished by the Mlecchas could be reclaimed by *śuddhi*. Not only Devala but also Vijñāneśvara in his Mitākṣarā gloss on Yājñavalkyasmṛti (III, 265) approvingly quotes many Smṛti texts on this point. That these injunctions were actually put into practice is clear from the re-conversion of all the persons, who had been forcibly converted to Islam in Sind, after the recall of Mohammad bin Qasim.[26]

A study of the sources available to Albīrūnī reveals that, although he mentions Devala as one of the six pupils of Vyāsa, he did not seem to have been familiar with Devala's work. This seems to be indicated by the tone of the following passage:

> Further, there are the books of the six pupils of Vyāsa, viz. *Devala, Śukra, Bhārgava, Vṛihaspati, Yājnavalkya,* and *Manu*. The Hindus have numerous books about all the branches of science. How could anybody know the titles of all of them, more especially if he is not a Hindu, but a foreigner?[27]

Moreover, in his list of *smṛti* works, Albīrūnī mentions Vṛhaspati, Yājñavalya, and Manu in common with the above list but not Devala, Śūkra, and Bhārgava.[28] So, apparently, he wasn't familiar with the *Devala Smṛti*. And as Vijñāneśvara lived subsequent to Albīrūnī,[29] his commentary on Yājñavalkya could not be available to Albīrūnī. So, Albīrūnī cannot be blamed for willful negligence in consulting the sources or for suppressing evidence; however, his account is clearly partial.

The partial nature of Albīrūnī's information on this point is further highlighted by an account which deals with Maḥmūd of Ghaznī's misadventure while returning from the sack of Somnath. It is important to bear in mind that the sack of Somnath took place in March 1024 AD,[30] Maḥmūd arrived back in Ghaznī in April 1026 AD,[31] and that *Albiruni's India* was finished in AD 1030.[32] Albīrūnī clearly refers to the destruction of Somnath.[33] He, however, does not allude to the incident mentioned below, which is said to have befallen Maḥmūd on his way back from Somnath in the desert regions of Rajputana.

> There is a curious passage relating to this defeat in an old chronicle in Persian, the *Tarikh-i-Sorath* (translated by Ranchodji Amarji, Bombay, 1882), p. 112: 'Shah Mahmud took to his heels in dismay and saved his life, but many of his followers of both sexes were captured. Turks, Afghans, and Mughal female prisoners, if they happened to be virgins, were accepted as wives by the Indian soldiers. . . . The bowels of the others, however, were cleansed by means of emetics and purgatives, and thereafter the captives were married to men of similar rank.' 'Low females were joined to low men. Respectable men were compelled to shave off their beards, and were enrolled among the Shekhavat and the Wadhel tribes of Rajputs; whilst the lower kinds were allotted to the castes of Kolis, Khantas, Babrias, and Mers.' I am not myself acquainted with the *Tarikh-i-Sorath* and do not know how far it can be considered as reliable. I have taken this quotation from K.M. Munshi's "The Glory that was Gurjardesa," Part III, p.140. What is especially interesting is the way foreigners are said to have been absorbed into the Rajput clans and even marriages having taken place. The cleansing process mentioned is novel.[34]

It is quite possible that Albīrūnī may not have been aware of the details that interest us, as they relate to what happened to Maḥmūd's men who couldn't make it back home. It is also perhaps not possible to verify this incident—[35]but what is significant is the readiness it indicates, in terms of Hindu psychology, to accept non-Hindus, not to speak of ex-Hindus, in the Hindu fold.

To conclude: Albīrūnī's description of the attitude of the Hindus towards ex-Hindus does not seem to be fully borne out by Hindu sources and may represent a regional fact, or his own limited experience.

In this section so far, we discussed two major encounters between Hinduism and Islam, which had taken place prior to the founding of the Delhi Sultanate. These were in the form of the Arab invasion of Sind in 712 AD and the iconoclastic raids of Maḥmūd of Ghaznī from 1001 AD to 1027 AD It was mentioned that these raids resulted in the conversion of Hindus to Islam but that the Hindus seemed, on the whole, quite willing to allow for the reconversion to Hinduism of those who had left or had been made to leave their fold. This is contrary to the generally held view on the matter, but one hopes that sufficient evidence has been offered to suggest the need for open-mindedness on the point, if not an alteration in the standpoint. It is also suggested by these accounts that the Hindus may not have been averse to accepting even Muslims into the Hindu fold.

III

The period of the Delhi Sultanate (1206–1526) saw the establishment of Muslim political power in North India and was marked by two main periods of persecution of the Hindus "under Firuz in the fourteenth century and under Sikander II and the Lodis in the fifteenth."[36] The period as a whole is also marked by greater oppression of the Hindus than during that of the Mughal Empire, which succeeded it.[37] Any evidence of missionary activity on the part the Hindus could only be regarded as striking, especially as the Hindus were "not usually allowed to make converts"[38] and "the re-conversion of Hindu converts to Islam was not usually permitted."[39]

Let us first examine cases of conversion to Hinduism. Under Fīrūz Tughluq (1351–1368) a "Brahman was burnt alive at the palace gates, for the crime of publicly worshipping in his own way and *attracting even Muslim devotees*."[40] Thus, the effort tragically failed but was made. Similarly, in the following passage, we find on the Sultan's own admission that the Muslims were beginning to mix with the Hindus:

> The Hindus and idol-worshippers had agreed to pay the money for toleration (*zar-i-zimmiya*), and had consented to the poll tax (*jizya*), in return for which they and their families enjoyed security. These people now erected new idol-temples in the city and the environs in opposition to the Law of the Prophet which declares that such temples are not to be tolerated. Under Divine guidance I destroyed these edifices, and killed those leaders of infidelity who seduced others into error, and the lower orders I subject to stripes and chastisement, until this abuse was entirely abolished. The following is an instance: In the village of Maluh there is a tank which they call *kund* (tank). Here they had built idol-temples, and on certain days the Hindus were accustomed to proceed thither on horseback, and wearing arms. Their women and children also went out in palankins and carts. There they assembled in thousands and performed idol worship. This abuse had been so overlooked that the *bazar* people took out there all sorts of provisions, and set

> up stalls and sold their goods. *Some graceless Musulmans thinking only of their gratification, took part in these meeting.* When intelligence of this came to my ears my religious feelings prompted me at once to put a stop to this scandal and offence to the religion of Islam. On the day of the assembling I went there in person, and I ordered that leaders of these people and the promoters of this abomination should be to death. I forbade the infliction of any severe punishments on the Hindus in general, but I destroyed their idol temples, and instead thereof raised mosques.[41]

It is true that the above case does not represent any missionary activity on the part of the Hindus, but it does show that the state was decidedly against the Muslims contacting the Hindus even peripherally. It would be difficult for Hindu missionary activity to proceed in such a situation. As a matter of fact, even the respectful attitude of Hindus towards other religions got them into trouble. Hindu "conversion" often proceeds by accepting the validity of the other person's point of view to begin with, but that this was a dangerous course to pursue with Islam as is exemplified by the case of Nawahun, a *darogha* of Uch. In the case below, he was not even out to convert a pious Muslim but his exercise in theological courtesy sealed his fate.

> When Sayyid Jalal-ud-din was on his death bed Nawahun called on him to enquire about his health and said, 'May God restore your health. Your holiness is the last of the saints as the Prophet Muhammad was the last of Prophets." Sayyid Jalal-ud-din Bokhari and his brother Sadr-ud-din Raju Qattal construed it as an expression of faith in Islam and therefore they demanded from Nawahun a formal declaration of his conversion to Islam. Nawahun firmly declined to make such a declaration and fled to the court of Firoz Shah Tughluq in search of asylum. When Sayyid-Jalal-ud-din Bokhari died, his younger brother Raju Qattal pursued the matter and reached Delhi in order to secure the execution of Nawahun according to the law of Islam, which punished apostasy with death. Although Nawahun was not a Muslim, he was put to death by Firoz's orders.[42]

An incident which occurred during the reign of Sikandar Lodi (1489–1517) also sheds light on the problems faced by Hinduism as a missionary religion. A *brāhmaṇa* named Bodhan (or Yodhan) declared that both Hinduism and Islam were true, a typically Hindu conclusion. He was put to death for making such an assertion "after the question had been discussed at length by the 'ulama.' "[43]

Two points need to be noted in general about this period. The constant harassment of the Hindus gave rise to a degree of militancy, and when a Hindu ruler had enough power, he tried to do to the Muslims what Muslim rulers had done to the Hindus. Thus "Rāṇā Kumbha claims to have imprisoned the *Yavanīs* (i.e. Muslim women) and also broken a mosque." When Medinī Rai was powerful in Mālwa, "Mussulmān and Sayyid women were taken by the Rājputs and were turned into slave girls. The massacre and raping of the Muslims by the Hindu kings of Vijayanagar are referred to by Firishta."[44] Whenever the Hindus got a chance they reconverted ex-Hindus or even non-Hindus, S.R. Sharma describes the situation:

> Conversion of Muslims to Hinduism or the re-conversion of Hindu converts to Islam was not usually permitted. Sometimes there were exceptionally tolerant rulers, like Zain-ul-'Abadin in Kashmir, who were prepared to allow all Hindu converts to Islam to return, if they wished, to their original faith. But this tolerant attitude was so exceptional that a story had to be invented proving him to be a Hindu recluse who had projected his own soul into the dead body of the king on his death-bed. Usually this prohibition must have been strictly enforced as it must have been considered highly objectionable in a Muslim king to encourage or tolerate apostasy, which was a capital offence. But Chaitanya reconverted the chief minister and the Mir Munshi Shah of Bengal (1493–1518) to Hinduism. He also reconverted Bijili Khan and Haridas to Hinduism. A group of Pathans was also admitted into the charmed circle of Hinduism.[45]

It is interesting to follow the fortunes of the Caitanya movement for the light they throw on the missionary character of Hinduism. In the beginning Caitanya, (1486–1533) had to face considerable difficulty, as is clear from a famous episode in the life of Caitanya mentioned in "the two great biographies of the great Vaishṇava saint," namely "the Chaitanya-charitāmṛta and the Chaitanya-bhāgavata."[46]

> He had introduced the system of public worship in the form of *kīrtan* (a sort of congregational song loudly sung together by a large number of men in public streets to

> the accompaniment of special musical instruments). This enraged the Muslim *qāzī*, and one day when Chaitanya's devotees were singing the name of God in the streets of Nadīyā (Navadvīpa in Bengal), he came out, struck blows upon everybody on whom he could lay hands, broke the musical instruments, and threatened with dire punishment all the Hindus who would dare join a *kīrtan* party in this way in his city of Nadīyā. To prevent the recurrence of public *kīrtan*, the *qāzī* patrolled the streets of Nadīyā with a party. The people of Nadīyā got afraid, but Chaitanya decided to defy the *qāzī*'s orders, and brought out a large *kīrtan* party which was joined by thousands. The *qāzī* was at first wild with anger and held out the threat that he would destroy the caste of all the Hindus of Nadīyā; but terror seized him when his eyes fell upon the vast concourse of people in a menacing attitude. He fled, and his house was wrecked by the angry crowd. The Chaitanya-Bhāgavata does not describe the sequel. But the other work, Chaitanya Charitāmrita describes how Chaitanya sent for the *qāzī* who was now in a more chastened mood, and the two had a cordial talk.[47]

In analyzing the Caitanya movement, some scholars like to emphasize its militant aspect and some its missionary aspect, though the two need not be necessarily dissociated. S.M. Ikram identifies "two very different attitudes which Hindu religious leaders had toward Islam" in the fourteenth and fifteenth centuries. Both reacted to Islam, but one was sympathetic while the outer was hostile." "The two trends," he thinks, "are similar to the growth of the tolerant, cosmopolitan Brahmo Samaj and the militant Arya Samaj, when Hinduism was confronted with Christianity in the nineteenth century. Kabir, Guru Nanak, Dadu, and other founders of syncretic sects are included in the first group, while the movement in Bengal, associated with Chaitanya, mirrors the latter tendency."[48] Ikram sees this militant aspect of the Caitanya movement as continuing right into Akbar's reign,[49] while R.C. Majumdar identifies a contemporary expression of it.[50]

Victor Turner compares the movement by Caitanya with that of St. Francis and notices that a cleavage developed in the movement between conservative and devotional wings: "One branch followed the lead of Caitanya's friend and intimate companion, Nityānanda, known as the 'casteless Avadhūta' (the Avadhūtas were ascetics), the other followed Advaita-ācārya, an early and leading devotee of

Caitanya, a Brahman of Santapura."[51] Nityānanda was not only casteless himself; he stayed with *Śūdras* and was "apostle to the Banyas" (both *Śūdras* and Banyas were low-caste Hindus); "he also allowed *thousands of Buddhist monks and nuns into the Vaiṣṇava fold*."[52] Unlike the more socially conservative group, "believing as he did that every man, regardless of caste or creed, could attain salvation by personal devotion to Krishṇa and Rādhā, he emphasized the missionary aspect of Vaiṣṇavism."[53] Caitanya and Nityānanda are also said to have "converted many Muslims—and thus antagonized the Muslim reigning power."[54] Turner concludes that "the successors of Caitanya failed because Advaita's group became absorbed in the caste system, and Nityānanda's group, exclusivist and full of missionary fervour, encountered persecution and, gradually lost heart."[55] The presence of the Hare Kṛṣṇa movement in the West in recent times may call for a reassessment of the extent of its failure.[56] But one continuity between the earlier and the modern forms of the movement is significant: the claim that it is the "one universal religion for today," which "everyone irrespective of caste, colour, creed, community, sex, age, space or time is allowed to enter or join."[57]

It is clear, therefore, both from historical evidence and present-day legacy that, even during the period of the Delhi Sultanate when Hindus were perhaps more demoralized than at any other time in their history, the missionary character of Hinduism continued to manifest itself, albeit in limited ways.

IV

The period of the Moghul Empire—when taken to cover the reigns of Bābur, Humāyūn, Akbar, Jahāngīr, Shāh Jahān, and Aurangzēb—extends from 1526 to 1707 AD.[58] By comparison with the previous period of Muslim rule, this period is generally regarded as having been less oppressive towards Hindus[59]—though with some exceptions, notably in the reign of Aurangzēb.[60] It is important to note, however—that except perhaps for that part of Akbar's reign when he adopted a liberal policy—the general atmosphere was not uniformly congenial from the Hindu point of view. Bābur (1526–1530) "inherited his religious policy from the Lodis,"[61] glimpses of which have been shown earlier, and his son Humāyūn (1530–1556) "had not much chance of developing any distinct policy of his own."[62] During the interregnum provided by the reign of Sher Shāh Sūrī (1540–1545), the situation hardly changed. He was a skilful administrator but hostile to the Hindus. A change did take place during Akbar's reign (1556–1605), but the tide changed again during the reigns of Jahāngīr (1605–1627)[63] and Shāh Jahān (1627–1658),[64] culminating in the long period of Aurangzēb's rule (1655–1707).[65]

Even Akbar commenced his reign in a way which gave little indication of the liberal approach he was to develop later.

> Almost his first act of state was to earn religious merit and the title of Ghazi (slayer of infidels) by striking at the disarmed and captive Hemu after his defeat at the second battle of Panipat. Akbar was not asked to whet his sword on Hemu because he was a rebel, but because he was a Hindu. He was to perform not the task of the official executioner, but that of a victorious soldier of Islam. Abu'l Fazl would have us believe that the boy Akbar was wiser than his years and refused to strike a defenseless enemy. But most other writers are agreed that he struck at Hemu and earned the title of the Ghazi thereby.[66]

Moreover, the "Akbar-Nama, the Ain-i-Akbari and Badayuni are all agreed that prior to 1593 some Hindus had been converted to Islam forcibly."[67]

Even Akbar's liberal policy was not shared by all. An incident illustrates this well. When the Battle of Haldighati took place in 1576,

> the historian Badauni had enthusiastically joined this campaign, because, as he put it, 'I have a presumption to desire to dye these black mustachios and beard in blood through loyalty to your Majesty's person.' He said to Asaf Khan, the chief under whom he fought, 'How are we in these circumstances, since there are Rajputs on either side, to distinguish between friendly and hostile Rajputs?" He answered, "Oh whichever side these may be killed, it will be a gain to Islam.' He records with great satisfaction: 'My hand prospered in the matter, and I attained the reward due to one who fights against infidels;' and that day through the generalship of Man Singh, the meaning of this line of Mulla Shir became known: *"A Hindu strikes, but the sword is Islam's.'* "[68]

Nevertheless, on the whole, the situation in Akbar's reign was essentially characterized by one of fair treatment of all religions. Hindu missionary activity seems to have benefited from this, especially when it came to taking ex-Hindus back into the fold, for "Akbar issued orders permitting the Hindus to reconvert to their faith such Hindus as had been forcibly compelled to accept Islam earlier. It is difficult to judge precisely the effects of this order. Contemporary accounts are silent as to the number of Hindus who went back to their faith as a result of this permission. Surely it could not have been an idle gesture."[69] The fact that conversions to Hinduism were taking place is also implied in the order against mixed marriages when "Akbar decreed that as such conversions to *Hinduism or Islam* were based on passion rather than on religion, they should not be permitted."[70] R.S. Sharma notes that Vincent Smith "rather unfairly omits to notice the provision in the Dabistan concerning such *conversions to Hinduism* notwithstanding the fact that Blochmann refers to it."[71]

There is evidence of conversion to Hinduism during the reign of Jahāngīr as well (1605–1627). "When Jehangir discovered in his fifteenth year that the Hindus at Rajauri converted and married Muslim girls of the locality, he had orders that this practice be put a stop to and the guilty be punished."[72] There is also evidence of such conversion continuing in the reign of Shāh Jahān (1627–1658).

> When Shah Jehan returned from Kashmir, in the sixth year of his reign, he discovered that Hindus of Bhadauri and Bhimbar were forcibly marrying Muslim girls and converting them to the Hindu faith. At death these women were cremated according to the Hindu rites. Jahangir had tried to stop this practice but with no success, and Shah Jahan also issued orders declaring such marriages unlawful. Four thousand such conversions are said to have been discovered. Many cases were also found in Gujarat and in parts of the Punjab. Partly to deal with such cases, and partly to conform to his early notions of an orthodox Muslim king, Shah Jahan established a special department to deal with conversions. After the tenth year of his reign, he seems to have ceased trying to prevent the proselytizing activities of the Hindus. There are several later cases of the conversion of Muslims, not recorded by the court historians. A number of Muslims—including at least two Muslim nobles, Mirza Salih and Mirza Haider—were converted to Hinduism by the vairagis, the wandering ascetics of the Chaitanya movement, which had become a powerful religious force in Bengal.[73]

The Vairāgīs seem to have been particularly active as missionaries. "Muhsin Fānī, who does not make any reference to the Bengal Vaishṇavas in his *Dabistān-ul-Majahab*, writing about the Vairāgīs, says: 'Whoever among the Hindus, Mussalmans or others wishes is received into their religion, none are rejected, but on the contrary all are invited.' He must have noticed this practice amongst the Vaishṇava ascetics of Upper India. He himself admits that he received the favor of a Hindu saint named Chatur Vāpāḥ. In 1642 AD, he met another saint, Nārāin Dās, in Lahore and wrote: 'A great number of Mussalmans adopted their creed, such as Mirza Saleh and Mirza Haidar, two noble Mussalmans who became Vairāgīs.'"[74]

There is also evidence of the manifestations of the Hindu tendency to assimilate other creeds within itself, which often characterizes its missionary activity. Thus, we learn that a Hindu saint Prānnāth,

> who acquired great influence with Chhatraśāl, the Raja of Bundelkhand . . . composed a book called *Mahitariyal* in which he placed texts from the holy Qur'ān and the Vedas side by side to prove that their tenets are not essentially different. He allowed his Hindu and Muslim disciples to follow the rituals and laws of their respective religions, but insisted on both the Hindus and Muslims dining together at the time of initiation.[75]

There is some evidence to suggest that Hindu missionary activity of a covert sort was in progress even in the time of Aurangzēb (1658–1707).

> On April 9, 1669, it was reported to the emperor, that the Brahmans of Sind, Multan and particularly Banaras were using their temples as schools, which attracted students, Hindus and Muslims alike, from great distances. Jehangir had not been able to tolerate even a young Muslim going to a Yogi for instruction in religious matters. It was but natural, therefore, that Aurangzeb should have been upset by such a report. But whereas Jehangir had held the two Muslims concerned guilty and punished them, Aurangzeb gave an order for the punishment of those whose only offence was the imparting of religious education to those who came to them.[76]

The case is instructive in several ways: (1) It is clear that Muslims were being attracted to Hindu religious doctrines and practices. (2) It is further clear that, notwithstanding all that is said about the Hindu attitude to the *mlecchas*, the Muslims were accepted as students. (3) The practice had not ceased even though efforts had been made to put a stop to it earlier. (4) As there is hardly any formal conversion to Hinduism, the kind of educational practices involved in the above case may well have been precisely the way in which non-Hindus gradually become Hindus. This must be borne in mind to prevent a premature dismissal of the evidence as of little consequence.

The following statement of S.M. Ikram needs to be taken seriously on the basis of these pieces of evidence:

> Hinduism is not generally thought of as a missionary religion, and it is often assumed that during Muslim rule conversions were only from Hinduism to Islam. This is, however, not true. Hinduism by now was very much on the offensive and was absorbing a number of Muslims.[77]

Even though one may not be quite certain whether Hinduism was on the "offensive," it is clear that it was rather defiant,[78] as the various rebellions Aurangzēb had to cope with clearly demonstrate. But above all it is clear that, even during Mughal rule, and even in Aurangzēb's time, it continued to exhibit tendencies of a missionary character.

V

One may now turn to South India for evidence of Hindu missionary activity or Hindu militancy in the face of the Islamic penetration of the South. Of supreme importance to the discussion here are the circumstances in which the foundation of the Vijayanagar Empire were laid, an empire whose significance lies in the fact that "for well nigh three centuries it stood for the older religion and culture of the country"—the Hindu—"and saved these from being engulfed by the rush of new ideas and forces," namely those of Islam.[79]

While the "early history of Vijayanagar is still shrouded in obscurity," the following picture has been pieced together by scholars.[80] The Sultan of Delhi captured Warangal in 1335 and the two brothers, Harihara and Bukka, fled to the Hindu kingdom of Kampili. They were however "taken captive by Muhammad Tughluq, embraced Islam" and were "entrusted by the Sultan to restore Muslim authority in the region" when he left for Delhi. In the meantime some of the other southern kingdoms had shaken off the Muslim yoke.

Harihara and Bukka, who must have followed closely the course of the war of independence, realized that it was impossible for them, under the changed circumstances, to maintain the authority of the Sultan in the province. They had, however, no desire to follow the example of Malik Maqbūl, the governor of Tiling; nor did they consider it wise to declare their independence and set up a Muslim dynasty at Kampilī. Hemmed in on three sides by the two powerful Hindu kingdoms of Karnataka and Andhra, and with no prospect of getting any help from Delhi, the chances of establishing an independent Muslim State on the banks of the Tuḥgabhadrā were remote. They decided, therefore, to throw in their lot with their Hindu subjects. Islam, which they were compelled to embrace, sat lightly on them, and they still cherished fondness for the faith of their fathers. Under the influence of sage Vidyāraṇya, whom they accepted as their guide both in temporal and spiritual matters, they came to believe that it was their duty to renounce Islam and champion the cause of the ancient Hindu *dharma*. Their path was not free from obstacles. The Hindu society was chary in re-admitting within its fold those who were forced to embrace Islām. Moreover, they were treated with suspicion on account of their connection with the Musulmāns. They, however, got over these difficulties with the help of Vidyāraṇya, who arranged for their re-conversion to Hindu religion. He convinced Vidyātīrtha, his own *guru* and the chief pontiff of the Advaita-maṭha at Śriṅgerī, that the re-conversion of his disciples was necessary for saving the Hindu *dharma*, and secured his approval. Harihara and Bukka were then taken back to Hinduism, and to mitigate any suspicion that might still lurk in the minds of the people, it was declared that Harihara was not ruling the kingdom in his own right but as a viceregent of the god Virūpāksha to whom it actually belonged. To lend colour to this declaration, Harihara was persuaded to adopt the name of the god Śrī Virūpāksha as his sign manual with which he had to sign all the state documents. Harihara was crowned in AD 1336 as the king of the new kingdom of Hampi-Hastināvatī; and to commemorate the event he laid the foundations of his new capital, Vijayanagara, on the same day.[81]

The above account has been reproduced in detail because the details of the founding of the Vijayanagar Empire, though known to students of Indian history, are often not known to students of Indian religions, and the blending of Hindu missionary activity and Hindu militancy produced such a unique mix that the details thereof are best not abbreviated.

Clear evidence of the missionary character of Hinduism in South India at the time is thus provided by the reconversion of Harihara and Bukka. Another interesting piece of evidence in support comes from a rather unlikely source, the *Pañcadaśī*, a popular manual of Advaita Vedānta,[82] composed by Vidyāraṇya (mentioned in the passage cited above). The verse runs:

> gṛhito brāhmaṇo mlecchaiḥ
> prāyascittam caranpunaḥ
> mlecchaiḥ saṅkīryate naiva
> tathābhāsaḥ śarīrakaiḥ

> Just as a brāhmaṇa seized by Mlecchas and afterwards undergoing the appropriate *prāyaścitta* does not become confounded with Mlecchas (but returns to the original status of being a brāhmaṇa) so the Intelligent Soul is not really to be confounded with the body and other material adjuncts.

According to P.V. Kane, who has drawn attention to this verse, "this establishes that the great Vidyāraṇya, who after Śaṅkarācārya, is the greatest figure among the ācāryas approved of the view that a brāhmaṇa even though enslaved by Mlecchas could be restored to his original status,"[83] i.e., get reconverted to Hinduism.

There is further evidence in support of reconversion to Hinduism to which attention may now be drawn: (1) Gangadhar Ranganatha Kulkarni of Harsul was forcibly converted to Islam but was administered appropriate *prāyascitta* and restored to his caste under orders from the Marattha king Sambhājī. (2) Khandu Jadhav was forced by the Muslims to eat their food and was restored to his caste for a fee of two rupees taken by the *brāhamaṇas*. (3) Aurangzēb forcibly converted one of Shivājī's commanders, Raje Netaji Palkar, to Islam, but he was reconverted to Hinduism by Shivājī. It is interesting that there are numerous such instances in which assemblages of *brāhamaṇas* are approached by the king, or the interested party, for determining the proper *prāyaścitta* for the restoration of caste.[84]

Chapter VI

Hinduism as a Missionary Religion

The Evidence from Modern India

I

One of the early representative figures of modern Hinduism is Raja Rammohun Roy (1772/74–1833). He is actually called a missionary by Richard Church, when Church writes that "Rabindranath Tagore carried on the great work begun 150 years ago by Rammohun Roy, *your first missionary to England.*"[1] Although the sense of the word here is obviously much more refined, and different from the usual one, it does serve to indicate that some sense of missionary zeal has to be associated with the work carried on by Rammohun Roy, although it was primarily directed toward reforming Hinduism[2] itself, rather than toward converting other people to it. As U.N. Ball has pointed out: "He felt the call within and would not deviate from his course in spite of the threats and frowns of others. He never despaired of his *mission* for want of support of others."[3] In this sense too, he was a missionary—also in the sense that he took the prime purpose of missionary activity to be moral rather than theological. This attitude he shared with his American Unitarian friends. As Rev. Robert Loring has remarked:

> The American liberals then, as now, did not share the orthodox zeal for missions, because they did not share the belief that the heathen needed a theological type of salvation . . . They entirely agreed with Rammohun Roy when he spoke of 'common-sense in religion,' of 'practical' religion, and when he explained that he omitted certain doctrines of Christianity in his selection of verses form the Gospels, 'first, that they are subjects of disputes and contentions;

> secondly, that they are not essential to religion.' Neither Rammohun Roy nor the American Unitarians denied the value of speculation, of philosophy, or argument in religion, but both wished to transfer the emphasis in religion from theological salvation, to moral salvation, from church creeds to personal character, from speculative knowledge to ethical and social inspiration.[4]

But what about Rammohun Roy as a missionary of Hinduism? Several points need to be noted here. First, inasmuch as it is not the goal of Hinduism to convert people necessarily to itself but to a more liberal and tolerant approach to religious pluralism in general, clearly Rammohun Roy was a missionary in this sense.[5] That he did indeed regard such tolerance as a vital element of Hinduism is clear from what he wrote in 1821: "It is well-known to the whole world, that no people on earth are more tolerant than the Hindoos, who believe all men to be equally within the reach of Divine beneficence, which embraces the good of every religious sect and denomination."[6] Second, that he did conceptually concede the possibility of formal conversion to Hinduism is clear from the speech he gave when Rev. Alexander Duff opened a school for imparting Western education in 1830. In relation to the fear that familiarity with the Bible may result in conversion to Christianity, he remarked: "Christians like Dr. H.H. Wilson have studied the Hindu sastras and you know that he has not become a Hindu."[7] Third, that he *may* have actually done something in the direction could perhaps be inferred from an interesting fact mentioned by Sir Brajendra Nath Seal—that he had adopted a Mohammadan child and called him Rajaram![8] It must, however, finally be noted, that already in Roy, one finds a clear anticipation of the standard neo-Hindu position that real conversion is vertical and not horizontal—that it consists in a Hindu becoming a better Hindu and a Christian a better Christian rather than in a Hindu becoming a Christian or vice versa.[9] Thus Roy wrote in the introduction to the *Kena Upanisad*:

> I have often lamented that in our general researches into theological truth we are subjected to the conflict of many obstacles. When we look to the traditions of ancient nations, we often find them at variance with each other; and when, discouraged by this circumstance, we appeal to reason as a surer guide, we soon find how incompetent it is alone to conduct us to the object of our pursuit. We often find that,

> instead of facilitating our endeavours or clearing up our perplexities, it only serves to generate a universal doubt, incompatible with principles, on which our comfort and happiness mainly depend. *The best method perhaps is neither to give ourselves up exclusively to the guidance of the one or the other; but endeavour to improve our intellectual and moral faculties,* relying on the goodness of the Almighty Power, which alone enables us to attain that which we earnestly and diligently seek for.[10]

Is such a point of view the negation of conversion, or the sublimation of conversion? The answer to that question will decide the extent to which we may regard Rammohun as a missionary.

Although Roy may, or may not, have been a missionary, considerable missionary zeal must be associated with another leading figure of the Brahmo movement, namely Keshub Chunder Sen (1838–1884). In his case, however, we find an interesting interaction of missionary and universal elements. What Sivanath Sastri regards as Keshub's fifth and sixth contributions to Brahmoism make interesting reading in this context:

> The fifth contribution was the infusion of *bhakti* or devotional fervour into the movement. Before his time the spiritual life of the Samaj partook more of the nature of thought and communion than of devotional fervour. Under Devendra Nath, who was a disciple of the Vedic *Rishis*, the piety of the Samaj occupied a high platform of elevating thought and spiritual communion, somewhat inaccessible to the common people. Mr. Sen partly changed that character by the infusion of *bhakti* into it. From Chaitanya's followers he introduced the practice of *Sankirtan* or devotional singing, which was an innovation in those days, but which opened the floodgates of devotional passion, making Brahmoism a practical religious culture, sweet and soothing to the human heart. During the course of the preceding two or three centuries the disciples of Chaitanya had fallen under popular contempt in Bengal, owing to the introduction of many objectionable practices amongst them. Mr. Sen rescued the name of the great prophet from that popular contempt by his warm advocacy of the methods of propagation introduced by him. Those new methods certainly brought Brahmoism nearer to the popular mind.

> The sixth was his sense of the universality of theism. It possessed him something like a passion. The conviction forced itself upon him from his study of the lives of the great religious teachings. He found a universal element in which all of them agreed. This conviction became further modified, in later times, into an ideal harmony of all religions, which led him into the rather novel doctrine that all religions were true. Many of us will certainly deny that position; but Mr. Sen's conception of the great and glorious mission of the theism of the Samaj to unify conflicting sects and creeds was certainly prophetic.[11]

Notwithstanding the manner in which Keshub combined "Brahmo nationalism, Vaiṣṇava emotionalism, Christian supernaturalism and Vedantic mysticism,"[12]—the vicissitudes the Brahmo Samaj underwent during his leadership and the unclear relationship of the Samaj with Hinduism make an assessment of his missionary activity in a Hindu context somewhat problematical.[13]

While we have to equivocate somewhat in describing Rammohun Roy of Bengal as a missionary—or would at least wish to clarify the sense in which the word *missionary* is being used before he may be called a missionary—such precautions are perhaps not necessary when one turns to the figure of Shree Swaminarayan (1781–1830), Roy's contemporary in Gujarat.[14] It is clear from the account of Bishop Heber's meeting with Swaminarayan[15] that one of the six persons who came to Bishop Heber's tent to convey Swaminarayan's greeting to him was "an old Mussulman, with a white beard." Was he merely an employee or a follower? Bishop Heber remarks: "The first spokesman told me that the young man now in the company of the eldest son of a Coolie Thakur, whose father was one of the Pundit's great friends, that he was himself a Rajpoot and ryot, that the old man in green was a Mussulman sepoy in the Thakoor's service, and sent to attend on his young master. He added that though of different castes, they were all disciples of Swaamee Narain, and taught to regard each other as bretheren."[16] This would seem to suggest that Swaminarayan had a Muslim follower, though the degree of conversion involved is not clear. But the fact that Swaminarayan movement was clearly missionary is supported by the Bishop's statement that, when the Bishop asked the Swami to expound his doctrine: "It was evidently what he came to do, and his disciples very visibly exulted in the opportunity of his, perhaps, *converting me*."[17] We also have Monier Monier-Williams personal testimony about the activity of the missionaries of the movement founded by Swaminarayan.[18]

The evidence provided by the attitude of Mahadev Govind Ranade (1842–1901) on the question of the missionary or non-missionary nature of Hinduism may now be considered. The importance of M.G. Ranade in this context consists of the fact that the theater of his activity was Maharashtra, which had a proximate history of a reformist devotional movement well into the eighteenth century.[19] This had an important implication for Hinduism as a missionary religion. Had Roy vigorously campaigned for the membership of the Brahmo Samaj as a group distinct from the Hindus, his efforts could have easily been labeled as missionary, although we have seen that this was hardly the case. A movement like the Prarthana Samaj, which was even less self-conscious of being distinct from Hinduism would, on account of such a reformist background, therefore hardly qualify as missionary. The work of Ranade, like that of Roy, "was more about the social and political aspects of religion than about its purely spiritual aspect," and this meant that a preoccupation with reform more or less precluded a concern with the missionary or otherwise nature of Hinduism, even to a greater extent than in the case of the Brahmo Samaj and specially the Arya Samaj. D.S. Sarma points out in this connection that many "members of the Arya Samaj in the Punjab and of the Brahmo Samaj in Bengal held the view that, when once people were converted to their own protestant religion, all the desired reforms would be automatically brought about. They found fault with Ranade and the Social Conference for confining themselves to social reform instead of *religious conversion*."[20]

It is clear then that conversion to the various new sects within Hinduism was an ongoing process, a process which did not quite cross the borders of Hinduism, though there was nothing in principle to prevent this from happening. Both the Brahmo Samaj and the Arya Samaj accepted non-Hindus, the former without and the latter with a purificatory rite. The Prarthana Samaj did not quite follow in their footsteps, but it is interesting to note that Ranade clearly associated a sense of mission with his calling. As D.S. Sarma remarks: "The great reformer must have startled his hearers when he said in his address at the Seventh Social Conference in Lahore in 1893:

> I profess implicit faith in two articles of my creed. This country of ours is the true land of promise. This race of ours is the chosen race.[21]

This sense of mission for the Indians is further confirmed when he remarks: "If the miraculous preservation of a few thousand Jews had a purpose, this more miraculous preservation of one-fifth of the human race is not due to mere chance."[22] But was he thinking here of the Indians or of the Hindus, or it did not quite matter?

One can speak with more confidence in the matter when one turns to Swami Dayananda Sarasvati (1824–1883). For Dayananda, Hinduism was clearly a missionary religion. V.S. Naravane seems to single out Dayananda for harboring such an attitude among the spokesmen of modern Hinduism.

> One point, however, should be noted here. Dayananda supported the idea of proselytization and told his followers that there should be no hesitation in converting non-Hindus to Hinduism. By doing this he seemed to set aside one of the characteristic features of Hinduism. Unlike the Judaeo-Christian and the Islamic faiths, Hinduism abstained from seeking converts. It regarded different religions as paths leading to the same goal. Historians of religion have always looked upon this characteristic as a mark of Hinduism's maturity and universalism. Dayananda, however, categorically asserted that Hinduism became non-missionary only in periods of decadence and weakness. Few progressive Hindus would accept this aspect of Dayananda's teaching. Mahatma Gandhi urged Christian missionaries to propagate the message of Jesus without seeking converts; and he invariably pointed to the example of Hinduism as worthy of emulation, so far as this aspect of religion was concerned.[23]

Whether Dayananda was alone in adopting such an attitude is for the reader to judge, but there is little doubt that the conception of Hinduism as a missionary religion is more pronounced in him than many others. This idea underlies Dayananda's doctrine of *śuddhi.* Three levels of the application of the word may be distinguished, which by itself means purification:[24]

1. "*the* quality of purity necessary for the proper performance of *dharma*";
2. "*the* rite by which pollution is removed and access to *dharma* restored," and
3. "the reinstatement of a 'lapsed" Hindu, perhaps somebody who had been converted to another religion."[25]

It is in this last sense that Svami Dayananda gave it currency,[26] and it has been a feature of the activities of the Arya Samaj ever since, though nowadays at a somewhat reduced level of intensity.[27]

One important point must be clarified here. The name *Śuddhi* (purification) might suggest that *only* a lapsed or former Hindu could be converted to Hinduism. It could also be suggested that this did not make Hinduism of the Arya Samaj brand, strictly speaking, a missionary religion as according to this doctrine of no conversion, only reconversion, to Hinduism was possible.[28]

This, however, is not the case for several reasons. First of all, Dayananda was in the Punjab, where the idea of *śuddhi* caught on, at the time of the inception of the idea that conversion to Hinduism is possible,. Thus, from its very inception the concept is associated with the conversion to Hinduism of not merely of former Hindus but of non-Hindus as well.[29] Second, it was pointed out in an earlier chapter how the *Manusmṛti* regards various peoples of the world (the Greeks and the Chinese included), as lapsed Hindus. Dayananda was a close student of the *Manusmṛti* and could easily have used the argument that those who appear to be non-Hindus are really lapsed Hindus.[30] Finally, the Arya Samaj has an explicitly global orientation. "In 1877 a list of 'Ten Principles' was formed by Dayananda which became the statement of faith all new members of the Samaj were expected to sign. It is still so used."[31] The sixth principle runs as follows:

> The *primary* object of this society is to do good in the *whole world*, that is, to look to its physical, social and spiritual welfare.[32]

The chapter seems to be developing a rhythm all its own in which one member of a pair seems to regard Hinduism only hesitantly as a missionary religion and the other enthusiastically so. Such is the situation if we pair Roy and Swaminarayan and Ranade and Dayananda. It also turns out to be the case with that famous pair of Ramakrishna (1833–1883) and Vivekananda (1863–1902).

Hinduism could hardly be regarded as a missionary religion from the point of view of Ramakrishna. As Arnold Toynbee writes in his preface to Swami Ghanananda's *Sri Ramakrishna and His Unique Message*:

> Sri Ramakrishna's message was unique in being expressed in action. The message itself was the perennial message of Hinduism. As Swami Ghanananda points out, Hinduism is unique among the historic higher religions in holding

> that neither Hinduism nor any other religion is a unique representation of the truth or a unique way of salvation. In the Hindu view, each of the higher religions is a true vision and a right way, and all of them alike are indispensable to mankind, because each gives a different glimpse of the same truth, and each leads by a different route to the same goal of human endeavours. Each, therefore, has a special spiritual value of its own which is not to be found in any of the others.[33]

If such be the case, where is the rationale for conversion?

This very insight, however, was informed with a sense of mission by his disciple Swami Vivekananda. "To the familiar argument that all religions were true, being but different pathways to the same goal, Vivekananda tended to add the suggestion that Hinduism was the only one of the great religions profound enough to recognize this fact. The insight of Hinduism meant that India had a spiritual secret that sharpened the contrast between her and the materialistic nations of the West."[34] It is in such a background that the following call for the conquest of the world by Indian thought, issued by Vivekananda to the young men of Madras, must be understood:

> This is the great ideal before us, and every one must be ready for it—the conquest of the whole world by India—nothing less than that, and we must all get ready for it, strain every nerve for it. Let foreigners come and flood the land with their armies, never mind. Up, India, and conquer the world with your spirituality! Aye, as has been declared on this soil first, love must conquer hatred, hatred cannot conquer itself. Materialism and all its miseries can never be conquered by materialism. Armies when they attempt to conquer armies only multiply and makes brutes of humanity. Spirituality must conquer the West. Slowly they are finding out that what they want is spirituality to preserve them as nations. They are waiting for it, they are eager for it. Where is the supply to come from? Where are the men ready to go out to every country in the world with the messages of the great sages of India? Where are the men who are ready to sacrifice everything, so that this message shall reach every corner of the world? Such heroic souls are wanted to help the spread of truth. Such heroic workers are wanted to go abroad and help; to disseminate the great truths of the

> *Vedanta*. The world wants it; without it the world will be destroyed. The whole of the Western world is on a volcano which may burst tomorrow, go to pieces tomorrow. They have searched every corner of the world and have found no respite. They have drunk deep of the cup of pleasure and found its vanity. Now is the time to work so that India's spiritual ideas may penetrate deep into the West. Therefore, young men of Madras, I specially ask you to remember this. We must go out, we must conquer the world through our spirituality and philosophy. There is no other alternative, we must do it or die. The only condition of national life, of awakened and vigorous national life, is the conquest of the world by Indian thought.[35]

Even though Vivekananda may have disowned the description, he was in a sense a missionary, perhaps the first major missionary of Hinduism in the West where "he made several devoted English converts, and laid the foundations of Neo-Vedantism in America which later captivated Aldous Huxley, Gerald Heard and other well-known literary figures."[36] This is well-known. What is less well-known is the fact that like Swami Dayananda, he also supported (though like Dayananda did not engage in) the reconversion of the non-Hindus in India to Hinduism.[37]

The attitude of the Theosophical Society to the issue of conversion has been discussed previously. By contrast to its opposition to conversion from Hinduism and even to conversion in general, one occasionally gets glimpses of a different viewpoint—one which is not averse to conversion to Hinduism. The American Theosophists wrote to Swami Dayananda about the willingness of the people in the West to convert to Indian religions. It may also be added that although it was Annie Besant (1847–1933) who declared that "A Hindu is born, he is not made"[38]; she herself was an Englishwoman who had virtually become a Hindu! As D.S. Sarma points out, after arriving in India in 1893, "she thereafter made India her home, wore Hindu costume, adopted Hindu ways of life and worked for the revival of Hinduism and the uplift of the Indian nation for forty years till she died."[39] He goes on to say: "One may well believe that Mrs. Besant possessed a Hindu heart beneath her European skin."[40] And asks: "who without possessing a Hindu heart could go on a pilgrimage, as Mrs. Besant did in 1901, to the cave temple of ice at Amarnath, 16,000 feet above the sea in the Himalayas, walking barefoot on the snow and bathing in the ice-cold stream beside the cave before entering the temple?"[41]

Thus, even if Hinduism does not seek converts, there is nothing to prevent one from converting to it. Do we in Annie Besant have the case of one who, while insisting that Hinduism does not allow conversion, converted to it?[42]

Even more striking then is the case of Sri Aurobindo (1872–1950), the anglicised Hindu who "converted" to Hinduism. His opposition to conversion has already been discussed. Yet, when one reads his life, and specially his account of his mystical experience in the Alipore jail, one finds him hearing the "voice of the Bhagvan or the Gita telling him that he was to fulfil a spiritual *mission*."[43] He was told:

> Something has been shown to you in this year of seclusion, something about which you had your doubts and it is the truth of the Hindu religion. It is this religion that I am raising up before the world, it is this that I have perfected and developed through rsis, saints and *avatars*, and now it is going forth to do my work among the nations. I am raising up this nation to send forth my word. . . . When you go forth, speak to your nation always this word, that it is for the *Sanatana Dharma* that they arise, it is for the world and not for themselves that they arise. I am giving them freedom for the service of the world.
>
> It is for the *Dharma* that India exists.[44]

Thus, once again one finds, paradoxically, a sense of mission among those very spokesmen of Hinduism who would deny that Hinduism is a missionary religion.

Mahatma Gandhi (1896–1948) was most explicit in his opposition to conversion in the usual sense, as has already been documented. But it is clear that he had a message for humankind, for he once wrote: "I believe my message to be universal, but as yet I feel that I can best deliver it through my work in my own country. If I can show visible success in India, the delivery of the message becomes complete."[45] Those writing about Mahatma Gandhi speak in term of his mission. Thus we read; "It was in South Africa that Gandhi became conscious of a life-*mission*; and throughout his life thereafter he made it his sole concern to be devoted to that *mission*, which was to champion the cause of the victimized and the oppressed as against the insolence and might of those who enslaved and oppressed them."[46] Thus, Mahatma Gandhi may not have been a missionary in the usual sense of the word, but he had a sense of mission and also a sense of conversion—of a Hindu becoming a better Hindu, a Muslim a better Muslim, a Christian a better Christian.

But, though Mahatma Gandhi was a missionary, even a crusader—in the best sense of the term, that is, of moral causes—he remained totally opposed to formal conversion from one religion to another. It was indicated earlier how Annie Besant virtually became a Hindu by adopting Hindu ways. An English follower of Mahatma Gandhi, Madeleine Slade, who was given the name Mirabai by Mahatma Gandhi, adopted Hindu ways, but Mahatma Gandhi strenuously denied that she had become a Hindu and wrote on 20.2.1930 in *Young India*:

> The English press cuttings contain, among many delightful items, the news that Miss Slade, known in the Ashram as Mirabai, has embraced Hinduism. I may say that she has not. I hope that she is a better Christian than when, four years ago, she came to the Ashram. She is not a girl of tender age. She is past thirty and has travelled all alone in Egypt, Persia and Europe befriending trees and animals. I have had the privilege of having under me Mussulman, Parsi and Christian minors. Never was Hinduism put before them for their acceptance. They were encouraged and induced to respect and read their own scriptures. It is with pleasure that I can recall instances of men and women, boys and girls having been induced to know and love their faiths better than they did before if they were also encouraged to study the other faiths with sympathy and respect. We have in the Ashram today several faiths represented. No proselytizing is practised or permitted. We recognize that all these faiths are true and divinely inspired, and all have suffered through the necessarily imperfect handling of imperfect men. Miss Slade bears not a Hindu name but an Indian name. And this was done at her instance and for convenience.[47]

We may call Mahatma Gandhi a missionary of Hinduism by the example he set, but he would never allow his sense of mission to be tainted by conversion, which for him amounted to little more than religious subversion! In other words, to use Weberian terminology, Mahatma Gandhi upheld exemplary—as opposed to emissary or missionary—activity.

If Mahatma Gandhi, who possessed a sense of mission, has not been described as a missionary, S. Radhakrishnan (1888–1975) has been openly described as such, at least by two scholars. Eric J. Sharpe, a comparative religionist, remarks, perhaps truly, if somewhat tartly, that what Radhakrishnan has said "may still lead to a more marked impatience with those believers—usually Christians—who conceive of their traditions as being in some sense unique in the world of religion, or who persist in conducting a mission to humanity (as though the Radhakrishnans of this world were not in their own way missionaries!)"[48] The other reference is more complimentary. R. Pierce Beaver, an expert in Christian missionary activities, described Radhakrishnan as "probably the most influential missionary of religion per se as well as the Hindu version of it."[49] What is more, Radhakrishnan clearly admits that at one time Hinduism was a missionary religion.

> In a sense, Hinduism may be regarded as the first example in the world of a missionary religion. Only its missionary spirit is different from that associated with the proselytizing creeds. It did not regard it as its mission to convert humanity to any one opinion. For what counts is conduct and not belief. Worshippers of different gods and followers of different rites were taken into the Hindu fold. Kṛṣṇa, according to the *Bhagavadgītā*, accepts as his own, not only the oppressed classes, women and Śūdras, but even those of unclean descent (*pāpayonayaḥ*), like the Kirātas and the Hūṇas. The ancient practice of Vrātyastoma, described fully in the *Tāṇḍya Brāhmaṇa*, shows that not only individuals, but whole tribes were absorbed into Hinduism.[50]

Thus, according to Radhakrishnan, Hinduism is a missionary religion; its missionary character tends to be obscured by the fact that its sense of mission is different from that of some other religions—in that "it is wholly free from the strange obsession of some faiths that the acceptance of a particular religious metaphysic is necessary for salvation, and non-acceptance thereof is a heinous sin meriting eternal punishment in hell."[51] The conclusion of his popular book *The Hindu View of Life* is also worth some consideration at this point.

> After a long winter of some centuries, we are today in one of the creative periods of Hinduism. We are beginning to look upon our ancient faith with fresh eyes. We feel that our society is in a condition of unstable equilibrium. There is much wood that is dead and diseased that has to be cleared away. Leaders of Hindu thought and practice are convinced that the time requires, not a surrender of the basic principles of Hinduism, but a restatement of them with special reference to the needs of a more complex and

> mobile social order. Such an attempt will only be the repetition of a process which has occurred a number of times in the history of Hinduism. The work of readjustment is in process. Growth is slow when roots are deep. But those who light a little candle in the darkness will help to make the whole sky aflame.[52]

As with most figures of modern Hinduism, the passage is still concerned with reform of Hinduism, but will not such a reformed Hinduism carry the impulse which transforms it beyond its own borders? The metaphor at the end of the passage has only to be slightly amended to show how naturally this can follow, if one reads *torch* in the place of the *little candle* and looks upon the Hindus as the torch-bearers!

The more missionary position of Radhakrishnan may be contrasted with that of Rabindranath Tagore (1861–1941) and Ramana Maharshi (1879–1950). But, even here, it may be noted that Tagore has been referred to as a "missionary" by implication, though in its more attenuated sense of having a mission to fulfil,[53] which in the context of India meant its destiny "to raise the history of man from the muddy level of physical conflict to a higher moral attitude."[54] Nor was his mission a total failure, for "Tagore was particularly popular in Europe and America around the time of World War I, and he did much to enlist sympathy for Hindu religious thought in the West."[55] It has even been suggested that the "synthesis he advocates, though today it is temporarily neglected, is still the one most likely to succeed."[56] It could be maintained in his case, as in the case of Ramana, that their outlook was so universal[57] as to leave little room for missionary activity of the kind associated with advancing the claims of a particular tradition[58] in howsoever gentle a manner. Missionary activity is normally based on the urge to universalize a particular statement of truth; in these cases, the recognition of the universality inherent in their concept of truth or goodness paradoxically dulled the missionary edge.[59] There seems to be a fair measure of agreement on the whole among scholars that Hinduism, by the beginning of the twentieth century, may be regarded as missionary in character. The work of Swami Vivekananda in this respect is considered something of a turning point. He has been variously described as a "Hindu missionary to the West," as a "missionary of Vedantic Hinduism," and as the "most zealous of Hindu missionaries." Although these titles are a trifle misleading, the foundation of Vedanta societies and other Hindu organizations in America and Europe certainly dates back to

Vivekananda. Vivekananda founded the Ramakrishna Mission after returning to India, which was destined to play a very significant role in the development of modern Hinduism. Here, we are more concerned with his role as a Hindu missionary. Scholars note that "from the first visit of Vivekananda to America, neo-Hinduism has been slowly making converts outside India"[60] and that there is a new missionary zeal evident from the time of Vivekananda to the present.[61] Hence, when we are dealing with the modern period, perhaps no extra effort needs be made to establish that Hinduism is a missionary religion.

I will conclude this section with the responses of two Western scholars to the Lakṣmī-Nārāyaṇa Temple in New Delhi, popularly known as the Birla Temple. After describing this temple, A.L. Basham concludes: "Birla Mandir is symbolic of the new Hinduism—a vigorous faith with a deep social conscience and *considerable missionary zeal*, willing to accept whatever it deems fit wherever it finds it."[62] A.C. Bouquet, after noting that the ancient Hindus did not call themselves Hindus but rather followers of Arya Dharma,[63] goes on to remark:

> and it is significant that the newest of all Indian temples, the Lakshmi-Narayan temple at New Delhi, was built as recently as 1938 by a rich merchant, Seth Raja Baldeolas Birla, "for the benefit" (as is expressly stated) "of the different branches of Arya Dharma," and that it aims at including under one roof not only orthodox Hindus but Buddhists, Jains, Sikhs, Arya-Samaj, Sanatanists or ultra-conservative Hindus, and even Harijans or outcastes, as well as "visitors from Europe and America who are Aryans in origins and are interested in Arya-Dharma." The enthusiasts of this new temple-foundation go so far as to say: "The spirit of Arya Dharma is . . . all comprehensive and as such it embraces even Christianity and Judaism, without meddling with their individual differences."[64]

II

While there is some measure of agreement among scholars that Hinduism in modern times must be considered a missionary religion, there are important differences of opinion among them on certain points. These will now be presented, along with the name of a scholar associated with these viewpoints.

1. According to the first position, Hinduism is a universal but *not* a proselytizing religion.

This position seems to be best represented by T.M.P. Mahadevan. He asserts in the following passage that Hinduism is a *universal* religion:

> All the great world-religions may be regarded as universal in spirit. Some of them were founded by individual prophets. The others are considered to have been revealed to a number of seers. Buddhism, Christianity and Islam are 'founded' religions. Hinduism has no single founder; the ancient seers served as but channels for the transmission of religious truths to humanity. All these religions are universal by virtue of their appeal to the spirit in man. None of them is professed by all the men in the world. There can be no such dictatorial religion. The universality of the world-faiths consists in the provision they make for the perfection of man. Each of them has a system of rituals which, besides shaping the artistic instincts of the individual on the right lines, exert (sic) a stabilizing influence over the institutions of the religion, a scheme of ethics to make man morally perfect, a path or paths to conduct the pilgrim to his destination, namely God, and a philosophy to satisfy the rigorous intellectual demands and serve as a portal to the intuitive experience of the Absolute.[65]

He also points out that the concept of universality in religion does not imply the idea of one religion:.

> Right from the beginning of her history, India has stood for the rule of co-existence in religion. There is no meaning in forced conversion. Mahatma Gandhi reflects the spirit of India and of Hinduism in this respect, as in every other, when he says: "I should like to see all men, not only in India but in the world, belonging to different faiths, become better people by contact with one another and, if that happens, the world will be a much better place to live in than it is today. I plead for the broadest toleration, and I am working to that end. I ask people to examine every religion from the point of the religionists themselves. *I do not expect the India*

> *of my dream to develop one religion,* i.e., to be wholly Hindu or wholly Christian or wholly Mussalman, but I want it to be wholly tolerant with its religions working side by side with one another.'[66]

On the question of conversion, he cites the following conversation between the late Śrī Chandraśekhara Bhāratī Swāmi of Sringeri *Pīṭha* and an American tourist as setting forth the correct Hindu attitude towards conversion.

> 'Why must it be,' impatiently demanded an earnest American tourist, 'that you will not convert other peoples to Hinduism? You have such a beautiful religion and yet you keep so many struggling souls out of it. If you say "yes," I will be the first to become a Hindu!' 'But why,' came the counter-question, 'do you want to change your religion? What is wrong with Christianity?' Taken aback, but not daunted, the tourist said: 'I cannot say what is wrong, but it has not given me satisfaction.' 'Indeed, it is unfortunate,' was the reply, 'but tell me honestly whether you have given it a real chance. Have you fully understood the religion of Christ and lived according to it? Have you been a true Christian and yet found the religion wanting?' 'I am afraid I cannot say that, Sir.' 'Then we advise you to go and be a true Christian first; live truly the word of the Lord, and if even then you feel unfulfilled, it will be time to consider what should be done.' To put the puzzled American at his ease, the sage explained: 'It is no freak that you were born a Christian. God ordained it that way because, by the *samskāra* acquired through your actions (*karma*) in previous births, your soul has taken a pattern which will find its richest fulfilment in the Christian way of life. Therefore your salvation lies there and not in some other religion. What you must change is not your faith but your life.' 'Then, Sir,' exclaimed the American, beaming with exhilaration, 'your religion consists in making a Christian a better Christian, a Muslim a better Muslim and a Buddhist a better Buddhist. This day I have discovered yet another grand aspect of Hinduism, and I bow to you for having shown me this. Thank you indeed.'[67]

Thus, according to T.M.P. Mahadevan, Hinduism is a world religion, a universal religion. It is, also according to him, *not* a proselytizing religion, as forced conversion is meaningless.[68] But what about voluntary conversion to Hinduism? The answer is not clear. The answer seems to be clearer to another question: "should Hindus seek voluntary converts?." It seems to be no.

On balance, however, it would seem fair to say that T.M.P. Mahadevan would regard Hinduism as a "missionary" religion in the sense that it has a mission to proclaim to the world—that of religious tolerance;[69] he would *not* regard it as "missionary" in the sense of seeking converts.[70]

2. According to the second position, Hinduism was not a missionary religion but has now become a missionary and universalist religion.

This position is represented by A.C. Bouquet, among others. Crucial to it is the understanding that the transformation of Hinduism from an ethnic to a universal religion, and specially a missionary one, in all probability represents the influence of Christianity. Thus, A.C. Bouquet writes:

> There is undoubtedly a tendency on the part of modern Hindus to try to present their religion as capable of being detached from the peculiar limitations of caste, food-regulations, idol-worship, and even polytheism. They seem to be trying to make it undergo a transformation similar to that which the popular nationalist religion of Israel underwent during the period 750 BC to AD 100, and which eventually led to its partial transformation into that universalist religion, which became known to the world as Christianity. Thus in a recent pamphlet issued in Delhi we read: "Arya Dharma is the common heritage of the entire human race. Its preservation and propagation are the sacred duty of every right-thinking and truth-loving man. . . . Social conditions and conventions have been given the status of religion by ignorant and foolish people. . . . They cannot however be called religion. . . . Idol-worship, in a temple or elsewhere, is not an end in itself. It is simply a means to an end that end being the concentration of the mind on God." The writer goes on to invite the peoples of Europe and America to embrace Arya Dharma, and claims that its principles could be held by anyone who yet remained and called himself a Christian. "Arya Dharma is the product of the pooling of all that is best in religious thought all over the world."

> There are critics who say that this competitive attempt to make Hinduism a universalist religion is provoked by the spectacle of Christian propaganda, and also by the very natural desire of a proud and ancient people not only to represent their religion as in no way inferior to that of other lands, but also to interpret it in such a manner as to make it *inclusive* of other religions. This may or may not be the case. Such a book as this one must express no opinion on the matter, but only record the fact of the attempt, and the criticism which it has provoked.[71]

It seems fair to say then that, according to some scholars, Hinduism has become, or is becoming, missionary.

3. According to the third position, Hinduism was and is a missionary religion. The issue is not the fact of its being one but rather how precisely it should ideally go about fulfilling its mission in the future.

This position is best represented by Louis Renou, who writes:

> Some people think that Hinduism should cease to be ethnical in character (*assuming that it ever has been so*), and become once more a missionary religion. There are already several organizations for spreading knowledge of Hinduism in the West, but very often their propaganda does not reach the right circles. When Hinduism is 'exported,' it tends to be regarded as a kind of theosophy—after all, the basic doctrinal principles of theosophy are rooted in Hinduism—or as a brand of Christian Science, tinged with pseudo-Vedantism. It can only become a force for good in the world when it emerges in India itself as a purified form of religion, free from primitivism and the cult of images. Extreme practices, such as *Haṭhayoga* and Tantrism 'of the left,' which often make such a deep impression on Europeans, never constitute the main strength of a religion; they are special features that should not be imitated outside the land of their origin.[72]

III

Out of these three positions, the first and the last are minority opinions at present. If T.M.P. Mahadevan implies that Hinduism is not a missionary religion in the sense of being actively involved in conversion even in modern times, then perhaps many would demur. And, if Louis Renou implies that Hinduism was always a missionary religion in the sense of actively seeking converts, many may demur again. In the present climate of opinion, the view represented by Bouquet about the nature of Hinduism—that, in our modern times, it has turned missionary—would perhaps meet with more widespread acceptance than the other two views, though all may not agree in attributing this new development to Christian influence.

It is, however, the main thesis of this book that Hinduism has always possessed a missionary character, and therefore, it is the aim of this book to persuade the reader that it is the third viewpoint—the one associated with Louis Renou—which is historically and logically more sound than the alternatives. This may be demonstrated by taking a fresh look at two figures of modern Hinduism, who are regarded as the least missionary in the sense of seeking converts: Ramakrishna Paramahamsa and Mahatma Gandhi.[73] Nevertheless, they were people with the profoundest sense of mission, had a large number of followers (but not converts) and have had an abiding influence on our times. Through them, numerous people have been brought to a recognition of both the greatness of Hinduism and of the value of religious tolerance—though themselves were not missionaries, they inspired numerous Hindus with a sense of mission. Thus, even in the case of those figures of modern Hinduism—who were *themselves*, in a sense, the least missionary and most opposed to conversion—their *impact* seems to have imparted a more pronounced missionary character to Hinduism. The sense of mission represented by them may make Hinduism unique, but Hinduism is hardly unique in the sense of not being a missionary religion.

Conclusions

I

One conclusion which emerges from the foregoing survey is the need to refine the religious vocabulary that is traditionally employed in discussing this issue. Three terms often come into play in such a context: a religion is sometimes described as a *missionary* religion, sometimes as a *proselytizing* religion, and sometimes as a religion which believes in *conversion*.

The case of Hinduism suggests that the semantic fields in the case of each need to be mapped out more clearly. Let us begin with the expression *missionary religion*. A missionary religion, by definition, is a religion which either has a *mission* or has a *sense of mission*. It is possible, in principle, for a religion to be performing a mission without a sense of doing so. Hanukkah, for instance, is an important Jewish festival. A standard textbook on religion offers the following description of it:

> Near the winter solstice, the darkest time of the year, comes Hanukkah, the Feast of Dedication. Each night for eight nights, another candle is lit on a special candle holder. The amount of light gradually increases like the lengthening of sunlight. Historically, Hanukkah was a celebration of the victory of the Maccabean Rebellion against the attempt by Antiochus to force non-Jewish practices on the Jewish people. According to legend, when the Jews regained access to the Temple, they found only one jar of oil left undefiled, still sealed by the high priest. It was only enough to stay alight for one day, but by miracle, the oil stayed burning for eight days. Many Jewish families also observe the time by nightly gift-giving, as rewards for Torah study. The

> children have their own special Hanukkah pastimes, such as "gambling" for nuts with the dreidel, a spinning top with four letters on its sides as an abbreviation of the sentence "A great miracle happened there."[1]

What this description does not tell us is that the Hanukkah, in the opinion of many scholars of religion, is an especially important festival for American Jewry because it falls around Christmas. Given the importance Christmas enjoys in a largely Christian country like the United States, it provides an important foil for it for the Jews and serves to maintain Jewish identity in what would otherwise be an overwhelming Christian environment. One cannot claim that this was done by conscious choice. It was not on account of a sense of "mission" on the part of Christianity, that this qualitative enhancement of the role of the Hanukkah holiday came about. Yet, the two phenomena cannot be dissociated. However, although related as cause and effect, no sense of mission can be attached to the situation because it was a case of causation brought about without consciousness of it.

Interaction between Hinduism and Islam provides at least two examples of influence exerted by a religion without any sense of mission. It has been argued that, under Islamic law, a Muslim is not allowed to covet a married woman, even if of another faith, but an unmarried woman even of another faith may be considered fair game for marriage. Some historians have argued that this was a factor in lowering the marriageable age of women in Hinduism, because, however young, the women's security in an otherwise politically inhospitable environment was enhanced by her having the status of being a "married woman." Now, surely, it was not Islam's mission in India to lower the age of marriage of Hindu women, although such a development is attributed by some to its presence in India. Similarly, it has been suggested that the idea—that Hindu law was immutable—may have been developed in the face of a similar claim made for the *Sharī'ah* in Islam. Once again, it is doubtful if Islam looked upon it as its mission to "freeze" Hindu law in time, although this could again have been a consequence of its presence. A third example is provided by the growth of purdah in Hindu circles, allegedly as a result of the prevalence of that practice in the Islamic environment in India. Again, it is doubtful if the achievement of such an effect was looked upon by Islam as its mission. A fourth example is provided by the possibility that the abolition of discriminatory punishments based on caste in medieval Hindu *nibandhas* may have come about, at least partly, on account of the egalitarian element in Islam. One might, of course, phrase these developments in such a way as to say that it was the "mission" of Islam to bring about such changes (if indeed it did bring them about), but this would only be so described in a rhetorical rather than a historical sense. The point, then, is that certain developments that even secure converts accidentally as it were cannot therefore be called "missionary." For instance, let us suppose a Jewish kibbutz is set up in a remote village, and as a result of this activity, electricity becomes available to the whole village in that remote area. The villagers are so comforted by this development that they all offer to become Jews. Since there was no conscious desire to secure such an outcome, these offers of conversion—even if accepted—would not be adjudged as resulting from "missionary activity." To be a missionary religion, one must have a *conscious* sense of that mission.

This sense of mission, however, in relation to bringing others into one's fold in the broadest sense, may take several forms. In the case of some religions, the mission may merely consist of achieving mutual understanding—as for instance, in the case of a meeting of Hindus and Jews. In other words—a sense of mission need not involve the goal of conversion. (One could argue, as an extreme case, that it is the mission of neo-Hinduism to put a stop to conversion among religions. So, the Hindu is trying to bring others in the fold—but not *his* particular fold as such. One might say that it amounts to trying to convert someone to a point of view against conversion. One could thus argue that the neo-Hindu sense of mission *also* involves conversion, but then, it is conversion of a very different kind than one usually associated with the word.) One could nevertheless claim that neo-Hinduism is also a missionary religion, like Christianity and Islam, provided one realizes that the nature of the conversion involved in the two cases is very different. In this manner, Hinduism may pass muster when described as a "missionary religion."

If, however, Hinduism does not seek converts to *itself* (as distinguished from a trans-Hindu point of view according to which all religions are valid), then it will be harder to characterize it as a *proselytizing* religion. A proselytizing religion, directly or indirectly, actively seeks converts. This is important, for this means that even if people converted on their own to a religion that was not seeking them as converts, then even in the face of such conversion, the religion could not be called a proselytizing religion. Perhaps a distinction needs to be drawn here between religions *seeking* converts and religions *accepting* converts. It is the seeking of converts to its own fold that makes a religion a proselytizing one—not just the act of accepting them. One could, of course, at this end of the spectrum, draw a further distinction between religions that don't accept converts (as was claimed for Hinduism by some) and those that do.

This means the belief in conversion can also take many forms. One may not believe in conversion at all. One may only believe in accepting converts and not seeking them. Or one may both seek them and accept them. For the sake of completeness, there is the hypothetical case where one may seek them but not accept them (although it is bound to leave those who were sought out but not accepted rather frustrated if not angry).

In terms of these explanations, Hinduism *could be described as a missionary religion* (with the proviso that its sense of mission may be very different from that of many other religions). It may, however, *not be described as a proselytizing religion*—as it does not seek converts to itself, but it may be said to accept *conversion* to it in the sense of the acceptance of a universal point of view—though, ironically, because it does not seek converts, it may be judged as being against conversion.

II

Another conclusion suggested by this survey is more substantive than nominal. It has to do with the process of conversion.

The point is best developed with a comparative analysis of how conversion to a religion might occur and the consequences of undergoing it. It might be useful to begin by describing the process of conversion to Islam. Mahmoud M. Ayoub explains:

> In practical implementation, a Muslim is often someone born to a Muslim family and thus a member of the Muslim community. Or one can become a Muslim by repeating before two Muslims witnesses the *shahadah,* or profession of faith: 'I bear witness that there is no god except God, and I bear witness that Muhammad is the messenger of God.' By so doing, such a man or woman becomes legally a Muslim with all the rights and responsibilities this new identity entails. Whether what this person publicly professes with the tongue is what he or she truly holds in the heart, Muslims assert, is only for God to judge. There is no other ceremony required for one to become a Muslim.[2]

It should be added that, once one has thus publicly embraced Islam, one cannot be denied the status of being a Muslim. Thereafter, the operational categories become "good" Muslim or "bad" Muslim, rather than "Muslim" or "non-Muslim." It may be further clarified, that according to formal classical *Sharī'ah*, one may not abandon Islam after having embraced it. The penalty for such apostasy may involve death.

The key elements to be borne in mind, which will also have considerable bearing on the ensuing discussion, are that, in the case of Islam, (1) there is one uniform mode of conversion (uttering the *shahadah* with the intention to embrace Islam in front of witnesses); (2) conversion is a one-way street; and (3) the adherence to Islam is exclusive. That is to say, one cannot, for instance, be a Jew and a Muslim at the same time. This point is important because Islam shares considerable common ground with both Judaism and Christianity, but this does not compromise the exclusivity demanded by conversion to Islam. Patrick Burke explains:

> Although non-Moslems view Islam as the youngest of the major religions, Islam does not think of itself like that. It sees itself as identical with the first revelation God gave to mankind. The Koran mentions some twenty-five individuals to whom God gave the Koranic message in earlier times. These are the prophets. A prophet in this sense is not necessarily a person who predicts the future, but one who speaks on behalf of God. They include Adam, Noah, Abraham (Ibrahim), Joseph (Yusuf), Moses (Musa), Aaron (Harun), David (Dawud), John the Baptist (Yahya), and Jesus (Isa). All of these were Moslems.
>
> A glance in the direction of Christianity clarifies the situation further. Conversion to Christianity consists of undergoing the baptism, so there is uniformity in the procedure of conversion in Christianity as in the case of Islam. Similarly, Christianity also insists on exclusive adherence. That is to say, one cannot be a Christian and a Muslim at the same time. One can however *cease* to be a Christian or lose the faith. One may go to hell for doing that but one's life on earth is spared.[3]

The case of Judaism is particularly interesting. One is typically a Jew by birth, as is the case with the Hindu. But there also exists a rite of conversion to Judaism.

> Rabbinic Judaism came to specify three conditions for conversion: Milah (circumcision for men), tevilah (ritual immersion or baptism), and kabbalat 'ol ha-mitzvoth (accepting the yoke of the commandments). There are many stories of conversions in rabbinic literature. The rabbis sought to determine which candidates for conversion were sincere in their aspirations, for insincere converts endangered the community. They verified that converts were willing to cast their lot with this unfortunate and endangered people. With a yes answer, one was accepted. Usually conversions involved a period of training during which the candidate learned the extent of an adult Jew's specific responsibilities.[4]

An important point of a comparative and common nature in terms of adherence to a one of the three Abrahamic religions—Judaism, Christianity, and Islam—is important here, namely, that it has to be exclusive. Thus, one can either be a Jew or a Christian or a Muslim, and this singularity supersedes the commonalities they might share.

The rite of conversion to Buddhism consists of reciting the Three Refuges thrice. So, in Buddhism, there is uniformity of procedure as far as conversion is concerned in common with the Abrahamic religions. However, there is a major distinction between being a lay follower or a monastic follower of the Buddha. Two points are worth noting in the case of Buddhism:

1. That adopting Buddhism does not *necessarily* mean abandoning the social rituals of one's earlier lifestyle, although they may be considerably modified, and
2. One is free to leave the monastic order and to reenter it.

In the case of the Abrahamic religions and Buddhism, then, there is a basic uniformity in the procedure of conversion. The severing of prior allegiance is strong in the case of the Abrahamic religions but more muted in the case of Buddhism. And freedom to move out of the tradition is least in Islam, less so in Christianity, much more in Judaism and most so in Buddhism.

It is in such a background that the problematic nature of the concept of conversion in Hinduism becomes evident. (1) There is no uniform procedure for becoming a Hindu. Typically one enters Hinduism by becoming a member of a sect or the follower of a guru, and each have their own process of initiation or none. Thus, conversion to Hinduism really boils down to self-affirmation, with few objective criteria to establish it. (2) Conversion to Hinduism does not entail the abandonment of one's previous allegiance (although it might entail a modification in the previous life style); one can be a Hindu in addition to one's existing lifestyle or religion. (3) There is hardly any regulation of movement into and out of Hinduism. However, there is strong sentiment against a Hindu, who was born as one, leaving the fold.

One might, on the basis of this survey, propose that (1) a conversion procedure to a religion may be (a) formal or (b) informal and (a) single or (b) multiple; (2) conversion to religion may or may not entail the severance of previous religious affiliation; (3) conversion to a tradition may be irrevocable or revocable.

One of the reasons why Hinduism appears as a non-missionary religion is that missionary religions typically possess a formal and uniform conversion procedure, insist on severance of all other forms of religious adherence, and favor continued membership once conversion has occurred. These features sit lightly on Hinduism and are even viewed with a certain ambivalence.[5] This does not mean, however, that Hinduism is not a missionary religion; although its sense of mission is different from that of other religions. Hinduism is, nevertheless, a missionary religion. It does *not* follow from this fact, however, that it is a proselytizing religion.

III

One final dimension remains to be explored: The relationship between missionary activity and religious tolerance. Missionary activity, specially when it involves proselytization, has often been associated with intolerance, though this not need necessarily be the case. The very fact that someone is targeted for conversion means that the person who has set its sights upon a candidate for conversion is not willing to tolerate that candidate in his or her present condition. Thus, while theological intolerance is necessarily involved, this may or may not involve legal intolerance. Islam and Christianity provide useful examples here. Non-Muslims living in an Islamic state are accorded well-defined rights if they are "people of a book," and many countries, where Christians are in the majority and Christianity is active even evangelically, have a secular legal culture which forbids discrimination on religious grounds.

However, while missionary activity may thus coexist with formal religious tolerance even in a proselytizing context, Hinduism tends to regard proselytizing missionary activity as inconsistent with actual (as opposed to formal) religious tolerance. So, while the question in the case of proselytizing missionary activity assumes the form: given that a group believes in proselytization, does it accord tolerance to others? in the case of Hinduism, the question gets reversed—given that Hinduism believes in religious tolerance, why does it have to be missionary at all? Or one can sharpen the question even further: Can a tolerant religion also be a missionary religion?

The example of Buddhism helps us edge towards an answer. Buddhism is usually considered a tolerant religion, but it has also obviously been a missionary religion. It, thus, illustrates the point that it is possible to be a tolerant as well as a missionary religion. In a sense, Buddhism is also a proselytizing religion, but it does not require its new votary to abrogate its previous allegiance, especially in its cultural dimension. Thus, unlike the Abrahamic religions of Christianity and Islam, conversion to which may often involve a replacement of existing culture and religion, Buddhism by contrast is satisfied by a placement within it.

The relationship of religious tolerance to missionary activity is, therefore, extremely complex. Hinduism has generally tended to follow the Buddhist example in this respect, only more so. It is clear, however, that, in accordance with its doctrine that all religions are valid or true, it possesses a very strong sense of mission in favor of religious tolerance. While, in the case of other religions, these two considerations provide points of tension or a call for coexistence—in Hinduism, they become integral to each other. But, if Hinduism believes in religious tolerance based on the equality of all religions, where would its missionary edge come from? It seems to stem from a desire to assist the world in making a transition from religious pluralism to religious universalism—or, in Sanskritic idiom, from *sarva-dharma-sama-bhāva* (all religions are the same) to *sarva-dharma-mama-bhāva* (all religions are mine, not just my own religion).

Notes

Preface

1. See Wilfred Cantwell Smith, *The Meaning and End of Religion: A New Approach to the Religious Traditions of Mankind* (New York: The MacMillan Company, 1962).

2. See Gunther D. Sontheimer and Herman Kulke, eds., *Hinduism Reconsidered* (New Delhi: Manohar, 1989).

Chapter I

1. See R.C. Majumdar, ed., *The Vedic Age* (Bombay: Bharatiya Vidya Bhavan, 1965) Chapter XI.

2. The evidence on the point suggests that the relations between the two branches of the Indo-Europeans may have become hostile. In such a situation, conversion by conquest would be logical procedure for a missionary religion to adopt, but there is no evidence of this happening.

3. See R.C. Zaehner, ed., *The Concise Encyclopedia of Living Faiths* (Boston: Beacon Press, 1959), 211.

4. Ibid., 210–11.

5. R.C. Majumdar, ed. *The Age of Imperial Unity* (Bombay: Bharatiya Vidya Bhavan, 1953) Chapter III, 39ff.

6. Ibid., 42.

7. Hemachandra Raychaudhuri, *The Political History of Ancient India with a Commentary by B.N. Mukherjee* (New Delhi: Oxford University Press, 1999), 586.

8. Quoted in R.C. Majumdar, ed., *The Age of Imperial Unity*, 567–68.

9. Ibid., 554–55.

10. Ibid., 554.

11. Arrian, as cited by Allan Dahlquist, *Megasthenes and Indian Religion* (Uppsala, Sweden: Almquist and Wiksell, 1962), 65.

12. Pliny; cited, ibid., 55.

13. Vincent A. Smith, *The Early History of India* (Oxford: Clarendon Press, 1924), 311.

14. James Legge, trans., *A Record of Buddhistic Kingdoms* (New York: Dover Publications Inc., 1965 [1886]) 97.

15. Ibid., 43.

16. Ibid., 46–47.

17. Ibid., 78.

18. Ibid., 79.

19. Ibid.

20. Ibid., 43.

21. Interesting sidelight is thrown on such birth-orientation by Faxian's friend Tao-ching, who decided to stay back in India rather than return to China. "When Tao-ching arrived in the Central Kingdom, and saw the rules observed by the Sramanas, and the dignified demeanor in their societies which he remarked under all occurring circumstances, he sadly called to mind in what a mutilated and imperfect condition the rules were among the monkish communities in the land of Ts'in, and made the following aspiration:—'From this time forth till I come to the state of Buddha, let me not be born in a frontier land.' He remained accordingly (in India) and did not return (to the land of Han). Fa-hian, however, whose original purpose had been to secure the introduction of the complete Vinaya rules into the land of Han, returned there alone." (ibid., 99–100). James Legge comments: "This then would be the consummation of the Sramana's being,—to get to be Buddha, the Buddha of his time in his Kalpa; and Tao-ching thought that he could attain to this consummation by a succession of births, and was likely to attain to it sooner by living only in India. If all this was not in his mind, he yet felt that each of his successive lives would be happier, if lived in India" (ibid., 100, fn. 1). The *content* of resolve is Buddhist, but its structure parallels the Hindu idea of improving one's caste-status through successive rebirths. There are hints *that* even conversion to Buddhism may depend on past karma. When Maitreya appears, it is said those will be converted "whose Karma in the past should be rewarded by such conversion in the present" (ibid., 110, fn 1).

22. Ibid., 62, 79.

23. Even when in Śrī Laṅkā, Faxian writes: "The king practices the Brahmanical purifications, and the sincerity of the faith and reverence of the people inside the city are great" (ibid., 104).

24. For a brief account of his life, see Percival Spear, ed., *The Oxford History of India* (Oxford: Clarendon Press, 1958), 182. For a biography, see Samuel Beal, trans., *The Life of Hiuen-Tsang by the Shaman Hwui Li* (London: Kegan Paul, Trench, Trübner & Co., 1914). Also see D. Devahuti, ed., *The Unknown Hsuan-Tsang* (New Delhi: Oxford University Press, 2001).

25. See Vincent A. Smith, op. cit., 14–15.

26. D. Devahuti, *Harsha* (Oxford: Clarendon Press, 1970) passim.

27. Percival Spear, ed., op. cit., 183–84.

28. R.C. Majumdar, ed., *The Classical Age* (Bombay: Bharatiya Vidya Bhavan, 1954), 113.

29. J. Takakusu, trans., *A Record of the Buddhist Religion as practiced in India and the Malay Archipelago (AD, 671–695) by I-tsing* (Delhi: Munshiram Manoharlal, 1976 [1896]), xxv, xxxviii.

30. Ibid., xxvi.
31. Ibid., 50–53, 70, 71.
32. Ibid., 52.
33. Ibid.
34. Ibid., xxiii, fn. 3.
35. Ibid., 182, emphasis added.
36. Ibid., 68. This passage and its implication is also noted by Jawaharlal Nehru, *The Discovery of India* (New York: The John Day Company, 1946), 190–91.
37. T.W. Rhys Davids and S.W. Bushell, eds., *On Yuan Chwang's Travels in India 629–645 AD by Thomas Watters* (London: Royal Asiatic Society, 1904).
38. Ibid., Vol. I, 234, 250, 265, 283, 299, 371; Vol. II, 25, 44, 59, 60, 77, 81, 115, 176, 178, 183–84,186–87, 190, 193, 198, 214, 224, 226, 228, 244–46, 248–50, 252, 254, 265, 269.
39. Ibid., Vol. I, 204–205.
40. Ibid., Vol. I., 320–21, 339, 360, 368–369, 377; Vol. II, 5, 12, 30, 34. 55, 68, 81, 98, 103, 109, 112, 119, 131–32, 144, 156, 171, 191, 200, 209, 280, 296,.
41. T.W. Rhys Davids and S.W. Bushell, eds., op. cit., Vol. II, 109–110.
42. Ibid., 165, emphasis added.
43. Ibid., Vol. I., 319. The place has not yet been identified. It lay north-east of modern Thanesar.
44. Ibid., Vol. I, 319.
45. Ibid., Vol. I. 349.
46. See R.C. Majumdar, ed., *The Classical Age*, 117.
47. See T.W. Rhys Davids and S.W. Bushell, eds., op. cit., Vol. I, 278, 287, 291, 299, 334, 348, 351, 355, 356, 364, 386, 396; Vol. II, 14, 20, 23, 35, 42–43, 51, 63, 84, 86, 130131, 162, 186, 200, 239, 241–42, 246–49, 251, 257, 262.
48. R.C. Majumdar, ed., *The Classical Age*, 117–18.
49. See Vincent A. Smith, op. cit., 15.
50. Edward C. Sachau, ed., *Alberuni's India* (Delhi: S.Chand & Co., 1964 [Indian reprint]) xxiii–xxiv.
51. S.M. Ikram, *Muslim Civilization in India* (New York: Columbia University Press, 1964), 27; Wilhelm Halbfass, *India and Europe: An Essay in Understanding* (Albany, N.Y.: State University of New York Press, 1988), 25–30.
52. Edward C. Sachau, ed., op. cit., Vol. I, 17.
53. Ibid., 19–20.
54. Ibid., Vol. II, 162–63.
55. The suggestion that foreigners seem to have been treated like untouchables would appear to further confirm this view. Thus, it has been pointed out that "People belonging to the higher castes in the Madhya-desa (Mid-India) did not, according to the testimony of Fa Hien, kill any living creature, nor drink intoxicating liquor, nor eat onions or garlic. Sharply distinguished from them were the Chandalas, who lived apart from others. When they entered the gate of a city or a market-place they struck a piece of wood to make themselves known so that men knew and avoided them, and did not come into contact with them. The existence of impure castes is

vouched for not only by Indian and Chinese records, but by Al-Biruni. *If the last-mentioned scholar is to be believed, the doctrine of impurity was extended to foreigners in the north-west towards the end of our period.* The Hindus of several provinces in the interior, however, did not share the views of their brethren about whom Al-Biruni wrote." (R.C. Majumdar, H.C. Raychaudhuri and Kalikinkar Datta, *An Advanced History of India* [New York: St. Martin's Press, 1967], 189, emphasis added).

56. R.C. Majumdar, ed., *The Delhi Sultanate* (Bombay: Bharatiya Vidya Bhavan, 1960), 8.

57. Ibid.

58. S.R. Sharma, *The Crescent in India* (Bombay: Hind Kitabs Ltd., 1954), 138–49.

59. R.C. Majumdar, ed., *The Delhi Sultanate*, 627–31.

60. See H.A.R. Gibb, trans., *Ibn Battuta Travels in Asia and Africa 1325–1354* (London: George Routledge and Sons, 1929), passim.

61. R.C. Majumdar, ed., *British Paramountcy and Indian Renaissance* (Bombay: Bharatiya Vidya Bhavan, 1965), Part II, 343ff.

62. S.R. Sharma, op. cit., 226–28.

63. See H.A.R. Gibb, trans., op. cit., 231, 232, 234, 238.

64. R.C. Majundar, ed. *The Delhi Sultanate*, 629. The page references in the citation are to Mahdi Husain, *The Rehla of Ibn Battuta* (India, Maldive Islands and Ceylon: Baroda, India: 1953).

65. R.C. Majumdar, ed., *The Delhi Sultanate*, 631.

66. S.M. Ikram, op. cit., 131–32. It should be noted, however, that, while according to Albīrūnī, even cow dung could not remove pollution caused by contact with Muslims; according to Ibn Batūtah it was regarded as efficacious, as is clear from the concluding lines of the following passage (cited by R.C. Majumdar, ed., op. cit., 630): "Occasionally we were compelled to ask some of the infidels in India to cook meat for us. They used to bring it in their own cooking pots and to sit at a little distance from us; they used to bring also leaves of banana tree upon which they placed rice—their principal food—pouring over the rice broth called *koshan* and subsequently they withdrew. Then we used to eat it, and, whatever remained would be eaten by the dogs and birds. If any innocent child happened to take anything from that remnant they would beat him and compel him to eat cow's dung which according to their belief purifies (xxxiv)."

67. For more about him, see K.A Nilakanta Sastri, *A History of South India* (Madras: Oxford University Press, 1966). 32.

68. See Robert Sewell, *A Forgotten Empire* (London: George Allen & Unwin, 1924 [first published 1900]), passim.

69. R.C. Majumdar, H.C. Raychandhurī and Kalikinkar Datta, op. cit., 370.

70. Ibid., 371.

71. See S.R. Sharma, op. cit., 231–32.

72. Robert Sewell, op. cit., 7.

73. K.A. Nilakanta Sastri, op. cit., 270–71.

74. See S.R. Sharma, op. cit., 201–202.

75. See accounts contained in Robert Sewell, op. cit., especially 245–46, 256, 390–91, 393–395. It should be noted, however, that the tolerance shown to Muslims could also have a pragmatic element in it (see S.R. Sharma, op. cit., 199); although it seems to have been genuine (See K.A. Nilakanta Sastri, *Development of Religion in South India* [New Delhi: Orient Longmans, 1963], 127).

76. See K.M. Panikkar, *A Survey of Indian History* (London: Meridian Books, 1947), 221–23.

77. See Ram Chandra Prasad, *Early English Travellers in India* (Delhi: Motilal Banarsidass, 1965).

78. Ibid., 57, 118, 264, 292, 340.

79. Ibid., 61.

80. e.g. Henry Lord, *Discoveries of the Sect of the Banians* (London: T.& R. Cotes,1630).

81. Ibid., 206. But see Sri Ram Sharma, *The Religious Policy of the Mughal Emperors* (London: Asia Publishing House, 1972), Chapter IV.

82. K.M. Sen, *Hinduism* (Baltimore: Penguin books, 1973) 35. K.M. Sen cites an interesting passage on the question of image worship, which is reproduced below: "In this connection a three-hundred-year-old conversation between the seventeenth-century French traveller Francois Bernier and some Hindu pandits of Banaras is perhaps worth quoting, since it will draw attention to the essence of these practices. Bernier was shocked by the ritualism and image-worship of popular Hinduism and asked the pandits how could they tolerate such things. The pandits said in reply: 'We have indeed in our temples a great variety of images. . . . To all these images we pay great honour; prostrating our bodies, and presenting to them, with much ceremony, flowers, rice, scented oil, saffron, and other similar articles. Yet we do not believe that these statues are themselves Brahma or Vishnu; but merely their images and representations. We show them deference only for the sake of the deity whom they represent, and when we pray it is not to the statue, but to that deity. Images are admitted in our temples, because we conceive that prayers are offered up with more devotion when there is something before the eyes that fixes the mind, but in fact we acknowledge that God alone is absolute, that He only is the omnipotent Lord.' This explanation did not convince Bernier, but it is in fact quite in line with Hindu philosophy" (ibid.).

83. Vincent A. Smith, ed., *Travels in the Moghul Empire AD 1656–1668* (London: Oxford University Press, 1916).

84. Ibid., 327.

85. Ibid., 327–28. A somewhat similar difficulty arises with respect to Islam whose missionary nature is scarcely in doubt. The observance of the *ṣalāt* and the *ramadān* in the polar regions would pose an obvious problem in terms of day and night and of the sighting of the moon.

86. P. J. Marshall, ed., *The British Discovery of Hinduism in the Eighteenth Century* (Cambridge: Cambridge University Press, 1970), 62.

87. Ibid., 64–65.

88. Ibid., 108–109.

89. Ibid., 110. Dow goes on to relate the ruse resorted to by Akbar to ferret out the mysteries of Hinduism. The account is not without interest (ibid., 110–11): "Not all the authority of Akbar could prevail with the Brahmins to reveal the principles of their faith. He was therefore obliged to have recourse to artifice to obtain the information which he so much desired. The Emperor, for this purpose, concerted a plan with his chief secretary, Abul Fazil, to impose him, then a boy, upon the Brahmins, in the character of a poor orphan of their tribe. Feizi being instructed in his part was privately sent to Benaris, the principal seat of learning among the Hindoos. In that city the fraud was practiced on a learned Brahmin, who received the boy into his house, and educated him as his own son. When Feizi, after ten years study, had acquired the Shanscrita language, and all the knowledge of which the learned of Benaris were possessed, proper measures were taken by the Emperor to secure his safe return. Feizi it seems, during his residence with his patron the Brahmin, was smitten with the beauty of his only daughter; and indeed the ladies of the Brahmin race are the handsomest in Hindostan. The old Brahmin saw the mutual passion of the young pair with pleasure, and as he loved him for his uncommon abilities, he offered him his daughter in marriage. Feizi, perplexed between love and gratitude, at length discovered himself to the good old man, fell down at his feet, and grasping his knees, solicited with tears for forgiveness, for the great crime he had committed against his indulgent benefactor. The Brahmin, struck dumb with astonishment, uttered not one word of reproach. He drew a dagger, which he always carried on his girdle, and prepared to plunge it in his own breast. Feizi seized his hand, and conjured him, that if yet any atonement could be made for the injury he had done him, he himself would swear to deny him nothing. The Brahmin, bursting into tears, told him, that if Feizi should grant him two requests, he would forgive him, and consent to live. Feizi, without any hesitation, consented, and the Brahmin's requests were, that he should never translate the Bedas, nor repeat the creed of the Hindoos. How far Feizi was bound by his oath not to reveal the doctrine of the Bedas to Akbar is uncertain; but that neither he, nor any other person, ever translated those books is a truth beyond any dispute. It is however well known, that the Emperor afterwards greatly favored the Hindoo faith, and gave much offence to zealous Mahomedans, by practicing some Indian customs which they thought savored of idolatry. But the dispassionate part of mankind have always allowed, that Akbar was equally divested of all the follies of both the religious superstitions, which prevailed among his subjects."

90. Ibid., 165.

91. Ibid., 147.

92. Ibid., 148–49.

93. Ibid., 148–49.

93. Henry K. Beauchamp, ed. *Hindu Manners, Custom's and Ceremonies by the Abbe S.A. Dubois* (Oxford: Clarendon Press, 1936).

95. Ibid., 12.
96. Ibid., 12.
97. Ibid.
98. Ibid., 41.
99. Ibid., 43.
100. Ibid.
101. Ibid., 43–44.
102. W.J. Wilkins, *Modern Hinduism: An Account of the Religion and Life of the Hindus in Northern India* (London: Curzon Press, 1975 [first published 1887]). W.J. Wilkins is, however, careful to add: "Where the aboriginal tribes have been absorbed into the Hindu community, they form only the very lowest caste; and have, as their chief hope, the possibility of rising in future births into the higher and more favoured ones. And so latitudinarian are the leaders of Hindu society in this wicked age, the Kali Yuga, that they believe they are only fulfilling the prophecies of degeneration made centuries ago, when they teach that it does not matter what a man believes so long as he observes the rules of the particular caste to which he may belong" (ibid.).
103. Ibid., 109.
104. Monier Monier-Williams, *Brahmanism and Hinduism* (London: John Murray, 1891), x–xi.
105. Ibid., 154, emphasis added.
106. See G.W, Trompf, *Friedrich Max Mueller: As a Theorist of Comparative Religion* (Bombay: Shakuntala Publishing House, 1976); Nirad C. Chaudhuri, *Scholar Extraordinary, The Life of Professor the Rt. Hon, Friedrich Max Muller, P. C.* (London: Chatto & Windus, 1974), Appendix II.
107. See Johannes N. Voight, *Max Mueller: The Man and His Ideas* (Calcutta: Firma K.L Mokhopadhyay, 1967).
108. See Ludo Rocher, "Max Mueller and The Vedas," in A. Destree, ed., *Melanges Armand Abel* (Leiden: E.J. Brill, 1978), Vol. III, 235.
109. Nirad C. Chaudhuri, op. cit., Appendix II.
110. F. Max Mueller, *Chips from a German Workshop* (London: Longmans, Green & Co., 1875), Vol. IV, 251ff.
111. Ibid., 251.
112. Ibid., 252.
113. Ibid., 253.
114. Ibid.
115. Ibid., 253–54.
116. Ibid., 262.
117. "The Jews, particularly in ancient times, never thought of spreading their religion. Their religion was to them a treasure, a privilege, a blessing, something to distinguish them, as the chosen people of God, from all the rest of the world. A Jew must be of the Seed of Abraham: and when in later times, owing chiefly to political circumstances, the Jews had to admit strangers to some of the privileges of their theocracy, they looked upon them, not as souls that had been gained, saved, born again into a new brotherhood, but as

strangers, as Proselytes, which means men who have came to them as aliens, not to be trusted, as their saying was, until the twenty-fourth generation.

A very similar feeling prevented the Brahmans from ever attempting to proselytize those who did not by birth belong to the spiritual aristocracy of their country. Their wish was rather to keep the light to themselves, to repel intruders they went so far as to punish those who happened to be near enough to hear even the sound of their prayers, or to witness their sacrifices" (ibid., p. 254).

Max Mueller also goes on to point out how Buddhism, by being missionary, represented a departure from Hinduism. He writes about Buddhist missionaries "that the fact that missionaries were sent out to convert the world seems beyond the reach of reasonable doubt; and this fact represents to us at that time a new thought, new, not only in the history of India, but in the history of the whole world. The recognition of a duty to preach the truth to every man, woman, and child, was an idea opposed to the deepest instincts of Brahmanism; and when, at the end of the chapter on the first missions, we read the simple words of the old chronicler, 'Who would demur, if the salvation of the world is at stake?' we feel at once that we move in a new world, we see the dawn of a new day, the opening of vaster horizons—we feel, for the first time in the history of the world the beating of the great heart of humanity" (ibid., 257–58).

118. Ibid., footnote 2.

119. Ibid., 255.

120. Ibid., 264–65.

121. See Eric J. Sharpe, *J.N. Farquhar* (Calcutta: Y.M.C.A. Publishing House, 1963).

122. J.N. Farquhar, *Modern Religious Movements in India* (Delhi: Munshiram Manoharlal, 1967), 445.

123. Ibid., e.g., 39, 125–28, 179, 271, 278, 343, 377–78, 415, 417, 424–29.

124. Ibid., 442.

125. See J.N. Farquhar, *The Crown of Hinduism* (Oxford: Oxford University Press, 1913), Introduction, passim.

126. J.N. Farquhar, *Modern Religious Movements in India*, 323–24.

127. Ibid., 393.

128. Ibid., 321–22.

129. T.M.P. Mahadevan, *Outlines of Hinduism* (Bombay: Chetana Ltd. 1960), 11.

Chapter II

1. Kenneth W. Morgan, ed., *The Religion of the Hindus* (New York: The Ronald Press Company, 1953), 42.

2. W. Theodore de Bary, ed., *Sources of Indian Tradition* (New York: Columbia University Press, 1958), Vol. II, 26.

3. Ibid.

4. Ibid. The criticism of this kind of conversion by Christians is not new; it was insinuated by the Moghul Emperor Jahāngīr (1605–1627); see Ram Chandra Prasad, *Early English Travelers in India* (Delhi: Motilal Banarsidass, 1965), 205.

5. Wm. Theodore de Bary, ed., op. cit., 26.

6. Ibid., 27.

7. D.S. Sarma, *Studies in the Renaissance of Hinduism in the Nineteenth and the Twentieth Centuries* (Benares: Benares Hindu University, 1944), 78

8. Ibid., 79, emphasis added.

9. Wm. Theodore de Bary, ed., op. cit., 20; D.S. Sarma, op. cit., 76.

10. Ibid., 93.

11. Roy was "a man whose habits and tastes in private life were those of a Mohammedan" (ibid., 77).

12. It now appears, in retrospect, that he was fairly successful in accomplishing this, as is clear from the following estimate (Wm. Theodore de Bary, ed., op. cit., 20): "The first Indian whose ideas were profoundly affected by contact with modern Western culture, Rammohun Roy was the first to give serious attention to the fundamental beliefs of the Christian religion. Although he rejected Christianity's doctrinal shell, he warmly welcomed its humanitarian message. At the same time he singled out for attention those classical Hindu scriptures which came closest in content to an ethical monotheism, thereby offering to his fellow Hindus a means of reforming certain corrupt beliefs and practices without losing their self-respect. This strategic reinterpretation of Hinduism forestalled the impending conversion of numbers of educated Hindus who recognized as Rammohun did the merits of Christian ethics, for they now began to claim that these merits were also the property of their ancestral faith. For this and his other contributions to the regeneration of Hindu society and religion, Rammohun Roy well deserves the title given him by later generations—'The Father of Modern India.' "

13. See D.S. Sarma, op. cit., 94; Wm. Theodore de Bary, ed., op. cit., 27. It is interesting that while most Britishers attributed the then wretched state of Hinduism (see R.C. Majumdar, *British Paramountcy and Indian Renaissance* ([Bombay: Bharatiya Vidya Bhavan,1965] Part II, 338) to a lack of civilization on the part of the Hindus, Roy attributed it to an "excess in civilization."

14. It could be argued though that, as casteism was a barrier to conversion to Hinduism and pacifism deprived Hinduism of the zeal to convert, Roy *was* implicitly criticizing Hinduism of declining as a consequence of being non-missionary. But such a line of argument is apparently far-fetched.

15. D.S. Sarma, op. cit., 93.

16. Ibid., 71.

17. Ibid., 71.

18. See Arvind Sharma, ed., *Modern Hindu Thought: The Essential Texts* (New Delhi: Oxford University Press, 2002), 75–76.

19. Ibid., 81.

20. D.S. Sarma, op. cit., 130.

21. Ibid.

22. Ibid.

23. Ibid., 131.

24. D.S. Sarma, op. cit., 136.

25. Ibid., 148.

26. See F. Max Mueller, *Chips from a German Workshop* (London: Longmans Green & Co., 1875), Vol. IV, 254.

27. D.S. Sarma, op. cit., 161–62.

28. Ibid., 161.

29. See J.T.F. Jordens, *Dayānanda Sarasvatī: His Life and Ideas* (Delhi: Oxford University Press, 1978).

30. Ibid., Chapter VI.

31. D.S. Sarma, *Hinduism Through the Ages* (Bombay: Bharatiya Vidya Bhavan, 1967), 97.

32. M.K. Gandhi, *Hindu Dharma* (Ahmedabad: Navajivan Publishing House, 1950), 15.

33. See Ainslie T. Embree, ed., *The Hindu Tradition* (New York: Random House, 1972), 307–309.

34. M.K. Gandhi, *Hindu Dharma*, 14.

35. J.N. Farquhar, *Modern Religious Movements in India* (New York: The Macmillan Co., 1915), 122.

36. K.C. Yadav, ed., *Autobiography of a Swami Dayananda Saraswati* (Delhi: Manohar, 1976), 7–10; R.C. Majumdar, H.C. Raychaudhuri, and Kalikinkar Datta, *An Advanced History of India* (New York: St. Martin's Press, 1967) 884.

37. K.C. Yadav, ed., op. cit., 7.

38. Ibid., 7–8. Also see Dayānanda Sarasvatī, *Satyārthaprakāśaḥ* (New Delhi: Sārvadeśika Ārya Pratinidhi Sabhā, 1996, 3.

39. Percival Spear's statement at one point that it was Dayananda who attended this meeting held in 1894 contains a double error *(India: A Modern History* [Ann Arbor: University of Michigan Press, 1961], 454), also see 294.

40. Haridas Bhattacharyya, ed., *The Cultural Heritage of India* (Calcutta: The Ramakrishna Mission Institute of Culture, 1937), Vol. IV, 635; K.C. Yadav, ed., op. cit., 7, fn. 23.

41. Ibid., 8.

42. K.C Yadav, ed., op. cit., 64. It may be noted that the illustration of universal maxim which he provides is a moral one. Those who seek the universal at a mystical rather than at the ethical level point out that the "moral virtues cannot provide the common core of religions" because "though they may be common they are not the core. From the religious point of view ethics is always derivative" (Huston Smith, "Introduction to Frithjof Schuon," in *The Transcendent Unity of Religions* [New York: Harper & Row, 1973], xxii).

43. Wm. Theodore de Bary, ed., Vol. II, op. cit., 83.

44. James Hastings, ed., *Encyclopedia of Religion and Ethics* (New York: Charles Scribner's Sons, 1909), Vol. II, 59.

45. What Swami Dayananda thought of conversion *from* Hinduism is easily surmised. He was opposed to it. What is more, he criticized even other

Hindu movements, such as the Brahmo Samaj, when he thought they were unduly influenced by Christianity (see D.S. Sharma, op. cit., 164).

46. D.S. Sarma, op. cit., 194.

47. Ibid., 196.

48. Ibid., 211.

49. Ibid., 195.

50. Ibid., 205, emphasis added.

51. Quoted in D.S. Sarma, ibid., 223.

52. Swami Saradananda, *Sri Ramakrishna: The Great Master* (Madras: Sri Ramakrishna Math, 1952), 295.

53. Ibid., 296.

54. Ibid., 260.

55. Swami Ghanananda, *Sri Ramakrishna and his Unique Message* (London: The Ramakrishna Vedanta Centre, 1970), 27.

56. Ibid., 61.

57. Ibid., 85–87.

58. Huston Smith, *The World's Religions* (San Francisco: Harper, 1991), 73.

59. Ibid., 74–75.

60. Ibid., 74.

61. *The Complete Works of Swami Vivekananda (Mayavati Memorial Edition)* (Calcutta: Advaita Ashrama, 1986), Vol. I, 3–4.

62. Ibid., 24.

63. See Rabindranath Tagore, *1861–1961 A Centenary Volume* (New Delhi: Sahitya Akademi, 1961).

64. Ainslie T. Embree, ed., op. cit., 326–27.

65. D.S. Sarma, op. cit., 364–65.

66. Thomas J. Hopkins, *The Hindu Religious Tradition* (Belmont, California: Dickinson Publishing Co., 1971), 124–26.

67. Rabindranath Tagore, *The Religion of Man* (London: Unwin Books, 1967 [first published 1931)], 12. Tagore goes on to add, however: "At the same time it must be admitted that even the impersonal aspect of truth dealt with by Science belongs to the human Universe." For more on Bauls, see K.M. Sen, *Hinduism* (Baltimore: Penguin Books, 1973 [first published 1961]), Chapter 19.

68. D.S. Sarma, op. cit., 336.

69. Ibid., 388.

70. "The idea of the humanity of God, or the divinity of Man the Eternal, is the main subject of the, book" (Rabindranath Tagore, op. cit., 11). This view is based on his mystical experience, ibid., 11–12, Chapter VI, 68.

71. Ibid., 34.

72. Ibid., 99–100: "Let me, in reference to this, give an instance from the history of Ancient India. There was a noble period in the early days of India when, to a band of dreamers, agriculture appeared as a great idea and not merely useful fact. The heroic personality of Ramachandra, who espoused its cause, was sung in popular ballads, which in a later age forgot their original

message and were crystallized into an epic merely extolling some domestic virtues of its hero. It is quite evident, however, from the legendary relics lying entombed in the story, that a new age ushered in by the spread of agriculture came as a divine voice to those who could hear. It lifted up the primeval screen of the wilderness, brought the distant near, and broke down all barricades. Men who had formed separate and antagonistic groups in their sheltered seclusions were called upon to form a united people."

73. Quoted in S. Radhakrishnan, *The Philosophy of Rabindranath Tagore* (London: Macmillan & Co., 1918), 170.

74. See Ibid., 281.

75. See Ibid., 43.

76. Rabindranath Tagore acknowledges the Hindu roots of such a universalistic attitude in the following passage: "Looking back upon those moments of my boyhood days, when all my mind seemed to float poised upon a large feeling of the sky, of the light, and to tingle with the brown earth in its glistening grass, I cannot help believing that my Indian ancestry had left deep in my being the legacy of its philosophy—the philosophy which speaks of fulfillment through our harmony with all things. The founding of my school had its origin in the memory of that longing for the freedom of consciousness, which seems to go back beyond the sky-line of my birth" (op. cit., 106).

77. M.K. Gandhi, *Hindu Dharma*, 4.

78. Ibid., 229. It is interesting to note that when Mahatma Gandhi tells us how "from my sixth or seventh year up to my sixteenth many things combined to inculcate in me a toleration of all faiths," he adds "only Christianity was at that time an exception" because "In those days Christian missionaries used to stand in a corner near the high school and hold forth, pouring abuse on Hindus and their gods." M.K. Gandhi, *An Autobiography: The Story of My Experiments with Truth.* Translated byMahadev Desai (London: Jonathan Cape, 1972 [first published in Great Britain 1949]), Part I, 27, 28–29. The tolerance for Christianity developed later.

79. This naturally meant that he was critical of evangelism, see K.L. Seshagiri Rao, *Mahatma Gandhi and Comparative Religion* (Delhi: Motilal Banarsidars, 1978) 127–32.

80. M.K. Gandhi, *An Autobiography*, Part II, Chapter XI.

81. Ibid., 113. The following passages are also of interest but are relegated to a footnote on account of their length. "My difficulties lay deeper. It was more than I could believe that Jesus was the only incarnate son of God, and that only he who believed in Him, would have everlasting life. If God could have sons, all of us were his sons. If Jesus was like God, or God Himself, then all men were like God and could be God Himself. My reason was not ready to believe literally that Jesus by his death and by his blood redeemed the sins of the world. Metaphorically there might be some truth in it. Again, according to Christianity, only human beings had souls, not other living beings, for whom death meant complete extinction; while I held a contrary belief. I could accept Jesus as a martyr, an embodiment of sacrifice, and a

divine teacher, but not as the most perfect man ever born. His death on the Cross was a great example to the world, but that there was anything like a mysterious or miraculous virtue in it my heart could not accept. The pious lives of Christians did not give me anything that the lives of men of other faiths had failed to give. I had seen in other lives just the same reformation that I had heard of among Christians. Philosophically there was nothing extraordinary in Christian principles. From the point of view of sacrifice, it seemed to me that the Hindus greatly surpassed the Christians. It was impossible for me to regard Christianity as a perfect religion or the greatest of all religions. I shared this mental churning with my Christian friends whenever there was an opportunity, but their answers could not satisfy me. Thus if I could not accept Christianity either as a perfect, or the greatest, religion neither was I then convinced of Hinduism being such. Hindu defects were pressingly visible to me. If untouchability could be a part of Hinduism, it could but be a rotten part or an excrescence. I could not understand the *raison d'être* of a multitude of sects and castes. What was the meaning of saying that the Vedas were the inspired Word of God? If they were inspired, why not also the Bible and the Koran? As Christian friends were endeavouring to convert me, even so were Musalman friends. Abdulla Sheth had kept on inducing me to study Islam, and of course he had always something to say regarding its beauty. I expressed my difficulties in a letter to Raychandbhai. I also corresponded with other religious authorities in India and received answers from them. Raychandbhai's letter somewhat pacified me. He asked me to be patient and to study Hinduism more deeply. One of his sentences was to this effect; 'On a dispassionate view of the question I am convinced that no other religion has the subtlety and profound thought of Hinduism, its vision of the soul, or its charity.' " (Ibid., 113–14).

82. M.K. Gandhi, *Hindu Dharma*, 14.

83. Ibid.

84. Ibid., 15.

85. T.M.P. Mahadevan, *Outlines of Hinduism* (Bombay: Chetana Limited, 1971), 20. This is a distinction traceable to S. Radhakrishnan, *The Hindu View of Life* (London: Unwin Books, 1965 [first published 1927]), 35.

86. M.K. Gandhi, *Hindu Dharma*, 232.

87. Ibid., 238. When accused of being a crypto-Christian, Gandhi responded by saying (ibid., 237–38): "The charge of' being a Christian in secret is not new. It is both a libel and a compliment, a libel because there are men who can believe me to be capable of being secretly anything, i.e. for fear of being that openly. There is nothing in the world that would keep me from professing Christianity or any other faith, the moment I felt the truth of and the need for it. Where there is fear there is no religion. The charge is a compliment in that it is a reluctant acknowledgement of my capacity for appreciating the beauties of Christianity. Let me own this. If I could call myself, say, a Christian, or a Mussulman, with my own interpretation of the Bible or the Quran, I should not hesitate to call myself either. For then Hindu, Christian and Mussulman would be synonymous terms. I do believe that in

the other world there are neither Hindus, nor Christians nor Mussulmans. They are all judged not according to their labels or professions but according to their actions irrespective of their profession. During our earthly existence there will always be these labels. I therefore prefer to retain the label of my forefathers so long as it does not cramp my growth and does not debar me from assimilating all that is good anywhere else."

88. T.M.P. Mahadevan, op. cit., 227–28.

89. M.K. Gandhi, *Hindu Dharma,* 235.

90. Ibid.

91. Ibid., 236.

92. Quoted in A.B. Purani, *Sri Aurobindo: Some Aspects of his Vision* (Bombay: Bharatiya Vidya Bhavan, 1966), 46–47.

93. For a recent edition, see Siri Aurobindo, *Essays on the Gita* (Pondicherry: Sri Aurobindo Ashram, 1959).

93. Robert Lawson Slater, *World Religions and World Community* (New York: Columbia University Press, 1963), Chapter III.

95. Ibid., 48.

96. Ibid., 83.

97. Ibid., 84.

98. For a good general introduction, see Robert A. McDermott, ed., *Radhakrishnan* (New York: E.P. Dutton and Company, Inc. 1970).

99. Ainslie T. Embree, ed., op. cit., 329.

100. A. McDermott, ed., op. cit., 13.

101. Vergilius Ferm, ed., *Religion in Transition* (London: George Allen & Unwin Ltd., 1937), 26–28.

102. Ainslie T. Embree, ed., op. cit., 343–44.

103. S. Radhakrishnan, *The Hindu View of Life* (London: Unwin Books, 1965 [first published 1927]), 40. Also see S. Radhakrishnan, *Religion in a Changing World* (London: George Allen & Unwin Ltd., 1967), 173–74. Also see 132.

104. See S.J. Samartha, *Introduction to Radhakrishnan the Man and his Thought* (New York: Association Press, 1964), 42.

105. S. Radhakrishnan, *The Hindu View of Life,* 26.

106. Ibid., 35. Also see T.M.P. Mahadevan, op. cit., 20–21.

107. S. Radhakrishnan did admit that Hinduism was once a missionary religion in some sense (see *The Hindu View of Life,* 28–29).

108. Robert A. McDermott, ed., op. cit., 38.

109. See Arthur Osborne, *Ramana Maharshi and the Path of Self-Knowledge* (New York: Samuel Weisner Inc., 1971 [first published 1954]). He is perhaps the best known among the lesser-known figures of modern Hinduism (see T.M.P. Mahadevan, op. cit., 240–48).

110. Arthur Osborne op. cit., 16–19, 25.

111. Ibid., 50.

112. T.M.P. Mahadevan, op. cit., 240.

113. Arthur Osborne, op. cit., 98.

114. Ibid., 106.

115. Ibid., 103.

116. See Sp. Annamalai, *The Life and Teachings of Saint Ramalingar* (Bombay: Bharatiya Vidya Bhavan, 1973); T. Dayanandan Francis, *Ramalinga Swamy* (Bangalore: Study of Religion and Society, 1972).

117. Ibid., 2.

118. Ibid., 1.

119. Ibid., 11.

120. Ibid.

121. Ibid., 1.

122. See V.T. Samuel, *One Caste One Religion One God: A Study of Sree Naraynna Guru* (New Delhi: Sterling Publishers Pty. Ltd., 1977).

123. Ibid., 126.

124. Quoted, ibid., 125–26.

125. Ibid., emphasis added.

Chapter III

1. See R.C. Majumdar, ed., *The Vedic Age* (Bombay: Bharatiya Vidya Bhavan, 1965), Chapter VIII.

2. Ibid., 148.

3. Ibid., 156.

4. Percival Spear, ed., *The Oxford History of India* (Oxford: Clarendon Press, 1958), 11, 42–43.

5. R.C. Majumdar, op. cit., 153.

6. Ibid., 154.

7. Ibid., 194. Also see Asko Parpola, *Deciphering the Indus Script* (Cambridge: Cambridge University Press, 1994).

8. Thomas J. Hopkins, *The Hindu Religious Tradition* (Belmont, California: Dickenson Publishing Company, 1971), 9.

9. R.C. Majumdar, ed., op. cit., 189–92. Also see R.C. Majumdar, H.C. Raychaudhuri, and Kalikinkar Datta, *An Advanced History of India* (New York: St. Martin's Press 1967), 20–21.

10. That the *ṚgVedic* Aryans immigrated into India is still the regnant view, although now increasingly under challenge. See Edwin Bryant, *The Quest for the Origins of Vedic Culture: The Indo-Aryan Migration Debate* (New York: Oxford University Press, 2001).

11. Pratima Bowes, *The Hindu Religious Tradition: A Philosophical Approach* (London: Routledge & Kegan Paul, 1977).

12. Ibid., 129, fn.7.

13. Ibid., 129–130.

14. Swami Dayananda says: "The word Arya means virtuous man, and Dassue a wicked man." (K.C. Yadav, ed., *Autobiography of Swarni Dayananda Saraswati* [Delhi: Manohar, 1976], 61). The expression *Arya Dharma*, which owes at least some of its popularity to him, also feeds into the meaning (see Malcolm Pitt, *Introducing Hinduism* ([New York: Friendship Press, 1958], 11)

15. K. Satchidananda Murty, *Vedic Hermeneutics* (Delhi: Motilal Banardass, 1933), 17. P.V. Kane is more sceptical in this respect. He writes (*History of Dharmaśāstra,* 2nd ed.) [Poona: Bhandarkar Oriental Research Institute, 1977], Vol. V, Part II, 1619–620): "Recently, some people appear to rely on the words 'kṛṇvanto viśvam-āryam' occurring in Ṛg.IX 63. 5–6 and hold that the Veda has put forward the mission of our country as making the whole world ārya. But there is hardly any foundation for this conceit. These words occur about the offering of Soma Juice (indavaḥ) to Indra. They only mean this—these Soma libations, brown in colour, (pressed from Soma plants) increase (the might of) Indra, making the waters to fall (from the sky), destroy hostile men coming to Indra, making all (the whole environment) noble they reach their proper sphere.' There is here no reference whatever to Vedic people making the whole world Ārya. At the most these verses may be interpreted as suggesting that Soma sacrifices to Indra would make the world Ārya. Then there is no message in it which modern Indians can give and spread. Soma plant itself became unavailable in Vedic times and substitutes had to be utilized. And hardly any solemn Vedic sacrifices have been performed for centuries in India and very rarely, if at all, Soma sacrifices."

16. On its importance in Vedic religion, see H. Aguilar, *The Sacrifice in the ṚgVeda (Doctrinal Aspects)* (Delhi: Bharatiya Vidya Prakashan, 1976), 7–8.

17. A.D. Pusalkar, "Aryan Settlements in India," in R.C. Majumdar, ed., *The Vedic Age* (London: George Allen & Unwin, 1952), 256. Unlike S. Radhakrishnan (in *The Hindu View of Life* [London: George Allen & Unwin Ltd., 1927], 38), A.D. Pusalkar did not refer to the rite by name.

18. R.C. Majumdar, ed., *The Vedic Age*, 253–54. Also see Monier Monier-Williams, *A Sanskrit-English Dictionary* (Oxford: Clarendon Press, 1976), 473.

19. Ram Sharan Sharma, *Śūdras in Ancient India* (Delhi: Motilal Banarsidass, 1958), 10–11.

20. Ibid., 21–22. For the meanings of the root *das*, see Monier Monier-Williams, op. cit., 473.

21. V. Kane, op. cit., Vol. II, part I, 386.

22. Ram Sharan Sharma, op. cit., 31–32.

23. Ibid., 19.

24. Ibid., 20.

25. Ibid., Chapter II. This is a debatable point. Many scholars do not distinguish between two, others hint at a distinction but do not follow up the point. A.D. Pusalker observes at one point that in "the Rigveda, Dāsa is not so reproachful a term as Dasyu" but goes on to say that "to the Rigvedic bards there was not much difference between the Dāsas and Dasyus" (see R.C. Majumdar, ed., *The Vedic Age*, 253, 254).

26. Ram Sharan Sharma, op. cit., 9.

27. Ibid.

28. Ibid., 11.

29. Ibid., 24. For linguistic and archaeological, evidence see Ibid. 23–24. It is useful to note in this connection the existence of words such as *Divodāsa* and so on.

30. Ibid., 69.

31. Ibid.

32. This verse has been cited by both Swami Dayananda (see Chirenjiva Bharadwaja, trans., *Light of Truth* [Madras: The Arya Samaj, 1932], 73), and Vivekananda (see R.C. Majumdar, ed., *Swami Vivekananda Centenary Memorial Volume* [Calcutta: Swami Vivekananda Centenary, 1963], 366) to prove that according to the Vedas themselves the *śūdras* were entitled to read the Vedas. Even after making allowance for its apologetic use, the verse quite clearly includes the *śūdras* among the listeners.

33. P.V. Kane, op. cit., Vol. II, Part I, 155.

34. Ibid.

35. R.S. Sharma, op. cit., 121.

36. A.L. Herman, *An Introduction to Indian Thought* (Englewood Cliffs, N.J.: Prentice-Hall, Inc., 1976), 26.

37. See R.C. Majumdar, ed., *The Vedic Age*, 373; A.A. Macdonell; *The Vedic Mythology* (Varanasi: Indological Book House, 1971 [Indian reprint]), 54ff; R.N. Dandekar, *Some Aspects of the History of Hinduism* (Poona: University of Poona, 1967), 41–43; R.C. Zaehner, *Hinduism* (London: Oxford University Press, 1962), 28ff.

38. Wm. Theodore de Bary, ed., op. cit., 3.

39. R.C. Majumdar et al., op. cit., 25–26. The concerned passage is *ṚgVeda*, VII.18.13.

40. R.S.Sharma, op. cit., 19–20.

41. Ibid., 19.

42. Benjamin Walker, *The Hindu World* (New York: Fredrick A. Praeger, 1968), Vol. II, 299, emphasis added.

43. R.S. Sharma, op. cit., 20. R.S. Sharma adds: "This also confirms the hypothesis that developed priesthood was a pre-Āryan institution, and implies that all the conquered people were not reduced to the position of the dāsas and śūdras. And hence, though the brāhmaṇa as such was an Indo-European institution, the priestly class of the Aryan conquerors may have been largely recruited from the conquered. Though there is nothing to indicate the proportion, it seems that some of the pre-Aryan priests found their way into the new society. It would be wrong to think that all the 'blacks' were reduced to the status of the śūdra helots, since there are some references to black seers. In the *ṚgVeda* the Aśvins are described as presenting fair-skinned women to black (śyāvāya) Kaṇva, who probably is named *kṛṣṇa* 'black' at another place and is the poet of the hymns (RV, VIII.85 and 86) addressed to the twin gods. It is perhaps again Kaṇva who is mentioned as *kṛṣṇa ṛṣi* in the first book of the *ṚgVeda*. Similarly Dīrgha-tamas, mentioned as a singer in one hymn of the *ṚgVeda*, may have been of dark colour, if his name was given to him on account of his complexion. It is significant that in several passages of the *ṚgVeda* he is known by his metronymic Māmateya alone, and a later legend says that he married Uśij, a slave girl and begot Kākṣīvant. Again in the first book of the *ṚgVeda* priestly Divodāsas, whose name suggests a dāsa origin, are described as composing new hymns, while in the tenth book the Aṅgiras

author of the RV, X.42–44 is called 'black.' Since most of the above references occur in the later portions of the *ṚgVeda* it would appear that towards the end of the ṚgVedic period some of the black seers and Dāsa priests were worming their way into the newly organized Āryan community."

44. Ibid., 15–17.

45. R.C. Majumdar, et al, op. cit., 26–27. This picture, however, fails to take adequate notice of another facet of Aryan policy, that of conciliation toward the Dāsas (see R.S. Sharma, op. cit., 9, 11, 16, 23–24) which may account for "the easy assimilation into the Aryan fold of their chiefs such as Divodāsa, Balbūtha and Tarukṣa. It is because of this that the Dāsas appear as frequent allies of the Aryans in their inter-tribal conflicts. Thus it would appear that the name *dāsa* in the sense of slave was derived not from the non-Aryan inhabitants of India but from a people allied to the Indo-Aryans. In the later period of the *ṚgVeda* the term *dāsa* may have been employed indiscriminately not only to cover the survivors of the original Into-European *dāsas* but also pre-Aryan peoples such as Dasyus and Rakṣasas, and also those sections of the Aryans who were impoverished or reduced to subjection on account of internal conflicts within their ranks" (Ibid., 24).

46. See Monier-Williams, *A Sanskrit-English Dictionary* (Oxford: Clarendon Press, 1960 [1899]), 457.

47. Benjamin Walker, op. cit., Vol. I, 384. S. Radhakrishnan provides an interesting perspective here when he writes (*The Hindu View of Life*) [London: Unwin Books, 1974, first published 1927] 87, emphasis added): "The struggle for equality has been with us from the beginning of India's history. We have one evidence of it in the feud between Vasiṣṭha, the pillar of orthodoxy and the enemy of all innovation, and Viśvāmitra, the leader of the progressives and the champion of freedom and liberty. While the conservative Vasiṣṭha wanted the Vedic religion be confined solely to the Aryans, Viśvāmitra tried to universalize it. The movement of the Upaniṣads was in spirit a democratic one. Buddhism, as is well known, undermines all hierarchical ideas. Śaṅkara's philosophy was essentially democratic, and Rāmānuja honoured members of the Śūdra and the Pañcama classes as Ālvārs."

48. This is perhaps one of the most quoted verses from the *ṚgVeda* in modern writings on or in Hinduism. See R.C. Zaehner, op. cit., 24; *D.S. Sarma, Studies in the Renaissance of Hinduism in the Nineteenth and Twentieth Centuries* (Benaras: Benaras Hindu University, 1944), 4; S. Radhakrishnan, op. cit., 22; Philip H. Ashby, Modern *Trends in Hinduism* (New York: Columbia University Press, 1974), 31; R.C. Majumdar et al, op. cit., 38; Louis Renou, *Religions of Ancient India* (New York: Schocken Books, 1968), 56.

49. See H. Aguilar, op. cit., 7.

50. See Thomas J. Hopkins, *The Hindu Religious Tradition* (Belmont, California: Dickenson Publishing Company, Inc. 1971), 11; Percival Spear, ed., *The Oxford History of India* (Oxford: Clarendon Press, 1958), 8; Louis Renou, *Hinduism* (New York: George Braziller, Inc. 1951), 17; S. Radhakrishnan describes the process thus (op. cit., 30–31): "It need not be thought that the Aryan was always the superior force. There are occasions when the Aryan yielded to the

non-Aryan, and rightly too. The Epics relate the manner in which the different non-Aryan gods asserted their supremacy over the Aryan ones. Kṛṣṇa's struggle with Indra, the prince of the Vedic gods, is one instance. The rise of the cult of Śiva is another. When Dakṣa, the protagonist of the sacrificial cult, conceives a violent feud against Śiva, there is disaffection in his own home, for his daughter Satī, who has become the embodiment of womanly piety and devotion, has developed an ardent love for Śiva.

The Vedic culture, which resembles that of the Homeric Greeks or the Celtic Irish at the beginning of the Christian era, or that of the pre-Christian Teutons and Slavs, becomes transformed in the epics into the Hindu culture through the influence of the Dravidians. The Aryan idea of worship during the earliest period was to call on the Father Sky or some other shining one to look from on high on the sacrificer, and receive from him the offerings of fat or flesh, cakes and drink. But soon *pūjā* or worship takes the place of *homa* or sacrifice. Image worship, which was a striking feature of the Dravidian faith, was accepted by the Aryans. The ideals of vegetarianism and non-violence (*ahiṁsā*) also developed. The Vedic tradition was dominated by the Agamic, and today Hindu culture shows the influence of the Āgamas, the sacred scriptures of the Jains, as much as that of the Vedas. The Aryan and the Dravidian do not exist side by side in Hinduism but are worked up into a distinctive cultural pattern which is more an emergent than a resultant. The history of the Hindu religious development shows occasionally the friction between the two strains of the Vedas and the Āgamas, though they are sufficiently harmonized. When conceived in a large historical spirit, Hinduism becomes a slow growth across the centuries—incorporating all the good and true things as well as much that is evil and erroneous, though a constant endeavor, which is not always successful, is kept up to throw out the unsatisfactory elements. Hinduism has the large comprehensive unity or a living organism with a fixed orientation. The Upanishad asks us to remember the Real who is One—who is indistinguishable through class or color and who by his varied forces provides as is necessary for the needs of each class and of all."

51. R.C. Majumdar, ed., *The Vedic Age*, 248.

52. Ibid., 265–66.

53. R.C. Majumdar et al, op. cit., 39.

54. R.C. Majumdar, ed., *The Vedic Age*. 266.

55. R.C. Zaehner, ed., *The Concise Encyclopedia of Living Religions* (Boston: Beacon Press, 1959), 178.

Chapter IV

1. See Percival Spear, ed., *The Oxford History of India*, 4th ed. (Delhi: Oxford University Press, 1994) 65; Louis Renou, ed., *Hinduism* (New York: George Braziller Inc., 1961), 18–19.

2. A.L. Basham, *Studies in Indian History and Culture* (Calcutta: Sambodhi Publications Private Ltd., 1964), 167–77.

3. S. Radhakrishnan, *The Hindu View of Life* (London: Unwin Books, 1974), 29–30.

4. R.C. Majumdar, ed., *The Vedic Age*, 48–50

5. See Percival Spear, ed., op. cit., 57–59.

6. K.A. Nilakanta Sastri, *Development of Religion in South India* (New Delhi: Orient Longmans, 1963), 16–17: "The gradual extension of the connotation of the term Āryāvarta (land of the Aryans) is also worth noting in this connection. The *Manusmṛti* (the code of Manu), the earliest of the metrical law books of India, probably assumed its present form in the early centuries before and after the Christian era. Some verses (17–23) in the second chapter of that work reveal the stages in the extension of Aryandom. The first of these defines Brahmāvarta (the land of the Vedas) as the region lying between the holy rivers of Sarasvatī and Dṛṣadvatī and affirms that it was created by the gods; the next verse states that the traditional usages (*ācārā*) of the region set the model for others to follow. Then there was the Brahmarṣideśa (the country of the Brahman seers) adjacent to Brahmāvarta and comprising Kurukṣetra (the field of the Kurus where the Great Battle of the *Mahābhārata* was fought, the historic Panipat plain) and the countries of the Matsyas, Pāñcālas and Śūrasenas; all men in the world should be instructed on their respective mores from the Brahman born in this region. The region between the Himālayas and the Vindhyas bounded by Vinaśanā (the place where the Sarasvatī river disappears in the sands of the Rajaputana desert) on the west and Prayāga (Allahabad) on the east is known as Madhyadeśa (21). Again the entire area between the two mountains already named and the seas on the west and east, (i.e. the whole of what we now call Northern India) is described as Āryāvarta by the learned (22). The name Āryāvarta is explained by the commentators as indicating that Āryas appear over and over again in this region; and Medhātithi, the earliest extant commentator (ninth century), states expressly that though the land may pass for a time under the rule of barbarians (*mlecchas*), yet it is soon restored to orthodoxy by the reappearance of Āryas—a comment full of historical import if we consider his date falling after the first Muslim impact on North India and on the eve of the definitive Muslim conquest of the North. Lastly, all lands where the black buck (spotted antelope) roams about naturally are fit places for the performance of the *yajña* (vedic sacrifice), i.e. places where Aryas could reside; all beyond is barbarian country (*mlecchadeśa*) (23). Here is a conscious extension of the limits of Āryadeśa to lands other than Northern India; and whether the test of the natural presence of the spotted antelope is literally fulfilled or not, there is little doubt that this last verse includes India south of the Vindhyas and is capable of application to Indonesia and Indochina as well. In this context we are forcibly reminded of the seven inscriptions from East Borneo engraved on stone *yūpas* (sacrificial posts to which the animal are tied before being sacrificed), and detailing many Vedic sacrifices by name which were preformed for the king Mūlavarman by Brahmins who had gone there specially for the purpose."

7. See Percival Spear, ed., op. cit., 42.

8. K.A. Nilakanta Sastri, op. cit., 13.

9. Ibid., 14.

10. Ibid., 15–16.

11. See John Brough, *The Early Brahmanical System of Gotra and Pravara* (Cambridge: Cambridge University Press, 1953), Chapter VIII.

12. K.A. Nilakanta Sastri, *Development of Religion in South India*, 14–15.

13. See Fred W. Clothey, *The Many Faces of Murukan: The History and Meaning of a South Indian God* (The Hague: Mouton, 1978).

14. K.A. Nilakanta Sastri, *Development of Religion in South India*, 21–22.

15. See K.A. Nilakanta Sastri, *A History of South India* (Oxford University Press, 1958), 55, 138, 355–56, 373, 422.

16. See K.A. Nilakanta Sastri, *Development of Religion in South India*, 22–26.

17. Ibid., 28.

18. See Arvind Sharma, "Classical Hinduism As A Missionary Religion," *Numen* 39:2 (November 1992):175–192.

19. See Padmanabh S. Jaini, "Śramaṇas: Their Conflict with Brahmanical Society," in Joseph W. Elder, ed., *Chapters in Indian Civilization* (Iowa: Kendall/Hunt Publishing Co., 1970), Vol. I, 39–82.

20.Percival Spear, ed., op. cit., 81.

21. Ibid., 137–138.

22. R.N. Dandekar, *Some Aspects of the History of Hinduism* (Poona: University of Poona, 1967), 92.

23. As a matter of fact, the performance of Aśvamedha in the Kaliyuga is forbidden by the Purāṇas; see P.V. Kane, *History of Dharmaśāstra* (Poona: Bhandarkar Oriental Research Institute, 1946), Vol. III, 962.

24. See Louis Renou, *Religions of Ancient India* (New York: Schocken Books, 1968), 100–102; Hemachandra Raychaudhuri, *Political History of Ancient India With A Commentary By B.N. Mukherjee* (New Delhi: Oxford University Press, 1999), 314–322.

25. R.N Dandekar, op. cit., 100.

26. Ibid., 102.

27. Ibid., 107.

28. Ibid., 107–108.

29. Louis Renou, *Religions of Ancient India*, 54–56. The extent to which the caste system hindered or surprisingly helped the Hinduisation process is not always clear (see K.A. Nilakanta Sastri, *The Development of Religion in South India*, 28). A parallel reflection is suggested by the question: to what extent did circumcision prove an obstacle to the missionary enterprise for the Semitic religions. It does not seem to have obstructed the spread of Judaism or of Islam but seems to have proven an obstacle in the way of Christianity.

30. Benjamin Walker, *The Hindu World* (New York: Frederick A. Praeger, 1968), Vol. II, 443.

31. See P.V. Kane, *History of Dharmaśāstra* (Poona: Bhandarkar Oriental Research Institute, 1941), Vol. II, Part I, 155–156.

32. Ibid., 155. "The scheme of classes and stages is helpful but not indispensable. Śaṅkara tells us that it is like a saddle horse which helps man to reach his goal easily and quickly, but even without it men arrive there"

(S. Radhakrishnan, *Eastern Religions and Western Thought* [Oxford: Clarendon Press, 1939], 382).

33. Ram Sharan Sharma, *Śūdras in Ancient India* (Delhi: Motilal Banarsidass, 1980) 195.

34. Ibid., 293.

35. B.R. Ambedkar, *Who Were the Shudras?* (Bombay: Thackers, 1970), passim.

36. G. Bühler, trans., *The Laws of Manu* (Oxford: Clarendon Press, 1886) 32–33, emphasis added.

37. See *Manusmṛti* II.172.

38. G. Bühler, trans. op. cit., 61.

39. Ibid., 412.

40. Ibid., 36–37, emphasis added.

41. Ibid., 406–407.

42. Ibid., 469.

43. Rameshvar G. Ojha, "Vrātystoma," in Harbilas Sarda, ed. *Dayanand Commemoration Volume* (Ajmer: Dayanand Nirvana Ardha Shatabdi Sabha, 1933) 169–80.

44. See Louis Renou, ed., *Hinduism* (New York George Braziller, 1962) 117; also see Julius Lipner, *Hindus: Their Religious Beliefs and Practices* (London and New York: Routledge, 1994) 74.

45. This point has not escaped the notice of some Western Indologists. Thus W.J. Wilkins writes in *Modern Hinduism* (London: Curzon Press, 1975) 263–64: "Concerning people not included in these four castes, such as the aborigines whom the Hindus found in India, and the inhabitants of countries bordering on their own, Manu has little to say. He affirms that the members of three castes, the Brahman, Kshatriyas, and Vaisyas, are twice-born; the fourth, the Sudra, once-born; there is no fifth. All others are outcastes. He enumerates a number of such tribes, and gives their pedigree, showing that they are the descendants of some who were once within the bounds of the Hindu castes. They have sunk to their low condition from the fact that their parents did not marry members of the caste. The common name Dasyus (slaves) is applied to them all, and it is taught that they ought to respect the Brahmanical institutions. In the Vishnu Purana is a story in harmony with Manu's teaching. Sagara, the son of a king in exile, raised an army and recovered his paternal estate. When he was about to exterminate his foes, they applied to Vasistha, his family priest, for protection, who interceded with the king, saying, 'You have done enough my son, in the way of pursuing these men, who are as good as dead. I have compelled them to abandon the duties of caste and all association with the twice-born.' Sagara compelled them to alter their costume. He made the Yavanas shave their heads, the Sakas shave half their heads, the Paradas to wear long hair, and the Pahlavas beards. These and other Kshatriyas he deprived of the study of the Vedas, in consequence of which, and of their desertion by the Brahmans, they became Mlechhas, or outcasts. From this and similar stories the writers evidently imagined that the people inhabiting the neighbouring countries were once part of their own

nation, who through their wickedness lost their position as members of one or other of the four great castes."

46. See Troy Wilson Organ, *Hinduism: Its Historical Development* (Woodbury, New York: Barron's Educational Series, Ind., 1974) 189–90.

47. See Milton Singer, ed., *Krishna: Myths, Rites, and Attitudes* (Honolulu: East-West Center Press, 1966) Chapter I.

48. A.C. Bhaktivedanta Swami Prabhupada, trans., *Śrimad-Bhāgavatam,* Second Canto, Part One (New York: The Bhaktivedanta Book Trust, 1972) p. 200. The gloss by Prabhupāda is not without interest as representing the Bhakti attitude to conversion in modern Hinduism with elements of traditional interpretation also represented (Ibid., 201): "*Kirāta*: A province of old Bhāratavarṣa mentioned in the *Bhīṣma Parva of Mahābhārata*. Generally the Kirātas are known as the aboriginal tribes of India, and in modern days the Santal Parganas in Bihar and Chota Nagpur might comprise the old province named Kirāta.

Hūṇa: The area of East Germany and part of Russia is known as the Province of the Hūṇas. Accordingly, sometimes a kind of hill tribe is known as the Hūṇas.

Āndhra: A province in Southern India mentioned in the *Bhīṣma Parva Mahābhārata*. It is still extant under the same name. *Pulinda*: It is mentioned in the *Mahābhārata*, (Ādi 174.39) viz., the inhabitants of the province of the name Pulinda. This country was conquered by Bhīmasena and Sahadeva. The Greeks are known as Pulindas, and it is mentioned in the *Vana Parva* of *Mahābhārata* that the non-Vedic race of this part of the world would rule over the world. This Pulinda Province was also one of the provinces of Bhārata, and the inhabitants were classified amongst the *kṣatriya* kings. But later on, due to their giving up the brahminical culture, they were mentioned as *mlecchas* (just as those who are not followers of the Islamic culture are called *kafirs*, and those who are not followers of the Christian culture are called heathens).

Abhīra: This name also appears in the *Mahābhārata*, both in the *Sabhā Parva* and *Bhīṣma Parva*. It is mentioned that this province was situated on the *River* Sarasvatī in Sind. The modern Sind Province formerly extended on the other side of the Arabian Sea, and all the inhabitants of that province were known as Ābhīras province of old Bhārata, mentioned in the *Mahābhārata*.

Yavanas: Yavana was the name of one of the sons of Mahārāja Yayāti who was given the part of the world known as Turkey to rule over. Therefore, the Turks are Yavanas due to being descendants of Mahārāja Yavana. The Yavanas were therefore *kṣatriyas*, and later on, by giving up the brahminical culture, they became *mleccha yavanas*. Descriptions of the Yavanas are in the *Mahābhārata* (*Adi* 85.34). Another prince of Tuvasu was also known as Yavana, and his country was conquered by Sahadeva, one of the Pāṇḍavas. The western Yavana joined with Duryodhana in the Battle of Kurukṣetra under the pressure of Karṇa. It is also foretold that these Yavanas also would conquer India, and it proved to be true.

Khasādaya: The inhabitants of the Khasadeśa are mentioned in the *Mahābhārata (Droṇa Parva)*. Those who have a stunted growth of hair on the upper lip are generally called Khasas. As such, the Khasādayas are the Mongolians and the Chinese and others who are so designated.

The above-mentioned historical names are different nations of the world. Even those who are constantly engaged in sinful acts are all corrigible to the standard of perfect human beings if they take shelter of the devotees of the Lord. Jesus Christ and Hajarat Mohammed, two powerful devotees of the Lord, have done tremendous service on behalf of the Lord on the surface of the globe."

49. Percival Spear. ed., *The Oxford History of India by the Late Vincent A Smith, C.I.E*, 4th ed. (Delhi: Oxford University Press, 1994) 178.

50. S. Radhakrishnan, *The Hindu View of Life* (London: George Allen & Unwin Ltd, 1927), Lecture 2; A.L. Basham, *The Wonder That Was India* (Delhi: Rupa & Co., 1999), 7.

51. See R.C. Majumdar, ed., *The Age of Imperial Unity* (Bombay: Bharatiya Vidya Bhavan, 1953), 438–39.

52. Ibid., 158.

53. Ibid., The full political background of the inscription is provided below (E.J. Rapson, ed., *Ancient India* [Cambridge University Press, 1922] 558): "The only Yavana king whose name has yet been found on a purely Indian monument is Antialcidas. The inscription on a stone column was erected in honour of Krishṇa (Vāsudeva) by the Yavana ambassador Heliodorus, son of Dio, an inhabitant of Takshaśilā, who had come from the Great King Antialcidas to King Kāśīpūtra Bhāgabhadra then in the fourteenth year of his reign. The inscription is full of interest. It testifies to the existence of diplomatic relations between the Yavana king of Takshaśilā and the king of Vidiśā (Bhīlsā); and it proves that already at this period some of the Yavanas had adopted Indian faiths, for Heliodorus is styled 'a follower of Vishṇu' (bhāgavata)."

54. See K.A. Nilakanta Sastri, ed., *A Comprehensive History of India* (Bombay: Orient Longmans, 1957), Vol. II, 473.

55. Percival Spear, ed., op. cit., 144.

56. Ibid., 158.

57. Milton Singer, ed., op. cit., 4–6

58. S. Radhakrishnan, op. cit., 29. That such connections may not be too far-fetched is suggested by the use of the *Bhagavadgītā* in the *Caitanya-Caritāmṛta* by Kṛṣṇadāsa to justify Caitanya's embracing certain defiled people. "Kṛṣṇadāsa draws upon two verses from the *Gītā* to explain Caitanya's willingness to embrace two allegedly defiling persons, Haridāsa, the Vaiṣṇava saint of Muslim background, and Sanātana, the brahman Vaiṣṇava who was disgraced in some circles for close association with Muslims and who was diseased. *Gītā* 6:8 says that a yogi sees no difference between a clod of earth and a piece of gold; *Gītā* 5:18 says that the wise look upon cow and dog, brahman and eater of dogs as equivalent. Caitanya's behaviour does not seem to have been part of an effort to do away with caste and ritual pollution altogether, as some modern enthusiasts have contended, but it was sufficiently liberal in these regards to gain for him a contemporary reputation for universal love of person whom others would dare not touch." (Joseph T. O'Connell, "Caitanya's Followers and the Bhagavad-gītā: A Case Study of Bhakti and

the Secular," in Bardwell L. Smith, ed., *Hinduism: New Essays in the History of Religions* [Leiden: E.J. Brill, 1976], 42).

59. W. Douglas Hill, *The Bhagavad Gītā*, 2nd ed. (Madras: Oxford University Press, 196623.

60. Louis Renou thinks, "there is nothing to indicate that . . . Hinduism had been deeply encroached upon by Buddhism" (ed., *Hinduism*, 48–49) and that Hinduism "never lost its hold over the masses" (Louis Renou, *Religions of Ancient India*, 54). On the other hand, E.J. Rapson thinks that it "widely extended" over "the greater part of the subcontinent" (ed., *Ancient India*, 55).

61. Louis Renou regards the eighth century as marking "the final decline of Buddhism in India" (ed., *Hinduism*, 49), while Richard Robinson seems to push it to the fifteenth century (see Richard H. Robinson and Willard L. Johnson, *The Buddhist Religion: A Historical Introduction*, 3rd ed. (Belmont, California: Wadsworth Publishing Company, 1982, 101).

62. K.A. Nilakanta Sastri, *Development of Religion in South India*, 45–47; also see K.A. Nilakanta Sastri, *A History of South India from Prehistoric Times to the Fall of Vijayanagar*, 425–26. In the latter book, K.A. Nilakanta Sastri seems to doubt the account of the theft of the Buddha image by Tirumangai (Ibid., 421) but adds that "it furnishes a clue to what his followers believed in later times" (Ibid.).

63. Ibid., 412.

64. Mariasusai Dhavamony, *Love of God According to Śaiva Siddhānta* (Oxford: Clarendon Press, 1971) 139. A more detailed account by K.A. Nilakanta Sastri (*A History of South India from Prehistoric Times to the Fall of Vijayanagar*, 423–24) shows clearly how not merely the individual but the family, the Jain community, and the royalty get caught up in religious tensions associated with his conversion. "Though born in a orthodox Śaiva family he was attracted to Jainism in his early years, and joined the Jaina monastery at Pātaliputra (Cuddalore) as a monk. His elder sister, who had watched his change of faith with untold regret, implored Śiva's help. Her prayer was answered: Dharmasena, for that was her brother's name in the monastery, became the victim of an incurable abdominal disorder. When all his fellow-Jains failed him, he was compelled to go and seek his sister's aid. She secured his cure by the grace of the God Tiruvadigai. The news of his defection greatly upset the Jaina monks of Pātaliputra who trumped up many false charges against Dharmasena to poison the mind of Mahendravarman against him. He was subjected to many trials and tortures which, however, by the grace of Śiva he easily surmounted. Finally, the king himself was convinced of the superiority of Śaivism, and embraced it. Whatever element of truth there may be in the life-story of Tirunāvukkaraśu or Appar which we have sketched above, a verse in the Trichinopoly inscription of Mahendravarman furnishes clear proof that the king did indeed turn to Śaivism from some other creed."

65. Mariasusai Dhavamony, op. cit., 139.

66. Ibid.

67. K.A Nilakanta Sastri (*A History of South India from Prehistoric Times to the Fall of Vijayanagar*, 424) who offers the following account of his career, does not give credence to this statement. "At that time the Pāndya country

was almost completely overrun by Jainism, and the Pāndyan queen, a princess from Chola country, and the minister Kulaccirai, both of whom were Śaivas, sent Samandar an urgent invitation to come and release the Pāndya and his country from the tightening grip of Jainism. Ñānasambandar betook himself to Madura, foiled all the conspiracies of the Jains against him, vanquished them in debate and converted the king and his subjects to Śaivism. The story goes that on this occasion 8,000 Jains were put to death by impalement, and a festival in the Madura temple is supposed to commemorate the gruesome event to this day. This, however, is little more than an unpleasant legend and cannot be treated as history. There is no reason to believe that, even in those days of intense religious strife, intolerance descended to such cruel barbarities." Elsewhere. the same author again cast doubt on the account (*Development of Religions in South India*, 42–43): "The story goes that on this occasion 8,000 Jains were put to death by impalement, and a festival in the Madurai temple is supposed even now to commemorate the event every year. This shocking legend can hardly be history. Religious antagonism was sharp at the time, and impalement as a punishment of felons is attested by more or less contemporary sculptures and otherwise. Still we can hardly believe that the intolerance of heresy on the part of the youthful and gentle saint—he did not live to be more that sixteen—descended to such cruel barbarities. The story is doubtless the product of orthodox imagination of a later time animated by a false scale of values. Sambandar had disputations also with Buddhists and visited many shrines which he praised in song. He was the saintliest of the *Nāyanārs* and had no past to regret. He may be placed in the middle of the seventh century or a little later and his Pāṇḍyan contemporary was most probably Māṛavarman Avaniśūlāmani." It is not impossible that Hindu missionary zeal may have taken such extreme forms. In any case, some works on Indian history refer to the episode without casting doubt on it. See Percival Spear, ed., *The Oxford History of India by the Late Vincent A. Smith, C.I.E.*, 4th ed. (Delhi: Oxford University Press, 1994) 227: "Persecution of the Jains. Very soon after Hieun Tsang's stay in the south, the Jains of the Pāndya kingdom suffered a terrible persecution at the hands of the king variously called Kūna, Sundara, or Nedumaran Pāndya, who originally had been a Jain and was converted to faith in Śiva by a Chola queen. He signalized his change of creed by atrocious outrages on the Jains who refused to follow his example. Tradition avers that 8,000 of them were impaled. Memory of the fact has been preserved in various ways, and to this day the Hindus of Madura, where the tragedy took place, celebrate the anniversary of the 'impalement of the Jains' as a festival (*utsava*)."

68. K.A. Nilankanta Sastri, *Development of Religion in South India*, 44.

69. Ibid.

70. Op. cit., 159.

71. R.C. Zaehner, op. cit., 170.

72. K.A Nilakanta Sastri, *A History of South India from Prehistoric Times to the Fall of Vijayanagar*, 423.

73. Ibid., 415.

74. Ibid., 416.

75. Ibid.

76. Ibid., 412.

77. Ibid.

78. Milton Singer, op. cit., 19–22.

79. D.S. Sarma, *Studies in the Renaissance of Hinduism in the Nineteenth and Twentieth Centuries* (Benares: Benares Hindu University, 1944), 38–39.

80. George Thibaut, trans., *The Vedānta Sūtras of Bādarāyaṇa with the Commentary of Śaṅkara* (New York: Dover Publications, Inc., 1962) Vol. I, 218.

81. Govind Chandra Pande, *Life and Thought of Śaṅkarācārya* (Delhi: Motilal Banarsidass, 1994), 87.

82. Legends suggest that he may have conceived of his mission early in life. Thus it is said that "much against his will his mother arranged a marriage for him, and all his efforts to persuade her to release him from the arrangement since he wished to become a *sannyasin* were of no avail. One day, the story goes, while mother and son were bathing in a river the boy's foot was caught by a crocodile. Thinking that his end was near he implored his mother once again to give him permission to become a sannyasin so that he might die in peace and the mother was obliged to accede to his request. The crocodile, it is said, was a deity in disguise who forthwith released the boy so that he might teach the truth to all the world." (Benjamin Walker, *The Hindu World* [New York: Frederick A. Praeger, 1968] Vol. II, 349).

83. See R.C. Zaehner, op. cit., 16; R.C. Zaehner, ed., *The Concise Encyclopedia of Living Faiths* (Boston: Beacon Press, 1959), 238.

84. Ainsile T. Embree, ed., *The Hindu Tradition* (New York: Random House, 1972) 198.

85. R.C Zaehner, ed., op. cit., 238.

86. Wm.Theodore de Barry, ed., *Sources of Indian Tradition* (New York: Columbia University Press, 1958), Vol. I, 310

87. Ainslie T. Embree, ed., op. cit., 198.

88. However, see Benjamin Walker, op. cit., Vol. II, 349.

89. K.A. Nilakanta Sastri, *Development of Religions in South India*, 85.

90. Benjamin Walker, op. cit., Vol. II, 349.

91. See P.V. Kane, *History of Dharmaśāstra* (Pooma: Bhandarkar Oriental Research Institute, 1941,) Vol. II, Part II, 907. This is further supported by the fact that "it is not until the ninth century that the first traces of a Hindu order appear, allegedly founded by Śaṅkara, with its ten brotherhoods, its regional directors, and its supreme head who bears the reverential title of *jagadguru*" (Louis Renou, *Religions of Ancient India*, 93).

92. P.V. Kane, op. cit., Vol. II, Part II, 948.

93. Ibid.

93. G.C. Pande, op. cit.,10ff.

95. "Śaṅkara studied under the guru Govindapāda who was himself a pupil of the famous philosopher Gauḍapāda (fl. AD 700). The young man dedicated his life to philosophy and early acquired a reputation as a formidable opponent in debate. He once had a famous controversy with a Pandit

named Maṇḍana (also known Maṇḍana Miśra, Sureśvara, or Viśvarūpa), with Maṇḍana's wife acting as judge. She awarded the victor's wreath to Śaṅkara, but just as he was about to ascend the throne that would signify his superiority over all contestants, she challenged him herself. Knowing that as a sannyāsin he would be ignorant of all matters pertaining to sex, she asked the philosopher what he knew of the science of love. Śaṅkara asked for a month's respite and retired to the banks of a stream with a few trusted disciples. Telling his followers to look after his body, he left his physical frame and occupied the body of a king named Amaru just after the latter's decease. Using the king's body he made love to the royal wives and concubines, and was soon so intoxicated with the pleasure of the flesh that in three weeks he forgot all about his controversy. His disciples, fearing just such a contingency, went around singing religious songs, one of which caught the ears of the voluptuary and immediately put him in mind of his mission. He left the body of the king, assumed his own fleshly form, continued the controversy and won, making converts of both Maṇḍana and his learned wife." (Benjamin Walker, op. cit., Vol. II, p. 349).

96. T.M.P. Mahadevan, *Outlines of Hinduism* (Bombay: Chetana Limited, 1971), 142–43.

97. Eliot Deutsh and J.A.B. Van Buitenen, *A Source Book of Advaita Vedanta* (Honolulu: The University Press of Hawaii, 1971), 314.

98. Benjamin Walker, op. cit., Vol. II, 350.

99. P.V. Kane, op. cit., Vol. II, Part I, 506.

100. Ibid., Vol. V, Part II, 1025.

101. P.V. Kane, op. cit., Vol. II, Part I, 716–17. Also see Thomas J. Hopkins, *The Hindu Religious Tradition* (Belmont, California: Dickenson Publishing Company, 1971), 119–21.

102. S. Radharkrishnan, *Eastern Religions and Western Thought,* 311.

103. Benjamin Walker, op. cit., Vol. II, 350.

104. Louis Renou, *Religions in Ancient India,* 58. According to some legends, probably to be accounted for by the fact that both upheld the cause of Hinduism, Kumārila and Śaṅkara met each other (Benjamin Walker, op. cit., Vol. II, 349).

105. Louis Renou, *Religions of Ancient India,* 58.

106. For a traditional account of Kumārila's life see Benjamin Walker, op. cit., Vol. I, 571–72: "Kumārila-bhaḥṭa or Kumārila-svāmī, was a celebrated teacher of Mīmāḥsā philosophy about whose life there is much uncertainty. He was educated, according to various claimants, in Bihar, Assam, Kashmir, Banaras, or South India, and was converted at an early age to Buddhism. But he still had a great reverence for the Hindu scriptures and was once observed to weep bitterly when his Buddhist teacher criticized the Vedas. Suspecting him of being a heretic and also jealous of the love his teacher had for him, his fellow students pushed Kumārila off a high terrace. In falling he cried out 'If the Vedas are true they will save me from harm.' He escaped with his life, but lost an eye for voicing doubt in his 'If.' Kumārila rejoined the Hindu fold, now an avowed enemy of Buddhism, and gave all his support

to the strengthening of Vedic ritualism and brāhminism. Few made a greater contribution to the strangulation of Buddhism in India. He used his influence with Hindu rulers to have Buddhists persecuted and killed wherever possible among them his own Buddhist guru had loved him so well. In his latter days Kumārila was filled with remorse, and tradition says that he committed himself to the flames because he could no longer endure the thought of the two great sins he had committed: in having abandoned and been responsible for the death of his Buddhist preceptor, and for having practically denied God in his sacrifices as a means of salvation. One legend has it that when Śaṅkara heard of Kumārila's intention to immolate himself he hurried to the aged philosopher but was unable to persuade him to change his mind and descend from the pyre, and actually witnessed the great sage end his life."

107. Oral communication from Pundits in India.

108. P.V. Kane, op. cit., Vol. II, 721–22.

Chapter V

1. See Percival Spear, ed., *The Oxford History of India By the Late Vincent A. Smith, C.I.E.*, 4th ed. (Delhi: Oxford University Press, 1994), Part IV.

2. See S. R. Sharma, *The Crescent in India* (Bombay: Hind Kitabs Ltd. 1954), Chapter IV and Chapter XVII.

3. See R. C. Majumdar et al, *An Advanced History of India* (New York: St. Martin's Press, 1967), Part II, Book I, Chapter III.

4. Thomas J. Hopkins, *The Hindu Religious Tradition* (Belmont, California: Dickenson Publishing Company, Inc. 1971), 132.

5. R.C. Zaehner, *Hinduism* (London: Oxford University Press, 1962), 177.

6. Ibid., 178–79.

7. R.N. Dandekar, *Some Aspects of the History of Hinduism* (Poona: University of Poona, 1967), 111.

8. P.V. Kane, *History of Dharmaśāstra* (Poona: Bhandarkar Oriental Research Institute, 1946), Vol. III 883.

9. Fazlur Rahman, *Islam* (New York: Anchor Books, 1968), xvii.

10. S. R. Sharma, op. cit., 45.

11. S.R. Sharma, op. cit., 226–28. Also See S. R. Sharma, *The Religious Policy of the Mughal Emperors* (London: Asia Publishing House, 1972 [1940]), Chapter I, XII.

12. R C. Majumdar, "Northern India During A. D. 650–750," in R. C. Majumdar, ed., *The Classical Age* (Bombay: Bharatiya Vidya Bhavan, 1970), 166ff.

13. Percival Spear, ed., op. cit., 39.

14. S.M. Ikram, *Muslim Civilization in India* (New York and London: Columbia University Press, 1965), 7.

15. S.R. Sharma, *The Crescent in India*, 40.

16. S. M. Ikram, op. cit., 11–12.

17. Percival Spear, ed., op. cit., 205–209.

18. Ibid., 209. "Alberuni, justly entitled the Master, a profoundly learned mathematician and astronomer, who entered India in the train of Mahmud of Ghazni early in the eleventh century, applied his powerful intellect to the thorough study of the whole life of the Indians. He mastered the difficult Sanskrit language, and produced a truly scientific treatise, entitled 'An Enquiry into India' (*Tahkik-i Hind*) which is a marvel of well-digested erudition. More than five centuries later that, great book served as a model to Abu-l Fazl, whose 'Institutes of Akbar' (*Ain-i Akbari*) plainly betray the unacknowledged debt due to Alberuni" (Ibid., 16).

19. Vincent A. Smith, *The Early History of India* (Oxford: Clarendon Press, 1962), 15.

20. Percival Spear, ed., op. cit., 209.

21. Edward C. Sachau, *Alberuni's India* (New Delhi: S. Chand & Co. [First Indian Reprint], 1954), Vol. I, 20.

22. Ibid., Vol. II, 162–63.

23. Many scholars have accepted the statement somewhat uncritically. Thus, K. M Panikkar remarks: "A further comment of Alberuni is also worth noting. He observes that the Hindus did 'not desire that a thing which has once been polluted should be purified and thus recovered.' Obviously this is very different from the time when even Huns could become Hindus and Greeks could be accepted into the Hindu fold as Heliodorus was, as worshippers of Vishnu. Hinduism had, through lack of contact, which shook its system, crystallized a leaden outer crust which enveloped its gold." (*A Survey of Indian History* [London: Asia Publishing House, 1964] 110).

24. Quoted in Buddha Prakash, *Some Aspects of Indian Culture on the Eve of Muslim Invasions* (Chandigarh, India: Secretary Publications Bureau, 1962), 37.

25. Ibid., 38.

26. lbid.

27. Edward C. Sachau, op. cit., Vol. I, 132.

28. Ibid., 131. Albīrūnī also mentions the name of Devala in an astrological context in a quotation from Varāhamihira's *Saṁhitā* (Ibid., Vol. II, 235).

29. R.C. Majumdar, H. C. Raychaudhri and Kalikinkar Datta, *An Advanced History of India* (London: Macmillan & Co., 1950), 189.

30. Percival Spear, ed., op. cit., 209.

31. Ibid.

32. Vincent A. Smith, op. cit., 15.

33. Edward C. Sachau, op. cit., Vol. II, 9, 103.

34. See Jawaharlal Nehru, *The Discovery of India* (New York: The John Day Company, 1946), 230, footnote.

35. It is also possible that the account of Maḥmūd's reverse is exaggerated, as according to the *Oxford History of India*, although Maḥmūd's army "suffered severely from want of water," when he returned through Sind, he "arrived at Ghazni about April 1026, loaded with plunder" (Percival Spear, ed. op. cit., 208).

36. Louis Renou, *Religions of Ancient India* (New York: Schocken Books, 1968), 104.

37. S.R. Sharma, *The Crescent in India,* 226–28; R. C. Majumdar, ed. *The Struggle for Empire* (Bombay: Bharatiya Vidya Bhavan, 1960), 497–502; R.C. Majumdar, ed., *The Delhi Sultanate,* (Bombay: Bharatiya Vidya Bhavan, 1990), 615–39.

38. S.R. Sharma, *The Religious Policy of the Mughal Emperors,* 7.

39. Ibid., 6.

40. S.R. Sharma, *The Crescent in India,* 227, emphasis added. A more detailed account is offered in R.C. Majumdar, ed., *The Delhi Sultanate,* 104: "Other instances are given by contemporary writers. 'Afif, gives a graphic description of one such case. A Brahman of Delhi was charged with "publicly performing the worship of idols in his house and perverting Muhammadan women, leading them to become infidels." The Brahman was told that according to law he must 'either become a Musulman or be burned.' The Brahman having refused to change his faith, 'was tied hand and foot and cast into a burning pile of faggots.' 'Afif, who witnessed the execution, ends his account by saying: 'Behold the Sultan's strict adherence to law and rectitude, how he would not deviate in the least from its decrees.' " A still more detailed account is found in R.C. Jauhari, *Firoz Tughlug (1351–1388 A. D.)* (Agra: Shiva Lal Agarwala & Company, 1968), 150–51, emphasis added: "Afif was an eye-witness to the burning of an old Brahman of Delhi who persisted in performing the worship of idols in his house. He had constructed a wooden seal on which were engraved the pictures of Hindu gods and demons. Large numbers of Hindus resorted to his house to worship the seal. *He was reported to have converted a Muslim woman to Hinduism.* For these faults the Sultan sent for him along with his idol. His case was placed before the judges, doctors and elders of Islam. Their unanimous verdict was that the Brahman must either become Muslim or be burnt to death. The Brahman refused to embrace Islam and therefore orders were issued for raising a pile of faggots in front of the royal court. The Brahman was tied hand and foot and cast into it. The wooden seal was thrown on the top of the pile and it was lighted in two places at his head and feet. The fire first reached his feet where the wood was dry and in a short while the crying Brahman was consumed by fire." (emphasis added).

41. R.C. Majumdar, ed., *The Delhi Sultanate,* 103–104, emphasis added.

42. R C. Jauhari, op. cit., 151.

43. Ibid., 147. Also see S. R. Sharma, *The Religious Policy of the Moghul Emperors,* 6.

44. R.C. Majumdar, ed., *The Delhi Sultanate,* 639 note 17.

45. S.R Sharma, *The Religious Policy of the Moghul Emperors,* 6.

46. R.C. Majumdar, ed., The Delhi Sultanate, 633.

47. Ibid., 633–34.

48. S.M. Ikram, op. cit., 126.

49. Ibid., 165: "At this time a great Hindu religious revival was sweeping the country. It commenced in Bengal, but under Chaitanya's successors,

Mathura in northern India became the great center of resurgent Hinduism. It was there that the great crisis had arisen over the wealthy Brahman who had taken building material collected for the construction of a mosque and used it for building a Hindu temple. It is possible that this particular incident occurred in connection with the large-scale Vaishnava temple building operations which were going on at Mathura at this time. Among the temple-builders was Raja Man Singh, Akbar's great Hindu general. The defiant spirit which had been inculcated by the new movement can be seen in the Brahman's action."

50. R.C. Majumdar, ed., *The Delhi Sultanate*, 634–35: "Sanātana, a trusted Hindu official of the Sultan, became an ardent devotee of Chaitanya. So he (Sanātana) spent his time in religious exercises in his house, and ceased to attend the court on plea of illness. One day the Sultān paid a surprise visit and found Sanātana hale and hearty, engaged in religious discourse with twenty to thirty Vaishṇavas. The Sultān got very angry and kept Sanātana in confinement. Sultān Husain Shāh was then making preparations for a military expedition against Orissa, and asked Sanātana to accompany him. But the latter refused, saying: 'You are going to torment our gods (i.e. destroy the images and temples); I cannot go with you.' This firm reply to the iconoclastic Sultan offers a striking contrast to the fulsome eulogies paid to him by some contemporary Bengali poets. One of them, Vijaya Gupta, mentioned above, describes Husain Shāh as an ideal king whose subjects enjoy all the blessings of life, and compares him to the epic hero Arjuna. Another goes even further and describes the Muslim Sultān, notorious for breaking Hindu temples, as the incarnation of Kṛishṇa in the Kali Age. All these merely indicate the degree of abject surrender and the depth of moral degradation of the Hindus of Bengal caused by three hundred years of political servitude and religions oppression. Evidently, a new spirit was infused into them by Chaitanya, at least for the time being."

51. Victor W. Turner, *The Ritual Process* (Chicago: Aldine Publishing Company, 1969), 159. Victor W. Turner has based his discussion on the work of Edward C. Dimock Jr. on the Vaiṣṇavas of Bengal.

52. Ibid., emphasis added.

53. Ibid., 160. A significant point, especially if we bear in mind Louis Renou's remark that "In fact, as a religion in the strictest sense of the term, Hinduism can almost be summarized as Viṣṇuism" (*Hinduism*, 37).

54. Victor W. Turner, op. cit., 161.

55. Ibid., 164. It may be added that the region of Mathura became an important center of this movement with the immigration of Bengali Gosvāmin priests, who "were missionaries of the Krishnaite devotional movement led by Caitanya in the sixteenth-century Bengal" (Milton Singer, ed., op. cit., 208).

56. Bardwell L. Smith, ed., *Hinduism: New Essays in the History of Religions* (Leiden: E. J. Brill, 1976) 25.

57. Ibid.

58. Percival Spear, ed., op. cit., Book VI.

59. Percival Spear, *India: A Modern History* (Ann Arbor: The University of Michigan Press, 1972) 132–33, 140.

60. Ibid., 143.

61. S.R. Sharma, The *Religious Policy of the Moghul Emperors*, 24.
62. Ibid., 25.
63. Ibid., 98.
64. Ibid., 119–20.
65. Ibid., 214–16.
66. Ibid., 30.
67. Ibid., 31.
68. S.R. Sharma, *The Crescent in India*, 405–406.
69. S.R. Sharma, *The Religious Policy of the Mughal Emperors*, 39. S.R. Sharma notes that the order "did not put an end to forcible conversions everywhere," but it can be "safely assumed that active persecution of the Hindus and the systematic conversion of the believers of other religions to Islam became rare" (Ibid.).
70. Ibid., 52, emphasis added.
71. Ibid., 71 note 140. Emphasis added.
72. Ibid., 83.
73. S.M. Ikram, op. cit., 232–33. He goes on to add: "There were also cases of conversions from Islam to Sikhism. When Guru Hargovind took up his residence at Kiratpur in the Punjab some time before 1645, he is said to have succeeded in converting a large number of Muslims. It was reported that not a Muslim was left between the hills near Kiratpur and the frontiers or Tibet and Khotan. His predecessor, Guru Arjan, had proselytized so actively that he incurred Jahangir's anger, and, as Jahangir mentions in his autobiography, the Hindu shrines of Kangra and Mathura attracted a number of Muslim pilgrims."
74. R.C. Majumdar, ed., *The Mughal Empire* (Bombay: Bharatiya Vidya Bhavan, 1974) 653–54.
75. Ibid. Prānnāth founded the Praṇāmī sect and Kasturba Gandhi, the wife of Mahatma Gandhi, is said to have belonged to it.
76. S.R. Sharma, *The Religious Policy of the Mughal Emperors*, 170–71.
77. S.M. Ikram, op. cit., 232.
78. See R.C. Majumdar, H.C. Raychaudhuri, and Kalikinkar Datta, *An Advanced History of India* (New York: St. Martin's Press, 1967) 488–97, 503–19. Therein, the revolts at the national level are discussed. Instances of defiance at the local level are also not wanting. See S.M. Ikram, op. cit., 233: "The Hindu position was so strong that in some places Aurangzeb's order for the collection of jizya was defied. On January 29, 1693, the officials in Malwa sent a soldier to collect jizya from a zamindar called Devi Singh. When he reached the place, Devi Singh's men fell upon him, pulled his beard and hair, and sent him back empty-handed. The emperor thereupon ordered a reduction in the jagir of Devi Singh. Earlier, another official had fared much worse. He himself proceeded to the jagir to collect the tax, but was killed by the Hindu mansabdar. Orders to destroy newly built temples met with similar opposition. A Muslim officer who [was] sent in 1671 to destroy temples at the ancient pilgrimage city of Ujjain was killed in a riot that broke out as he tried to carry out his orders."

79. R. C. Majumdar et al, op. cit., 360.

80. See Robert Sewell, *A Forgotten Empire* (New Delhi: Publications Division, Government of India, 1962) Chapter III.

81. R.C. Majumdar, ed., *The Delhi Sultanate*, 271–72, also see 321–23; on account of the somewhat controversial nature of the issue, also see R. C. Majumdar et al, op. cit., 417–18; Percival Spear, ed., 302–305, S. R. Sharma, *The Crescent in India*, 197–200; K. A. Nilakanta Sastri, *A History of South India from Prehistoric Times to the Fall of Vijayanagar* (Oxford University Press, 1958), 226 ff.

82. T.M. Mahadevan, *The Pañcadaśi of Bhāratītīrtha-Vidyāraṇya: An Interpretive Exposition* (Madras: University of Madras, 1969), xi.

83. P.V. Kane, *History of Dharmaśāstra* (Poona: Bhandarkar Oriental Research Institute, 1974), Vol. II, Part I, 391.

84. Ibid., See Vol. II, Part II, 973–74. P.V. Kane comments, however, that though under "Shivaji and the Peshwas it appears that several persons that had been forcibly made Moslems were restored to caste after undergoing prāyaścitta. But this was done, in only a few instances" (Ibid. 391). The statement is somewhat self-contradictory, but there can be little doubt that some measure of re-conversion was going on in Maharastra as well, during the period under review and beyond (see Ibid., 973–74). Kane seems to underplay the significance of the evidence he provides because of his commitment to the view that Hinduism is tolerant and non-missionary (Ibid., Vol. II, Part I, 367).

Chapter VI

1. Richard Church, "The Universal Man," in *Rabindranath Tagore 1861–1961: A Centenary Volume* (New Delhi: Sahitya Akademi, 1961), 127, emphasis added.

2. See Sivanath Sastri, *History of the Brahmo Samaj* (Calcutta: R. Chatterjee, 1919), Chapter I.

3. U.N. Ball, *Rammohun Roy* (Calcutta: University of Calcutta, 1933), 339, emphasis supplied.

4. Quoted, Ibid., 340. As he wrote in the preface to the English translation of the *Kuth-Opunishud* in 1819: "It seems to me that I cannot better employ my time than in an endeavour to illustrate and maintain Truth, and to render service to my fellow-labourers, confiding in the mercy of that Being to whom the motives of our actions and secrets of our hearts are well-known." (Cited in Satis Chandra Chakravarti, ed., *The Father of Modern India: Commemoration Volume of the Rammohun Roy Centenary Celebrations 1933* [Calcutta: Rammohun Roy Centenary Committee, 1935], Part II, 91).

5. See Wm. Theodore de Bary, ed., *Sources of Indian Tradition* (New York: Columbia University Press, 1958), Vol.II, 28.

6. Satis Chandra Chakravarti, ed., op. cit., Part II, 91.

7. Cited in D.S. Sarma, *Studies in the Renaissance of Hinduism in the Nineteenth and the Twentieth Centuries* (Banaras: Benares Hindu University, 1944), 79.

8. M.C. Kotnala, *Raja Ram Mohun Roy and Indian Awakening* (New Delhi: Gitanjali Prakashan, 1975), 140–41.

9. Satis Chandra Chakravarti, ed., op. cit., Part II, 91.

10. Quoted in D.S. Sarma, op. cit., 93, emphasis added.

11. See D.S. Sarma, op. cit., 102–103; Sivanath Sastri, op. cit., 225–31.

12. Ibid., 299–300.

13. D.S. Sarma, op. cit., 109.

14. See Leslie Shepard, ed., *Life and Philosophy of Shree Swaminarayan 1781–1830 by H.T. Dave* (London: George Allen & Unwin Ltd., 1974).

15. M.A. Laird, ed., *Bishop Heber in Northern India* (Cambridge: Cambridge University Press, 1971), 303–311.

16. Ibid., 303.

17. Ibid., 304, emphasis added.

18. Ibid., 308.

19. Ainslie T. Embree, ed., *The Hindu Tradition* (New York: Random House, 1972), 251.

20. D.S. Sarma, op. cit., 157–58, emphasis added.

21. D.S. Sarma, op. cit., 161.

22. Ibid.

23. V.S. Naravane, *Modern Indian Thought* (New Delhi: Orient Longman Limited, 1978), 52. Dayananda's position is expressed more trenchantly by Vishwa Prakash (*Life and Teachings of Swami Dayananda* [Allahabad: Kala Press, 1969], 113–14): "For ten centuries, Hinduism was a prey to foreign domination. Mohammedans came and conquered this country. Later they began their conversion work. By threats of life, or baits of officialdom they succeeded in converting more than a quarter of the Hindu population. When English came to this country they brought Christian missionaries. These Christian missionaries were educated people, and they had a sufficient backing from their countries. They obtained little success amongst the educated classes, so they shifted their energies to the people of lower strata of society. Untouchables and hill tribes were converted to their faith. But what for Hinduism. Hinduism was not a proselytizing religion. It could easily lose its own men, but no one could be brought back into its fold. Swami Dayanand saw that this was the weakest point of Hinduism. A society, however large it may be, will surely be extinct from the face of the earth, if it allows its people to go away, but do not allow others to come in. So he opened the portals wide, he began the conversion work which was taken up by his disciples and today it is settled fact that Hinduism has become a proselytizing religion. Now millions of non-Hindus have been converted back into Hinduism. The tide has turned."

24. For a slightly sceptical view, see Julius Lipner, *Hindus: Their Religious Beliefs and Practices* (London and New York: Routledge, 1994), 118.

25. Monier Monier-Williams, *A Sanskrit-English Dictionary* (Oxford: Clarendon Press, 1976), 1082.

26. J.T.F. Jordens, *Dayānanda Sarasvatī: His Life and Ideas* (Delhi: Oxford University Press, 1978), 169.

27. R.C. Majumder, ed., *British Paramountcy and Indian Renaissance* (Bombay: Bharatiya Vidya Bhavan, 1965), Part II, 111.

28. For instance, this is the impression generated by the following passage from R.C. Zaehner (*Hinduism* [New York: Oxford University Press, 1962], 209–10): "The Arya Samaj thus became intolerant, dogmatic, and aggressive. By the institution of a ceremony called Suddhi it made it possible for untouchables to be invested with the sacred thread and thereby to become (in the eyes of the Samaj but not of orthodoxy) the equals of caste Hindus; and the same ceremony was used to re-admit apostate Hindus into their ancestral faith." He also adds, however, that the "progressive" regard the Samaj "as the nucleus of a world religion not confined to India" (Ibid., 209).

29. See J.F. Seunarine, *Reconversion to Hinduism through Śuddhi* (Madras: The Christian Literature Society, 1977).

30. He does not seem to do so actually, but his insistence that the Aryans once ruled over the entire world and his use of the *Manusmṛti* in this context are highly suggestive;, see Chiranjiva Bharadwaja, trans., *Light of Truth* (Madras: The Aryan Samaj, 1932), 309–10.

31. Troy Wilson Organ, *Hinduism: Its Historical Development* (Woodbury, N.Y.: Barron's Educational Series, Inc., 1974), 348.

32. Ibid., 349, emphasis added.

33. Swami Ghanananda, *Sri Ramakrishna and his Unique Message* (London: Ramakrishna Vedanta Centre, 1970), vii.

34. Ainslie T. Embree, ed., op. cit., 223.

35. As cited in Louis, Renou, ed., *Hinduism* (New York: George Braziller, Inc., 1961), 228–29. Also cited in Wm. Theodore de Bary, ed., op. cit., Vol. II, 100.

36. R.C. Zaehner, op. cit., 223.

37. *The Complete Works of Swami Vivekananda (Mayavati Memorial Edition)* (Calcutta: Advaita Ashrama, 1979), Vol. V, 233–35:

> Having been directed by the Editor, writes our representative, to interview Swami Vivekananda on the question of converts to Hinduism, I found an opportunity one evening on the roof of a Ganga houseboat. It was after nightfall, and we had stopped at the embankment of the Ramakrishna Math, and there the Swami came down to speak to me.
>
> Time and place were alike delightful. Overhead the stars, and around—the rolling Ganga; and on one side stood the dimly lighted building, with its background of palms and lofty shade-trees. "I want to see you, Swami," I began, "on this matter of receiving back into Hinduism those who have been perverted from it. Is it your opinion that they should be received?"
>
> "Certainly," said the Swami, "they can and ought to be taken." He sat gravely for a moment, thinking, and then resumed. "Besides," he said, "we shall otherwise decrease in numbers. When Mohammedans first came, we are said—I think on the authority of Ferishta, the oldest Mohammedan historian—to have been six hundred millions of Hindus. Now we are about two hundred

millions. And then every man going out of the Hindu pale is not only a man less, but an enemy the more. Again, the vast majority of Hindu perverts to Islam and Christianity are perverts by the sword, or the descendants of those. It would be obviously unfair to subject these to disabilities of any kind. As to the case of born aliens, did you say? Why, born aliens have been converted in the past by crowds, and the process is still going on. In my own opinion, this statement not only applies to aboriginal tribes, to outlying nations, and to almost all our conquerors before the Mohammedan conquest, but also to all those castes who find a special origin in the Puranas. I hold that they have been aliens thus adopted. Ceremonies of expiation are no doubt suitable in the case of willing converts, returning to their Mother-Church, as it were; but on those who were alienated by conquest—as in Kashmir and Nepal—or on strangers wishing to join us, no penance should be imposed."

"But of what caste would these people be Swamiji?" I ventured to ask. "They must have some, or they can never be assimilated into the great body of Hindus. Where shall we look for their rightful place?"

"Returning converts," said the Swami quietly, "will gain their own castes, of course. And new people will make theirs. You will remember," he added, "that his has already been done in the case of Baishnavism. Converts from different castes and aliens were all able to combine under that flag and form a caste by themselves—and a very respectable one too. From Ramanuja down to Chaitanya of Bengal, all great Vaishnava Teachers have done the same."

And where should these new people expect to marry? I asked. "Amongst themselves, as they do now," said the Swami quietly. "Then as to names," I enquired, "I suppose aliens and perverts who have adopted non-Hindu names should be named newly. Would you give them caste-names, or what?" "Certainly," said the Swami, thoughtfully, "there is a great deal in a name!" and on this question he would say no more.

But my next enquiry drew blood. "Would you leave these new-comers, Swamiji, to choose their own form of religious belief out of many-visaged Hinduism, or would you chalk out a religion for them? "Can you ask that?" he said. "They will choose for themselves. For unless a man chooses for himself, the very spirit of Hinduism is destroyed. The essence of our Faith consists simply in this freedom of the Ishta."

I thought the utterance a weighty one, for the man before me has spent more years than any one else living, I fancy, in studying the common bases of Hinduism in a scientific and sympathetic spirit—and the freedom of the Ishta is obviously a principle big

> enough to accommodate the world. But the talk passed to other matters, and then with a cordial good night this great teacher of religion lifted his lantern and went back into the monastery, while I, by the pathless paths of the Ganga, in and out amongst her crafts of many sizes, made the best of my way back to my Calcutta home.

38. Quoted in D.S. Sarma, op. cit., 205.

39. Ibid., 202. Also see 213–14.

40. Ibid., 202.

41. Ibid., 203. The following extract which D.S. Sarma cites on the authority of Jinarajadasa is not without interest (op. cit., 202, fn. 1): "From the first year of her coming to India she not only lived with Indians, but she lived as one of them. She wore a sari, the Indian woman's robe, she sat cross-legged on the ground or on a chowki (a kind of divan) at work, she ate seated on the ground in Hindu fashion and not at a table, using the right hand and not a spoon or a fork. Of course, in Europe she reverted to European ways, but in her own mind the Indian ways were the natural ways. She has herself explained one reason for this instinctive feeling, that she has had of late several Indian incarnations, and that her last one, before the birth as Annie Wood, was in India, and that, from the close of that Indian life and the beginning of the present one, there was only a gap of three years. She recollected incidents of that life and particularly how she was then the grand-daughter of the Adept, who is now her Guru." Also see L.A. Wickremeratne, "An American Bodhisattva and an Irish Karmayogin: Reflections on Two European Encounters with Non-Christian Religious Cultures in the Nineteenth Century," *Journal of the American Academy of Religion* 50:2 (June 1982): 237–52

42. It may also be noted that one of the objects of the Theosophical Society was "to make known to Western nations the long suppressed facts about Oriental religious philosophies, their ethics, chronology, esoterism, symbolism, to counteract as far as possible the efforts of the missionaries to delude the so-called 'Heathens' and 'Pagans' as to the real origin of the dogmas of Christianity" (cited in D.S. Sarma, op. cit., 195). On the positive side, it was "to disseminate a knowledge of the sublime teachings," among other times of that "pure esoteric systems of the archaic period which are mirrored in the oldest Vedas" (Ibid.). In other words, the Theosophical Society could be considered missionary at least by implication if not intention.

43. T.M. Mahadevan, *Outlines of Hinduism* (Bombay: Chetana Limited, 1971), 232, emphasis added.

44. Ibid., 232.

45. Quoted in T.M. Mahadevan, op. cit., 229.

46. Ibid., 223–24, emphasis added. Elsewhere, we again find a reference to his life-mission (Ibid., 228, emphasis added).

47. Quoted in M.K. Gandhi, *Hindu Dharma* (Ahmedabad: Navajivan Publishing House, 1958), 230.

48. Eric J. Sharpe, *Universal Religion for Universal Man* (Melbourne: Charles Strong Memorial Trust, 1978), 28.

49. Quoted in J.F. Seunarine, op. cit., 7.

50. S. Radhakrishnan, *The Hindu View of Life* (London: Unwin Books, 1974), 28–29, emphasis added.

51. Ibid., 28.

52. Ibid., p. 92.

53. *Rabindranath Tagore 1861–1961 A Centenary Volume*, 127. As a matter of fact some of his statements seem to be a call to India, significantly not Hinduism, to come out of its shell (see Ainslie T. Embree, ed., op. cit., 330–31): "So, for ourselves, we must bear in mind that India is not engaged in recording solely our story, but that it is we who are called upon to take our place in the great Drama, which has India for its stage. If we do not fit ourselves to play our part, it is we who shall have to go. If we stand aloof from the rest, in the pride of past achievement, content with heaping up obstacles around ourselves, God will punish us, either by afflicting us with sorrow unceasing till He has brought us to a level with the rest, or by casting us aside as mere impediments. If we insist on segregating ourselves in our pride of exclusiveness, fondly clinging to the belief that Providence is specially concerned in our own particular development; if we persist in regarding our dharma as ours alone, our institutions as specially fit only for ourselves, our places of worship as requiring to be carefully guarded against all incomers, our wisdom as dependent for its safety on being locked up in our strong rooms; then we shall simply await, in the prison of our own contriving, for the execution of the death sentence which in that case the world of humanity will surely pronounce against us."

54. Quoted in Troy Wilson Organ, *Hinduism: Its Historical Development* (Woodbury, New York: Barron's Educational Series, Inc., 1974), 360.

55. *The New Encyclopaedia Britannica* (Chicago: Helen Hemingway Benton, 1974), Vol. 8, 918.

56. Louis Renou, *Religions of Ancient India* (New York: Schoken Books, 1968), 108.

57. B.K. Ahluwalia and Shashi Ahluwalia, eds., *Maharshi Ramana: His Relevance Today* (Delhi: Vivek Publishing Company, 1980), 5–7.

58. Ibid., 22–32.

59. Ibid., 108.

60. A.L. Basham, "Hinduism," in R.C. Zaehner, ed., *The Concise Encyclopedia of Living Faiths* (Boston: Beacon Press, 1967), 260.

61. Stephan Hay, ed., *Sources of Indian Tradition*, 2nd ed. (New York: Columbia University Press, 1988), Part II, 37.

62. R.C. Zaehner, ed., *The Concise Encyclopaedia of Living Faiths* (Boston: Beacon Press, 1959), 260.

63. A. C. Bouquet, *Hinduism* (New York: Hutchinson's University Library, 1949), 10.

64. Ibid.

65. T.M. Mahadevan, op. cit., 11.

66. Ibid., 293–94, emphasis supplied.

67. Ibid., 294–95.

68. Ibid., 16–21.

69. Ibid.

70. Ibid.

71. A.C. Bouquet, op. cit., 12–13.

72. Louis Renou, *Religions of Ancient India* (New York: Schocken Books, 1968), 109, emphasis added.

73. This is also the viewpoint of D.S. Sarma (op. cit., 112): "The greatest prophets of our age—Ramakrishna Paramahamsa and Mahatma Gandhi—do not mean by harmony of religions any such bloodless cosmopolitanism as is indicated by the creed of the Sadharan Brahmo Samaj. They mean, on the other hand, firm adherence to own's own religion as well as tolerance and respect for other religions. In fact, these two principles taken together have even been the motto of Hinduism. The Bhagavad-Gita, for instance, says not only, 'Howsoever men approach me, even so do I accept them,' but also, 'Better death in one's own Dharma, the Dharma of another is fraught with fear.' The one is the complement of the other. The former saves us from narrowness and bigotry, the latter from diffuseness and superficiality."

Conclusions

1. Mary Pat Fisher, *Living Religions, 4th* ed. (Upper Saddle River, N.J.: Prentice Hall, 1999 [1991]), 262–63.

2. Mahmoud M. Ayoub, "The Islamic Tradition," in Willard G. Oxtoby, ed., *World Religions: Western Traditions,* 2nd ed. (Toronto: Oxford University Press, 2002), 342.

3. Patrick Burke, *The Major Religions: An Introduction with Texts* (Oxford: Blackwell Publishers Ltd., 1996), 247.

4. Alan G. Segal, "The Jewish Tradition," in Willard G. Oxtoby, ed., op. cit., 129–30.

5. The case of Zoroastrianism provides an interesting example here: "In the Zoroastrian diaspora today, small numbers and decentralized patterns of residence mean that the majority of most young Zoroastrians' close acquaintances are likely to come from outside their own religious community. Such a setting demonstrably increases intermarriage and brings to the fore the definition of Zoroastrian identity. Neither in India nor in Iran was Zoroastrianism accustomed to receiving converts. The reasons were different in the two cases—a caste structure in Indian society and a theologico-legal ban on defection from Islam in Iranian society—but the net effect was parallel. Since neither of these inhibiting structures obtains in the English-speaking world, the conversion question is discussed anew. Recent Indian and Iranian experience are precedents, to be sure, but it is also clear that in its Sasanian heyday, Zoroastrianism was a religion for everyone" (Willard G. Oxtoby, "Zoroastrianism" in Willard G. Oxtoby, op. cit., 194).

Bibliography

Aguilar, H. 1976. *The Sacrifice in the ṚgVeda*. Delhi: Bharatiya Vidya Prakashan.

Ahluwalia, B.K. and Shashi Ahluwalia, eds. 1980. *Maharshi Ramana: His Relevance Today*. Delhi: Vivek Publishing Company.

Ambedkar, B.R. 1970 [1946]. *Who Were the Shudras?* Bombay: Thackers.

Annamalai, Sp. 1973. *The Life and Teachings of Saint Ramalingar*. Bombay: Bharatiya Vidya Bhavan.

Ashby, Philip H. 1974. *Modern Trends in Hinduism*. New York: Columbia University Press.

Aurobindo, Sri. 1959. *Essays on the Gita*. Pondicherry: Sri Aurobindo Ashram.

Ball, U.N. 1933. *Rammohun Roy*. Calcutta: University of Calcutta.

Basham, A.L. 1999 [1954]. *The Wonder That Was India*. Delhi: Rupa & Co.

———. 1964. *Studies in Indian History and Culture*. Calcutta: Sambodhi Publications Private Ltd.

Beal, Samuel, trans. 1914. *The Life of Hiuen-Tsang by the Shaman Hwui Li*. London: Kegan Paul, Trench, Trübner & Co.

Beauchamp, Henry K., ed., 1936. *Hindu Manners, Customs and Ceremonies by the Abbe S.A. Dubois*. Oxford: Clarendon Press.

Bharadwaja, Chirenjiva, trans., 1932. *Light of Truth*. Madras: The Arya Samaj.

Bhattacharyya, Haridas, ed. 1937. *The Cultural Heritage of India*. Calcutta: The Ramakrishna Mission Institute of Culture.

Bouquet, A.C. 1949. *Hinduism*. New York: Hutchinson's University Library.

Bowes, Pratima. 1977. *The Hindu Religious Tradition: A Philosophical Approach*. London: Routledge & Kegan Paul.

Brough, John. 1953. *The Early Brahmanical System of Gotra and Pravara*. Cambridge: Cambridge University Press.

Bryant, Edwin 2001. *The Quest for the Origins of Vedic Culture: The Indo-Aryan Migration Debate*. New York: Oxford University Press.

Bühler, G., trans. 1886. *The Laws of Manu*. Oxford: Clarendon Press.

Burke, Patrick. 1996. *The Major Religions: An Introduction with Texts*. Oxford: Blackwell Publishers Ltd.

Chakravarti, Satis Chandra, ed. 1935. *The Father of Modern India: Commemoration Volume of the Rammohun Roy Centenary Celebrations 1933*. Calcutta: Rammohun Roy Centenary Committee.

Chaudhuri, Nirad C. 1974. *Scholar Extraordinary, The Life of Professor the Rt. Hon. Friedrich Max Mueller, P.C.* London: Chatto & Windus.

Church, Richard. 1961, "The Universal Man," in *Rabindranath Tagore 1861–1961: A Centenary Volume.* New Delhi: Sahitya Akademi.

Clothey, Fred W. 1978. *The Many Faces of Murukan: The History and Meaning of a South Indian God.* The Hague: Mouton.

Dahlquist, Allan. 1962. *Megasthenes and Indian Religion.* Uppsala: Almquist and Wiksell.

Dandekar, R.N. 1967. *Some Aspects of the History of Hinduism.* Poona: University of Poona.

Davids, T.W. Rhys and S.W. Bushell, eds. 1904. *On Yuan Chwang's Travels in India 629–645 A.D. by Thomas Watters.* London: Royal Asiatic Society.

Dayānanda, Svāmī. 1932. *Light of Truth.* Trans. Chirenjiva Bharadwaja. Madras: The Arya Samaj.

de Bary, Wm. Theodore, ed. 1958. *Sources of Indian Tradition.* New York: Columbia University Press.

Destree, A., ed., 1978. *Melanges Armand Abel.* Vol. III Leiden, The Netherlands: E.J. Brill.

Deutsh, Eliot and J.A.B. Van Buitenen. 1971. *A Source Book of Advaita Vedānta.* Honolulu, Hawaii: The University Press of Hawaii.

Devahuti, D., ed. 2001. *The Unknown Hsuan-Tsang.* New Delhi: Oxford University Press.

———. 1970. Harsha. Oxford: Clarendon Press.

Dhavamony, Mariasusai. 1971. *Love of God According to Śaiva Siddhānta.* Oxford: Clarendon Press.

Embree, Ainslie T., ed. 1972. *The Hindu Tradition.* New York: Random House.

Farquhar, J.N. 1967. *Modern Religious Movements in India.* Delhi: Munshiram Manoharlal.

———. 1913. *The Crown of Hinduism.* Oxford: Oxford University Press.

Ferm, Vergilius. 1937. *Religion in Transition.* London: George Allen & Unwin Ltd.

Fisher, Mary Pat. 1999 [1991]. *Living Religions.* 4th ed. Upper Saddle River, N.J.: Prentice Hall.

Francis, T. Dayanandan. 1972. *Ramalinga Swamy.* Madras: The Christian Literature Society.

Gandhi, M.K. 1972. *An Autobiography: The Story of My Experiments with Truth.* Trans. Mahadev Desai. London: Jonathan Cape.

———. 1950. *Hindu Dharma.* Ahmedabad: Navajivan Publishing House.

Ghanananda, Swami. 1970. *Sri Ramakrishna and His Unique Message.* London: The Ramakrishna Vedanta Centre.

Gibb, H.A.R., trans. 1929. *Ibn Battuta Travels in Asia and Africa 1325–1354.* London: George Routledge and Sons.

Halbfass, Wilhelm. 1988. *India and Europe: An Essay in Understanding.* Albany, N.Y.: State University of New York Press.

Hastings, James, ed. 1909. *Encyclopedia of Religion and Ethics.* New York: Charles Scribner's Sons.

Hay, Stephan, ed. 1988. *Sources of Indian Tradition*. 2nd ed. New York: Columbia University Press.
Herman, A.L. 1976. *An Introduction to Indian Thought*. Englewood Cliffs, New Jersey: Prentice-Hall, Inc.
Hill, W. Douglas P. 1966 [1928]. *The Bhagavad Gītā* second edition. Madras: Oxford University Press.
Hopkins, Thomas A. 1971. *The Hindu Religious Tradition*. Belmont, California: Dickinson Publishing Co.
Husain, Mahdi. 1953. *The Rehla of Ibn Battutah*. (India, Maldive Islands and Ceylon). Baroda, India: Publisher not mentioned.
Ikram, S.M. 1964. *Muslim Civilization in India*. New York: Columbia University Press.
Jaini, Padmanabh S. 1970. "Śramaṇas: Their Conflict with Brahmanical Society," in *Chapters in Indian Civilization*. Ed. Joseph W. Elder. Iowa: Kendall/Hunt Publishing Co.
Jauhari, R.C. 1968. *Firoz Tughlug 1351–1388 A.D.* Agra: Shiva Lal Agarwala & Company.
Jordens, J.T.F. 1978. *Dayānanda Sarasvatī: His Life and Ideas*. Delhi: Oxford University Press.
Kane, P.V. 1977. *History of Dharmaśāstra*. 2nd ed. Poona: Bhandarkar Oriental research Institute.
Kotnala, M.C. 1975. *Raja Ram Mohun Roy and Indian Awakening*. New Delhi: Gitanjali Prakashan.
Laird, M.A., ed. 1971. *Bishop Heber in Northern India*. Cambridge: Cambridge University Press.
Legge, James, trans. 1965 [1886]. *A Record of Buddhistic Kingdoms*. New York: Dover Publications Inc.
Lipner, Julius. 1994. *Hindus: Their Religious Beliefs and Practices*. London and New York: Routledge.
Lord, Henry. 1630. *Discoveries of the Sect of the Banians*. London: T. & R.
McDermott, Robert A., ed. 1970. *Radhakrishnan*. New York: E.P. Dutton and Company, Inc.
Macdonell, A.A. 1971. *The Vedic Mythology*. Varanasi: Indological Book House.
Mahadevan, T.M.P. 1969. *The Pañcadaśī of Bharatītīrtha-Vidyāraṇya: An Interpretive Exposition*. Madras: University of Madras.
Mahadevan, T.M.P. 1960. *Outlines of Hinduism*. Bombay: Chetana Ltd.
Majumdar, R.C., ed. 1974. *The Mughal Empire*. Bombay: Bharatiya Vidya Bhavan.
———, ed. 1965. *British Paramountcy and Indian Renaissance*. Bombay: Bharatiya Vidya Bhavan.
———, ed. 1965. *The Vedic Age*. Bombay: Bharatiya Vidya Bhavan.
———, ed. 1963. *Swami Vivekananda Centenary Memorial Volume*. Calcutta: Swami Vivekananda Centenary.
———, ed. 1990 [1960]. *The Delhi Sultanate*. Bombay: Bharatiya Vidya Bhavan.
———, ed. 1960. *The Struggle for Empire*. Bombay: Bharatiya Vidya Bhavan.
———, ed. 1954. *The Classical Age*. Bombay: Bharatiya Vidya Bhavan.

———, ed. 1953. *The Age of Imperial Unity*. Bombay: Bharatiya Vidya Bhavan.

Majumdar, R.C., H.C. Raychaudhuri and Kalikinkar Datta. 1967. *An Advanced History of India*. New York: St. Martin's Press.

Marshall, P.J., ed. 1970. *The British Discovery of Hinduism in the Eighteenth Century*. Cambridge: Cambridge University Press.

Monier-Williams, Monier. 1976. *A Sanskrit-English Dictionary*. Oxford; Clarendon Press.

———. 1891. *Brahmanism and Hinduism*. London: John Murray.

Morgan, Kenneth W., ed. 1953. *The Religion of the Hindus*. New York: The Ronald Press Company.

Mueller, F. Max. 1875. *Chips from a German Workshop*. London: Longmans, Green & Co.

Murty, K. Satchidananda. 1933. *Vedic Hermeneutics*. Delhi: Motilal Banardass.

Naravane, V.S. 1978. *Modern Indian Thought*. New Delhi: Orient Longman Limited.

Nehru, Jawaharlal. 1946. *The Discovery of India*. New York: The John Day Company.

The New Encyclopaedia Britannica. Vol. 8. 1974. Chicago: Helen Hemingway Benton.

O'Connell, Joseph T. 1976. "Caitanya's Followers and the Bhagavad-gītā: A Case Study of Bhakti and the Secular," in *Hinduism: New Essays in the History of Religions*. Ed. Bardwell L. Smith. Leiden: E.J. Brill.

Ojha, Rameshvar G. 1933. "Vrātystoma," in *Dayanand Commemoration Volume*. Ed. Harbilas Sarda. Ajmer: Dayanand Nirvana Ardha Shatabdi Sabha.

Organ, Troy Wilson. 1974. *Hinduism: Its Historical Development*. Woodbury, New York: Barrons' Educational Series.

Osborne, Arthur. 1971. *Ramana Maharshi and the Path of Self-Knowledge*. New York: Samuel Weisner Inc.

Oxtoby, Willard G. 2002. *World Religions: Western Traditions*. 2nd ed. Toronto: Oxford University Press.

Pande, Govind Chandra. 1994. *Life and Thought of Śaṅkarācārya*. Delhi: Motilal Banarsidass.

Panikkar, K.M. 1964. *A Survey of Indian History*. London: Asia Publishing House.

———. 1947. *A Survey of Indian History*. London: Meridian Books.

Parpola, Asko. 1994. *Deciphering the Indus Script*. Cambridge: Cambridge University Press.

Pitt, Malcolm. 1958. *Introducing Hinduism*. New York: Friendship Press.

Prabhupada, A.C. Bhaktivedanta Swami, trans. 1972. *Śrimad-Bhāgavatam*. New York: The Bhaktivedanta Book Trust.

Prakash, Buddha. 1962. *Some Aspects of Indian Culture on the Eve of Muslim Invasions*. Chandigarh, India: Secretary Publications Bureau.

Prakash, Vishwa. 1969. *Life and Teachings of Swami Dayananda*. Allahabad: Kala Press.

Prasad, Ram Chandra. 1965. *Early English Travellers in India*. Delhi: Motilal Banarsidass.

Purani, A.B. 1966. *Sri Aurobindo: Some Aspects of his Vision*. Bombay: Bharatiya Vidya Bhavan.
Rabindranath Tagore 1861–1961: A Centenary Volume. 1961. New Delhi: Sahitya Akademi.
Radhakrishnan, S. 1967. *Religion in a Changing World*. London: George Allen & Unwin Ltd.
———. 1965 [1927]. *The Hindu View of Life*. London: Unwin Books.
———. 1939. *Eastern Religions and Western Thought*. Oxford: Clarendon Press.
———. 1918. *The Philosophy of Rabindranath Tagore*. London: Macmillan & Co.
Rahman, Fazlur. 1968. *Islam*. New York: Anchor Books.
Rao, K.L. Seshagiri. 1978. *Mahatma Gandhi and Comparative Religion*. Delhi: Motilal Banarsidass.
Rapson, E.J., ed. 1922. *Ancient India*. Cambridge, U.K.: Cambridge University Press.
Raychaudhuri, Hemachandra. 1999. *The Political History of Ancient India with a Commentary by B.N. Mukherjee*. New Delhi: Oxford University Press.
Renou, Louis. 1968. *Religions of Ancient India*. New York: Schocken Books.
———. 1951. *Hinduism*. New York: George Braziller, Inc.
Robinson, Richard H. and Willard L. Johnson. 1982 [1970]. *The Buddhist Religion: A Historical Introduction*. 3rd ed. Belmont, Calif.: Wadsworth Publishing Company.
Rocher, Ludo 1978. "Max Mueller and the Vedas," in *Melanges Armand Abel*. Ed. A. Destree, Vol. III. Leiden, The Netherlands: E.J. Brill.
Sachau, Edward C., ed. 1964. *Alberuni's India*. Delhi: S. Chand & Co.
Samartha, S.J. 1964. *Introduction to Radhakrishnan the Man and his Thought*. New York: Association Press.
Samuel, V.T. 1977. *One Caste One Religion One God: A Study of Sree Narayana Guru*. New Delhi: Sterling Publishers Pty. Ltd.
Saradananda, Swami. 1952. *Sri Ramakrishna: The Great Master*. Madras: Sri Ramakrishna Math.
Sarasvatī, Dayānanda. 1996. *Satyārthaprakāśaḥ*. New Delhi: Sārvadeśika Ārya Pratinidhi Sabhā.
Sarma, D.S. 1967. *Hinduism Through the Ages*. Bombay: Bharatiya Vidya Bhavan.
———. 1944. *Studies in the Renaissance of Hinduism in the Nineteenth and the Twentieth Centuries*. Benares: Benares Hindu University.
Sastri, K.A. Nilakanta. 1966. *A History of South India from Prehistoric Times to the Fall of Vijayanagar*. Madras: Oxford University Press.
———. 1963. *Development of Religion in South India*. New Delhi: Orient Longmans.
———. 1957. *A Comprehensive History of India*. Bombay: Orient Longmans.
Sastri, Sivanath. 1919. *History of the Brahmo Samaj*. Calcutta: R. Chatterjee.
Sen, K.M. 1973. *Hinduism*. Baltimore, Md.: Penguin Books.
Seunarine, J.F. 1977. *Reconversion to Hinduism Through Śuddhi*. Madras: The Christian Literature Society.

Sewell, Robert. 1962. *A Forgotten Empire*. New Delhi: Publications Division, Government of India.

———. 1924. *A Forgotten Empire*. London: George Allen & Unwin.

Sharma, Arvind, ed. 2002. *Modern Hindu Thought: the Essential Texts*. New Delhi: Oxford University Press.

———. 1992. "Classical Hinduism as a Missionary Religion," *Numen* 39 (November 1992): 2:175–192.

Sharma, Ram Sharan. 1958. *Śūdras in Ancient India*. Delhi: Motilal Banarsidass.

Sharma, S.R. 1954. *The Crescent in India*. Bombay: Hind Kitabs Ltd.

———. 1972 [1940]. *The Religious Policy of the Mughal Emperors*. London: Asia Publishing House.

Sharpe, Eric J. 1978. *Universal Religion for Universal Man*. Melbourne, Austalia: Charles Strong Memorial Trust.

———. 1963. *J.N. Farquhar*. Calcutta: Y.M.C.A. Publishing House.

Shepard, Leslie, ed. 1974. *Life and Philosophy of Shree Swaminarayan 1781–1830 by H.T. Dave*. London: George Allen & Unwin Ltd.

Singer, Milton, ed. 1966. *Krishna: Myths, Rites, and Attitudes*. Honolulu: East-West Center Press.

Slater, Robert Lawson. 1963. *World Religions and World Community*. New York: Columbia University Press.

Smith, Bardwell L. 1976. *Hinduism: New Essays in the History of Religions*. Leiden, The Netherlands: E.J. Brill.

Smith, Huston. 1991. *The World's Religions*. San Francisco, Calif.: Harper.

———. 1973. "Introduction," in *Transcendent Unity of Religion and Ethics*. Ed. Frithjof Schuon. New York: Harper & Row.

Smith, Vincent A. 1924. *The Early History of India*. Oxford: Clarendon Press.

———. 1916. *Travels in the Moghul Empire A.D. 1656–1668*. London: Oxford University Press.

Smith, Wilfred Cantwell. 1962. *The Meaning and End of Religion: A New Approach to the Religious Tradition of Mankind*. New York: The Macmillan Company.

Sontheimer, Gunther D. and Herman Kulke, eds. 1989. *Hinduism Reconsidered*. New Delhi: Manohar.

Spear, Percival, ed. 1994. *The Oxford History of India by the Late Vincent A. Smith, C.I.E.* 4th ed. Delhi: Oxford University Press.

———. 1961. *India: A Modern History*. Ann Arbor, Mich.: University of Michigan Press.

———, ed. 1958. *The Oxford History of India*. Oxford: Clarendon Press.

Tagore, Rabindranath. 1967 [1931]. *The Religion of Man*. London: Unwin Books.

Takakusu, J., trans. 1976 [1896]. *A Record of the Buddhist Religion as Practiced in India and the Malay Archipelago AD 671–695 by I-tsing*. Delhi: Munshiram Manoharlal.

The Complete Works of Swami Vivekananda Mayavati Memorial Edition. 1986. Calcutta: Advaita Ashrama.

Thibaut, George, trans. 1962 [1896]. *The Vedānta Sūtras of Bādarāyaṇa with the Commentary of Śaṅkara*. New York: Dover Publications, Inc.

Trompf, G.W. 1976. *Friedrich Max Mueller: As a Theorist of Comparative Religion*. Bombay: Shakuntala Publishing House.

Turner, Victor W. 1969. *The Ritual Process*. Chicago, Ill.: Aldine Publishing Company.

Voight, Johannes N. 1967. *Max Mueller: The Man and His Ideas*. Calcutta: Firma K.L. Mokhopadhyay.

Walker, Benjamin. 1968. *The Hindu World*. New York: Fredrick A. Praeger.

Wickremeratne, L.A. 1982. "An American Bodhisattva and an Irish Karmayogin: Reflections on Two European Encounters with Non-Christian Religious Cultures in the Nineteenth Century," *Journal of the American Academy of Religion* 50 (June 1982): 2:237–52.

Wilkins, W.J. 1975 [1887]. *Modern Hinduism: An Account of the Religion and Life of the Hindus in Northern India*. London: Curzon Press.

Yadav, K.C., ed. 1976. *Autobiography of a Swami Dayananda Saraswati*. Delhi: Manohar.

Zaehner, R.C. 1962. *Hinduism*. London: Oxford University Press.

———, ed. 1959. *The Concise Encyclopedia of Living Faiths*. Boston: Beacon Press.

Index of Terms

Index of Names

Index of Subjects